Shakespearean
Performance
as Interpretation

Shakespearean Performance as Interpretation

H. R. Coursen

DELAWARE

Newark: University of Delaware Press
London and Toronto: Associated University Presses

Associated University Presses
440 Forsgate Drive
Cranbury, NJ 08512

Associated University Presses
25 Sicilian Avenue
London WC1A 2QH, England

Associated University Presses
P.O. Box 39, Clarkson Pstl. Stn.
Mississauga, Ontario,
L5J 3X9 Canada

The paper used in this publication meets the requirements of the American National Standard for Permanence of Paper for Printed Library Materials Z39.48-1984.

Library of Congress Cataloging-in-Publication Data

Coursen, Herbert R.
   Shakespearean performance as interpretation / H.R. Coursen.
      p.   cm.
   Includes bibliographical references and index.
   ISBN 0-87413-432-3 (alk. paper)
   1. Shakespeare, William, 1564–1616 Stage history.   2. Shakespeare, William, 1564–1616—Film and video adaptations.   3. Shakespeare, William, 1564–1616—Criticism and interpretation—History.
   I. Title.
PR3091.C68   1992
792.9′5—dc20   90-50933
                                                                          CIP

PRINTED IN THE UNITED STATES OF AMERICA

Contents

This book is for Homer and Laura Swander
and their Theatre in England program

Acknowledgments

I wish to thank Helen Carson for a splendid job of typing the manuscript, Miriam Gilbert and Phillip McGuire for making many useful suggestions for revision, Carmen Greenlee for helping me so much with video cassettes, the students in my several Shakespeare on TV seminars at Bowdoin College for sharpening my own perceptions, the National Endowment for the Humanities for permitting me to develop techniques with secondary school teachers in summer seminars, Bruce Brandt, editor of the *Marlowe Society Newsletter,* Bernice Kliman and Kenneth Rothwell, editors of *The Shakespeare on Film Newsletter,* Jim Lusardi and June Schlueter, editors of *Shakespeare Bulletin,* in whose journals some of this material originally appeared, The Ohio Shakespeare Conference and The Shakespeare Association of America, where some of this material was originally presented, James Bulman, co-editor of *Shakespeare on Television,* Karen Bush of Washington and Jefferson College, Sam Crowl of Ohio University, the Bowdoin College Faculty Research Fund for helping me to travel to many meetings over the years, and many funding agencies who had the confidence that I could complete this work without their assistance.

Introduction

When Jones and Partridge finally reach London, they go to Drury Lane, where Garrick is playing Hamlet. Partridge asks, "What man is that in the strange dress?" Jones identifies the Ghost, much to Partridge's disdain. "Persuade me to that, sir, if you can. Though I can't say I actually saw a ghost in my life, yet I am certain I should know one, if I saw him, better than that comes to." But Partridge, having refused to suspend his disbelief, soon falls "into so violent a trembling, that his knees knocked against each other." When Jones remonstrates, Partridge replies, "Nay, you may call me coward if you will; but if that little man there upon the stage is not frightened, I never saw any man frightened in my life." During the Ghost's "I could a tale unfold" speech, Partridge sits "with his eyes fixed partly on the ghost and partly on Hamlet, and with his mouth open; the same passions which succeeded each other in Hamlet succeeding likewise in him."[1]

While we, like the spectators around him, laugh at Partridge—a spectator version of Quince and company—he makes a number of points about Shakespearean drama, even as served up in an eighteenth-century playhouse in the edited and rewritten vehicles of David Garrick. The Ghost, for example, is not meant to confront the spectator directly. Its appearance is prepared for. We watch Horatio respond. Marcellus's "Thou art a scholar" should be mocking, not abjectly fearful. Marcellus has seen the Ghost already. He offers an attitude that mediates our response. Horatio offers another. Seldom does Shakespeare attempt directly to arouse *our* response to the supernatural. Exceptions may be act 1, scene 1, parts of act 1, scene 3, and parts of act 4, scene 1 of *Macbeth*, since the Weird Sisters appear by themmselves, even if they make no direct appeal to us.*

---

*Subsequent citations to Shakespeare will appear in parentheses and in accordance with the Craig-Bevington edition III (Glenview, Ill.: Scott, Foresman, 1980).

Garrick, who used a wig that stood up when he pulled a string under his Macbeth costume, convinces Partridge: not the Ghost, but Garrick's response to it. Even as Partridge knows "it is but a play,"[2] he identifies completely with Garrick. "When I saw the little man so frightened himself, it was that which took hold of me."[3] From "overdistance," Partridge is suddenly yanked to "underdistance,"[4] demonstrating in his naiveté that aesthetic distance from a Shakespearean production is a variable. A chorus, aside, or soliloquy can address us directly. A soliloquy can be "stream of consciousness" (Claudius's soliloquy in 3.3, even as another interpolating soliloquy—Hamlet's "Now, might I do i't"—can be directed to us). Segments of the plays are suited to the "fourth wall" treatment, while others are metadramatic, saying, we know this is a play and so do you, so share the experience with us. Even when the metadramatic invitation is tendered, however, the illusion takes over and we become convinced at some level—that of the imagination or the psyche—that what we are experiencing is "real." As Partridge shows us, our suspension of disbelief is not necessarily automatic, but often gradual.

Partridge manifests the distinctions that Michael Goldman makes in *Acting and Action in Shakespearean Tragedy*. *Praxis* is the action the characters perform. By the time Partridge experiences 1.5 of *Hamlet*, *poesis*—the actors' creation and projection of their roles—has subsumed *praxis*. Partridge believes in the Ghost because Garrick's Hamlet does. Partridge, then, represents an extreme example of *theoria*—the action of the audience or spectator in possessing the dramatic experience.[5] The energy exchanged between *poesis* and *theoria* constitutes the dramatic experience, "because what matters," as Peter Brook says, "is for us [actors and spectators] to have a living contact with one another. If this contact isn't there, then everything we can possibly say about the theatre in theory just falls to pieces."[6]

II

While Goldman provides useful distinctions, and while Partridge exemplifies them, I do not believe that any satisfactory "theoretics of performance" will ever emerge.

In a recent analysis of "performance criticism," Richard Levin says, "once we acknowledge that the plays of Shakespeare were written for the stage, then it necessarily follows that any interpretation of them that cannot be conveyed on the stage could not have been intended by the author." Levin finds this an "eminently reasonable principle."[7] While I will debate Levin on his equation that intention equals consensus, here we certainly agree. I will use feminist, psychoanalytic, and cultural materialist formulations as a basis for examining performance. It is not just that a certain critical theory may inform performance but that theory can also help us understand our response to performance. Indeed, theory can help us "individuate" our response, if I may use a word and concept of Jung's. Few practitioners have used critical theory as a means of evaluating *theoria*—the ways in which we *possess* production.

Levin goes on to argue that

> If a play exists only in performance, then, since there would be no way to determine *which* performance (since that would bring us back to the author's text, and so confer "reality" upon it as well), it would have to mean *any* performance. This would mean that any alterations made in the text during any performance, even including actors' errors, would become parts of the "real" play. Then there would be no "real" play, but only the aggregate of all the different performances, which would all be equally legitimate, since the author's text, and hence his meaning, could no longer be relevant, and the sole criterion for judging them would be whether each one "worked" in its own terms. But it then would make no sense to say that a play can be really understood only in performance, because there would be no independent "reality" apart from the performance that could be understood.[8]

The concept of *script*, however, assumes a "text" subject to variables ("solid," "sullied," "sallied," or, as Cleopatra would have it— "salad"). Performance criticism works from that "reality," obviously, using the record and recording of actual performances as a reference point, not as a "reality," as Levin would suggest with an assumed literalness. Levin's insistence on definition and "author's meaning" suggests that either an Ur-performance exists or that a proliferation of performances erases any possibility for meaning or reality. The point is that performance itself is a variable, often based on an edited and possibly equivocal reality known as a script, or *praxis*. If Shakespeare's scripts, however, represent inscriptions of ongoing narratives, then we are free of a priori assumptions.

What we have are options based upon variables. Take, for example, the opening scene of *Antony and Cleopatra*. It is a play-within-a-play framed by Philo's disapproval at the outset and Demetrius's grudging agreement with Philo at the end. In the

Trevor Nunn version (ABC-TV, 1975), Philo's description of "this dotage of our general's" cuts from a line of black-and-white grim-faced Roman soldiers in helmets to Antony and Cleopatra cavorting in front of a vaseline-smeared lens looking at soft colors and filmy fabrics. Janet Suzman's Cleopatra plays Richard Johnson's Antony off against her Egyptian audience, making a smaller and extemporaneous play within the frame. Jonathan Miller's BBC version (1981) is set in total Renaissance opulence—Veronese—and provides no distinction between Rome and Egypt. Philo is a courtier whose objection is mild, at most. As no conflict seems to exist between Rome and Egypt, none exists between Antony and Cleopatra, who conduct a pleasant private conversation in the midst of a sixteenth-century court. In the film version with Charlton Heston and Hildegard Neil (1972), a messenger arrives on a ship and rides pell-mell through the huddled streets of Alexandria, knocking shops apart and scattering civilians. He finds Antony intent on making love to Cleopatra, who is merely a compliant vessel for his lust. The Bard version (1983, directed by Lawrence Carra) finds Lynn Redgrave consistently pleased with herself and Timothy Dalton mostly histrionic. That tendency is accentuated by the lack of an audience for a "stage" production. We have neither Rome nor Egypt but only Tudor facades meant to resemble the Globe, but with only the camera as audience.

Of these versions, the Nunn strikes me as superior, but the *praxis* in each case is virtually identical.

In another discussion of the issue of performance as criterion, William Worthen says that

> Our ability to read a text as "drama" . . . is enabled by the practices that allow us to read it both as literature and as theatre. Such a sense includes not only the strategies that allow us to read the text as instigating the behaviors we recognize as "acting," but also the inter-pretive habits that guide our performance as readers and critics. . . . Like the *mise-en-scène*, the *mise-en-page* places the text and its production at issue; in this regard performance criticism might take Shake-spearean textual criticism as a paradigm. For not only does the controversy locate the act of reading as a social behavior potentially related to other performances, it raises in a cogent and powerful manner the central issue still eluding performance criticism: the prob-lematic relation between the text's origin, its initial production, and its reproduction through history.[9]

While Worthen focuses on variability rather than fixedness, we still find the issue of "the text's origin" raised as if "the text" were somehow independent of performance and "the act of reading" somehow isolated from the *theoria* involved in hearing a play. I do not dispute that the concept of "the text" has grown up since plays were first printed, or that the concept of text bears Ben Jonson's powerful imprimatur.[10] Nor do I dispute that reading the plays has, in various places and at various times, replaced performance. I do assert, however, that "text" and "reading" are hardly a paradigm but a secondary and derivative epiphenomenon or activity.

No audience, however, assembles for a play without a sense of "meaning," not necessarily in the script per se, but in the signifiers—the spoken word, the gesture, the fineness or meanness of costumes, for example—whereby a production conveys its specific variation on the given *praxis*. Those meanings depend in part upon the elements that Worthen lists, and also on *zeitgeist*, that ever-changing constant from which Shakespeare's scripts invariably draw energy and through which that energy gets transmitted, augmented, and reprojected to, within, and by the spectator, whether the latter is conscious of the process or not.

III

I hope, herein, to account for three variables that I believe are crucial to "performance as interpretation." They are space, script, and the subjectivity of the individual spectator.

The space defines what can happen within it. The proscenium arch tends to create a "fourth wall," so that we spectators gaze in upon a version of "reality" in which the actors live, unaware of the audience. Shakespeare's plays can be played under the arch, and as recently as 1964, I witnessed a superb *Hamlet* at the Lunt/ Fontane Theater in New York. While Richard Burton was laceratingly ironic with his characterization, he made few if any gestures towards his live audience, seemingly unaware that he *had* an outer audience. This approach was in marked contrast to more recent Hamlets, like those of Michael Pennington, Roger Rees, and Mark Rylance. Newer spaces—rake-thrust stages and the long platform of the Swan in Stratford, for example, create new possibilities for what can occur there. Film and television are also spaces that create and limit the possibilities of what can be contained within the expanding cone of light emanating from the projector or within the more limited dimensions of the cathode-ray tube.

The script encountering the space creates a further set of variables. Television, a close-up medium, can handle small scenes well, as witness the Northumberland, Ross, Willoughby scenes in the BBC-TV *Richard II* or the several confrontations in the BBC-TV *Measure for Measure*. Few, however, would argue that the BBC's depiction of the orations in *Julius Caesar* is as effective as that in the Mankiewitz 1954 film, where a black-and-white and unwidened screen created a spectacle we expect of cinema, and which cinema can deliver as television never will. Shakespeare's "larger" scenes, the scenes in courts and courtrooms, forums and city centers, are often minimized by the television screen. This diminution occurs even when the editing is skillful, as in Trevor Nunn's *Antony and Cleopatra* (ABC-TV, 1975), David Giles's *Richard II* (BBC-TV, 1980), and Desmond Davis's *Measure for Measure* (BBC-TV, 1979). Ironically, film can do what Shakespeare claims he cannot do—in the opening Chorus of *Henry V*—create Agincourt, make Bosworth Field and a thousand eager horses emerge from Richard III's drawing on the earth, and have a hundred quivering arrows pierce the tunic of a Japanese "Macbeth." Films do not have to rely on "a crooked figure . . . attest[ing] in little place a million." Films have "casques" of thousands. The ample space of film, however, demands visual imagery, not dialogue. The filmmaker, then, pares the script down to the minimum of words. "Dialogue? We had faces!" as Gloria Swanson says in *Sunset Boulevard*. Some scripts may be more "filmic," "televisual," or even "stageworthy" than others. The degree of difficulty of a given script as it translates itself onto a given space cannot be calculated with any precision, but it must be considered before judgment is rendered about the success or lack of success of a given production.

The spectator, of course, is not merely an inevitably subjective element in the evaluation of performance. I believe that no debate can exist about the fact that Shakespeare appeals to our subjectivity, which is not the same as someone else's subjectivity. The appeal to what is latent, unconscious, and unique in each of us is the secret of Shakespeare's endurance, along with the uncanny ability of Shakespeare's scripts to capture *zeitgeist*. It follows then that no two people will agree about a given production, which itself is an interpretation of a given script fitted to a specific space. What I intend to do, then, is set up the criteria for disagreement. That is one reason why I treat many productions available on cassette. Several other productions I examine have already gathered a significant critical history about them. This book, then, is an effort to challenge people into viewing and *re*-viewing the

many versions available and to sharpen and question their memories of productions they may have seen. Beyond that, this book
aims at the goal of my classroom teaching—to develop a better
audience for Shakespeare, one that in turn demands better Shakespeare from actors and directors.

A Shakespearean script exists only in performance. Period.
Performance sharpens "the text" necessarily in this or that direction. We are free to debate or enjoy the choices a director and his
actors make. But the debate has relevancy only as it responds to
performance. Otherwise, the "text" becomes a spaceship filled
with tinkerers and dial-watchers, but with no destination. When a
crew comes aboard, it wants to take the ship somewhere. Actors
and directors want to take the script somewhere—with the coop-
eration of that energy field known as an audience. Having said
that, however, let me add that many of the newer modes of
criticism—psychological, feminist, and cultural materialist (which
is *not* the same as "new historicism"), for example—can be re-
phrased in the context of performance.

The most exciting approach to Shakespeare is the feminist. Like
cultural materialism, which emerges from Marx-Engels, feminism, which often finds its roots in Freud, is *political*. As deployed
by its best practitioners, feminism creates convincing links between the Shakespearean script and contemporary thought. This
is not to say that the feminists make "Shakespeare our contemporary." They are usually conscious of the patriarchal assumptions
of most of Shakespeare's contemporaries and of Shakespeare's
exploration of those Elizabethan commonplaces. The feminists
share with Ann Thompson a belief that "In some sense all future
readings could be said to be already 'there' in the text, but we
have to wait for the historical circumstances that will make them
visible."[11] Feminist critics make visible the very issues ignored by
the patriarchs who once exclusively inhabited academe. The approach allows us to go back and reexamine still-existing productions on the basis of feminist insights.

The ways in which perceptions about what a play *is* shift almost
unnoticeably can be illustrated by quoting Dover Wilson: "Apart
from the play, apart from his actions, from what he tells us about
himself, and what other characters tell us about him, there *is* no
Hamlet."[12] But this is to put all meanings into the text and to
ignore it as a *script*. I, the auditor, may share Coleridge's "smack of
Hamlet." I, the actor, may agree with Richard Monette, who
played the role at Stratford, Canada, in the late 1970s, that the
story of *Hamlet* is "about me!" John Styan adds the vital dimension

to Wilson's analysis and, indeed, to any critique of a play that treats the text as only text: "What we call a play has no existence except in the minds of its audience, because it is the audience which puts it all together. A play text is written in words, but they are not the same sort of words we find in novels. . . . They are a code which waits to be projected and deciphered."[13]

While I would suggest that the play may also exist in the mind of a director who creates the circumstances for that exchange of the unique energy created by live performance, and while I agree that explorations of the script are basic to the process, I suggest and will argue that the exploration of performance—the way the words weigh on stage (and, obviously, in other media)—is basic to the understanding of the words as they appear, deceptively, on the pages of a big book. Their "decoding," as Styan suggests, can occur only within the medium for which they were written. Now, of course, we can add as we must the media of film and television. If the text is "repressed," it is so by some remarkably inept directors and by the imposition of nondramatic or extradramatic criteria upon it—that is, that criticism which sees the script *only* as text, an artifact leading back into the mirroring regress of criticism, as opposed to a script leading to the performance that sets a mirror up to the spectator.

If the text is a version of psyche, it is so because the life of performance vibrates beneath the inherited words. Those words yearn for actors to play out the dream ready to be presented and interpreted by the audience, the sharers and shapers of the dream-scenario—assuming they have *not* "but slumber'd here." Media other than the stage, of course, impose other patterns of response. What can happen on television or in film becomes a central component of any theory of production as interpretation, particularly since so much of our Shakespeare comes to us via cassette.

IV

I will use examples gleaned from my own experience and will lean heavily on productions that are available on film or cassette. In those instances, I will employ the present tense, particularly since my insights can be debated as these productions move on into time and find inevitable perches for reinterpretation. We are now in a position, for example, to apply new insights against old productions, to "re-view" Shakespeare, as Miriam Gilbert suggests.[14] We may find those productions dated in technique but possibly ahead of their times in the attitudes they discern in the script and share with us, the latter-day audience. I will use only a few plays for my specific applications, plays that have several different productions available for comparison and contrast, but I suggest that the applications are infinite, mine being but a few tentative scratchings at the surface of what may become an expanding corpus of Shakespeare in Production.

With obvious exceptions—as when I quote responses to many productions of *Shrew*—I deal herein with productions I have seen, sometimes in more than one format, as when a stage production has been translated to television. While I can be indicted, I suppose, for not having seen more productions, I hope that some of the questions I raise can be asked by spectators and auditors about *their* experiences, particularly of those moments when a play is happening in front of their eyes, to be recorded and remembered via the "rewind" and "pause" that accurate observation may permit. As many readers will know, the Royal Shakespeare Company (RSC) takes the most successful of its Stratford productions to London. The BBC productions appeared earlier on British television than on American. I have tried to be as accurate as I can be in identifying productions. In the case of stage productions, the year I give may not be the year that coincides with that in which other theater-goers saw the same production. I am responding in the case of stage production to *my* memory. Even the same production can change over the course of a run, sometimes squeezing fifteen minutes from the original running time, and productions that appeared as revivals or in different venues—like the Hands or Nunn *Henry V* or *Macbeth*, for example—will evoke different responses from the same spectator. While film and television versions can't "change," time does march on. The spectator changes, perhaps growing more discriminating and demanding. Conventions change as well, so that what we applauded once we now may find hopelessly dated and riddled with clichés that were deemed highly original in their time. But—to use a cliché—all of that suggests the continuing vitality of that quality known as Shakespeare.

The examples I adduce from productions not available on film or cassette are intended to suggest what a specific performance can show us about a particular script. Performance is a gestalt, a bringing together of many elements into a profound concentration that may induce a different interpretation of the archetype in different spectators but that will show us much more than any reading can do. Performance appeals to the imagination and the psyche, not merely to the intellect. The intellect that is primary in the act of reading is, for the spectator, an agency for ordering other than merely intellectual responses. We must understand the words and their syntactical relationships, but when we listen to a play we comprehend much more. When I deal with failures here, as I do occasionally, I have in mind the potentiality of the script that weak performances betray. The energy remains, awaiting a Terry Hands, as *Henry V* did, or a Deborah Warner, as *Titus Andronicus* did. We learn from failures, however, because they force us back to the script and back to productions we have seen and back to the theater again, back to that composite "reality" that lies behind every production.

The script is made up of words. Those words may be peopled by a reader. But the act of reading is only preliminary or secondary when dealing with a script. The words of the script are signals—often stage directions—awaiting the response of actors, directors, and audience. The reader does not engage in the communal act of theater nor does he or she participate in and contribute to the continuum of energy that is created by performance. No matter how he or she attempts to "imagine the play," that activity occurs only fitfully at best as the reader reads.

V

Since I suggest that no theoretics of performance criticism is likely to come along to baffle the uninitiated with jargon and obscurity, I must rest the initial argument on examples. I suggest simply that production shows us what the text never will, even if the many beats of a production are emerging from the text. Production can help us to say, "Ah, now I see what those lines mean!" even if we later recognize that we are experiencing *how* they mean within the dynamic of a specific experience of the script. But—to examples.

At the end of the sweaty duel scene in *Romeo and Juliet* (3.1), Zeffirelli's Tybalt (Michael York) exits with the arm of a Capulet retainer under his elbow. It is a nice allusion to the way Mercutio had been wounded and a precise visualization of the Gerome painting *After the Masquerade*, in which the successful swordsman moves away from the clown he has just killed. For Zeffirelli death is elegant, if ironic—the uninvited guest who ends the masquerade. Caviar for the general, no doubt, but a reward for those who know the Jerome, and a vivid picture for those who do not.

In the 1975 Theatre at Monmouth production of *King Lear*, director Earl McCarroll achieved a fine moment as Goneril and Regan stripped Lear of his retinue. Goneril asks Lear, "What need you five and twenty, ten or five, / To follow in a house where twice so many / Have a command to tend you?" (2.4.160). The Fool was seated downstage, right, his back to his master's humiliation. Regan's "What need one?" bit into the Fool's back and registered in his wince.

The BBC *Julius Caesar* (1979) is creative with the so-called double revelation of Portia's death. We know that Brutus knows the specifics of Portia's death before Messala delivers the news again, with Brutus's prompting. Director Herbert Wise has Brutus play the scene for Messala's benefit:

> Why farewell, Portia. We must die, Messala.
> With meditation that she must die once,
> I have patience to endure it now.
>
> (4.3.189–91).

Messala is impressed: "Even so great men great losses should endure." Brutus and Cassius debate about the site of the coming battle. After all that moisture—tides, voyages, and shallows—Brutus glances at Messala. The latter, still stunned by Brutus's calculated display of greatness, nods. Cassius capitulates. Brutus has been for once, and only ironically, an effective politician. Left in, the lines give us a glimpse of "Shakespeare's intention." The BBC production supports Thomas Clayton's assertion that "the nature and effects of the double revelation, whether part of the original composition or of later addition, are well integrated and deeply revealing, and this much remains a matter of consensus: whether and however they came to be as they are, they came from Shakespeare's hand."[15]

At the end of John Barton's *Dream*, which I saw at the Aldwych in 1978, all the characters except those of the fairy world lay in a dim semicircle around the stage as the spirits performed their final ministrations. At Puck's lines, "Now it is the time of night / That the graves, all gaping wide, / Every one lets forth his sprite, / In the churchway paths to glide," the other characters, Duke and Amazon, lovers and artisans, identities erased in the twilight, rose and joined hands in a harmonious closing dance. The orchestration of word, action, and lighting gave the ending the quality of dream—even of Bottom's fathomless vision. It seemed to be not merely Barton's vision but Shakespeare's as well.

Toward the end of a lackluster BBC *Tempest* (1980), Miranda

(Pippa Guard) emerges from her game of chess and looks at the group Prospero has assembled. She recognizes the family resemblance between her father and Antonio and delivers her "How beauteous mankind is!" to/at Antonio. Prospero's sour "'Tis new to thee" is perfectly set up. We see how Shakespeare might have directed the moment.

In the Camden Shakespeare Company's production of *Hamlet* (1981), Hamlet (Casey Kizzah) uttered the First Folio stage directions for "The Murder of Gonzago": "She seems loath and unwilling awhile, but in the end accepts his love," for example. Hamlet's cynical detachment was transformed into a fascination and from that declension into a magnetic attraction to the mimesis, so that he ended up as not just "chorus" but as an actor who had forgotten his role in the outer play and who had no lines to speak in "Gonzago." The interpolation may have been slightly extra-textual, a speaking of "cues and all," but it built powerfully toward what was, in this production, the climax of *Hamlet*.

In Camden's 1981 *Othello*, Julian Bailey's Iago stroked his beard with the handkerchief Emilia had just delivered and pondered his use of it. He suddenly looked at what he was doing and cued his concupiscent suggestion to Othello about the handkerchief and Cassio's beard.

Richard Sewell's otherwise undistinguished *Twelfth Night* at Monmouth in 1983 achieved a brilliant instant. Malvolio has been mortified but insists on his sanity in a mad world, my masters. Thus his mortification continues. As he exited from the madhouse at the end of 4.1—a scene that on the modern stage does not demand an exit—Malvolio heard a few lines of "O, Mistress Mine, Where Are You Roaming?" We had heard it already, of course. Malvolio had felt himself to be on the veriest brink of the fulfillment of his fantasies: wealth, luxury, power, Olivia's daybed any time of day. But Olivia is roaming with a Sebastian who has eased into Malvolio's dream. Malvolio is headed downstairs again. The strains of the song captured in a crystalline instant the dream and its bitter refutation. The day had slipped free of the hold that Malvolio had believed was his certain seizure.

As Polanski's Macbeth (Jon Finch) battles Macduff, Macbeth gets a sword between the plates. He staggers away as Macduff retrieves his sword. Macbeth stumbles up the steps and falls. Macduff raises his sword and swings it down. The camera makes a 90 degree jump-cut as the sword chunks off Macbeth's head, even as his hands grope for it and for the crown on top of it. The head falls away as the body clatters down the steps. Malcolm rationalizes his horror with "Such a day as this is cheaply bought." Macduff stands on the platform and says, "Hail, King, for so thou art. Behold where lies the usurper's cursed head." The head, meanwhile, has splatted onto a lower platform. The camera follows a stain of blood until it finds the head, crown in place, eyes wide open. "The time is free," Macduff says, as we look at the head. Ross removes the crown and carries it towards Malcolm. The latter removes his helmet as all shout "Hail!" Ross shouts, "Hail, King of Scotland!" and Malcolm dons the crown.

An eerie chord sounds as Macbeth's head is placed upon a pike. The camera tracks past cheering soldiers, blurred, mouths open but silent, as if time passes in some strange, slow-motion sequence. The head bleeds, the eyes are open. The camera creates a quick montage—three times to the head, twice to the silent roar of the soldiers, and then to the cheers from the courtyard balconies, which resemble an amphitheater, or the galleries of an Elizabethan theater. Macbeth's head rises on the other side, subject of the victorious cheering.

The head, of course, observes all of this—honor, love, obedience, troops of friends, all glimpsed through the profoundly ironic transparency of death. There is speculation in the eyes, which seem merely to glare. But instead of being the destroyer of a would-be ceremony of amity, as is Banquo's half-corpse, half-apparition, Macbeth's head is the focal point of such a celebration. But his audience cheers him as a "poor player" to be "heard no more."

It may be that Polanski borrows from Camus's quotation of Father Devoyod's description of an execution by guillotine:

> His head fell into the trough in front of the guillotine and the body was immediately put into the basket; but by some mistake, the basket was closed before the head was put in. The assistant who was carrying the head had to wait a moment until the basket was opened again; now, during that brief space of time we could see the condemned man's eyes fixed on me with a look of supplication, as if to ask forgiveness. Instinctively we made the sign of the cross to bless the head, and then the lids blinked, the expression of the eyes softened, and finally the look, that had remained full of expression, became vague.[16]

Polanski could have done more with his remarkable exercise in point of view.[17] While the film tries too often to edge into the genre of "horror film," the effect here is brilliant.[18] Polanski takes what we used to call "the theme of time" and forces us to experience that theme. The time is not as free as Macduff and Malcolm would make it. As Jorgens says, "The time is not free at the end of Polanski's melodrama, for there will be no end to the chain of ambitious killings, repression, and fear."[19]

I remain unconvinced that the script offers this interpretation as an option, but Polanski's camera has suggested that time is not necessarily what the Elizabethan world picture would insist that it be. For an instant Polanski escapes to the imagination that the script invites even with the closed "worldview" that the script imposes. For once, Polanski makes the "Macbeth leap." For the most part, however, I agree with Jorgens that, for all of the virtues of the film as film, it remains "a naturalistic portrait of meaningless violence acted out in a wasteland."[20]

These briefly noted "spots of time" suggest what rides beyond the text but what may be inherent in the script. The latest critical approaches must be, where they can be, employed as a means of evaluating production. This book takes a few tentative steps in that direction. The fact of a spectator—me, in this instance—casts an inevitable subjectivity over what follows. But insofar as my discussion engenders disagreement and rebuttal—most claim to have liked the Papp-Antoon *Much Ado About Nothing,* and many celebrate Jonathan Miller's *The Taming of the Shrew,* for example, two productions that I excoriate—the debate will occur in the proper place—or theater—for such debate. Deconstruction may tell us what is not there. Production tells us what is, though we are invited to disagree about our interpretation of what a production has told us. The action imitated depends upon the action of our own deepest reflexes, which create some unique imitation of an action that is ours to discern.

1

Preliminaries

I wish here to consider three attacks on the primacy of "the script," one indirect, one "from within," and one explicit. These are Richard Levin's concepts of "intention" and "consensus," the tendency of directors to embrace "the bright idea," which itself is often an attack against the script rather than an attempt to accept the terms in which it becomes comprehensible for actors and audience, and Harry Berger's argument for the primacy of the text.

The purpose of these preliminaries is to clear the way for consideration of the approaches that *are* helpful—to melt the occlusion from in front of the mimetic transparency, as they say. I will, however, attack the "bright idea" again in the chapters that follow.

I

"Meaning" as it pertains to Shakespeare emerges from the script—from the words wherein the psychology of the characters is revealed: their meanings, their intentions, and their misconceptions. The script is the latent energy that awaits the kinesis and articulation of production. It may be true, as Malcolm Evans argues, that the text must "signify not 'in its own terms' but in the context of a discourse—feminist, Marxist, or anti-colonialist, for example—which recognizes that any production of the text is *for* a particular interpretation of history [and] not simply a disinterested chronicle." [his ital.].[1] If so, production takes the same compensatory, even adversarial, stance toward the text—or script—that specific critical approaches adopt. Production, then, is a mode of interpretation.

Professor Levin has demolished a frightening number of bizarre, wildly idiosyncratic, and simply wrongheaded readings of the plays.[2] But as Levin's attack obliterates thematics, it emerges

from premises that must be challenged. Rejecting the points of
view so brilliantly put forward by a generation of young critics,
Levin reflects the *zeitgeist*—the numbness of consensus. That
stance isolates recent critical theories as "radical" and therefore
marginalizes them, when they deserve to be incorporated into our
point of view as we watch productions of the scripts. His conclusions rest on two orthodoxies that lead to two highly questionable attitudes about the plays. Levin argues that if Shakespeare
"made his meaning clear, then whenever a traditional interpretation has grown up around the play over the generations, it is very
likely to be very close to his real intentions."[3] I question whether
(1) Shakespeare intended to "make his meaning clear" and (2) any
consensus has grown up about the meaning of most of Shakespeare's plays.

I would argue for irony in the endings of many of Shakespeare's
plays but not for its preeminence over other "final impressions."
Irony is, after all, neither a genre nor an emotion. But irony is a
valid dramatic device, not merely the invention of overingenious
critics. Irony complicates response and, if we are alert to it, helps
individuate response. It validates dramatic experience by allowing
us to recognize that Shakespeare doesn't "cheat" with his endings. Even Feste's final song can be interpreted as a pointing back
over the shoulder at the sunlit, unchanging, and "resolved" world
of Illyria, and as a pointing out at the afternoon darkening above
the Thames and the city across the river, the city where "comic
endings" are more difficult than they have seemed in "our play."
Barbara Hodgdon describes the ending of Adrian Noble's 1984
Henry V (RSC): "As Chorus speaks the concluding sonnet, the
flickering candle-lit battlescape is once again revealed—both as
backdrop for the marriage treaty joining France with England and
as a prefiguring of future war. In this final image, past, present,
and future occupy the stage simultaneously."[4] I agree with Levin
that a heavy-handed *imposition* of irony can confuse issues, as I felt
it did at the end of the Polanski film version of *Macbeth*, where the
implication that Donalbain will recycle evil into the world has
been canceled in advance by the infinite progress of kings the
Weird Sisters have shown Macbeth. Do we assume that the Sisters
have been wrong? Or is it that Donalbain wants to learn how to
play Martin Bormann to his brother's Hitler? In suggesting an
endless chain of treachery, Polanski carried forth one pattern of
his film that refuted other parts of his presentation. I would
defend other "ironic" endings, however. The aloof Malcolm of the
John Gorrie Classic Theatre television version suggestion that *this*

Malcolm, while he will reward his "thanes and kinsmen," will not allow any of them within knifing distance. That ending carried through the shrewdness of Malcolm's catechism of Macduff in 4.3. The exhausted Malcolm of Trevor Nunn's RSC *Macbeth* showed that a great energy, however malign, had been excised, and perhaps that no comparable positive power could replace it. Production concepts are as debatable as critical responses are. A critic or a director must make choices, recognizing that a "total understanding" of the "text" will never be realized. The question of interpretation is only confused by a theory of "clarity" based on a consensus that reveals intention. Levin's view denies the element of subjectivity, rather than merely setting reasonable limits around the inevitably individual responses of critic, director, and spectator.

An example of Levin's appeal to intention and clarity will suggest how production corrects the seeming certainty of criticism. Levin argues against any debunking of the marriages at the end of *The Merchant of Venice, All's Well that Ends Well,* and *Measure for Measure:*

> Such marriages were firmly established as a final comic solution by one of the oldest and most potent of dramatic conventions, so that if the author really intended to overcome our conventional reaction and make us doubt the permanence of the marriages, he would surely, unless he were hopelessly incompetent, have taken special pains to emphasize this in the closing dialogue. But instead we find that, as with the reformations, all of these marriages are accepted as final by all of the characters who comment on them at the end, and no one raises any doubts about their future. (The objection would apply even more strongly to the special variant of this attack deployed against *Measure for Measure,* where, it has recently been argued, we cannot even be sure that the marriage of the Duke to Isabella will take place, since she never actually accepts the proposal. But in this case the comic convention of marital resolutions—reinforced here by the other two marriages arranged at the same time—plus the Duke's authority, both dramatic and political, to manage this resolution, plus the proverbial assumption that "silence gives consent" all points so unmistakably to her acceptance that, if Shakespeare had intended us to think otherwise, he would certainly have indicated this.)[5]

I suggest that Shakespeare *will* jar an audience's expectations, and would cite the entrance of Mercade, and the alteration of the ancient and potent convention of marriage as comic resolution in Shakespeare's suggesting a "sixth act" to *Love's Labours Lost,* in which the Gentlemen of Navarre must learn the lessons they have glibly avoided during the play per se. The ending suggests a conscious reaching "beyond convention."[6] Further, to argue from convention is to impose a "formula" approach that Levin, at other times, opposes effectively. To "reinforce" the marriage of Isabella and Vincentio with those of Angelo and the Mariana Angelo has previously jilted and to whom, in the dramatic sequence, Angelo would seem to prefer death, and of Lucio and his whore seems a dubious reinforcement indeed.

Directors have glimpsed latitude where Levin sees "unmistakable" clarity of intention. John Barton left his Isabella "puzzling about what she should do" in his 1970 RSC production, although, as Levin suggests, her attitude implied rejection.[7] At the end of Jonathan Miller's 1975 Greenwich production, Vincentio was also left alone on the stage, having watched Penelope Wilton's Isabella (in this production very like a nun) shake her head not merely to his proposal but at his misunderstanding of *her*. The Duke's public relations coup in exposing then pardoning Angelo and in resurrecting Claudio had succeeded brilliantly. But the inner man had found no reward. He could only shrug and return to the lonely world of rule. I found this ending remarkably convincing. It focused the consistent Shakespearean concern with the political as opposed to the personal man. I had never linked *Measure for Measure* and its Duke with characters like Henry VI, Richard II, the later Antony, and Coriolanus, who elevate personality at the price of worldly success, or, conversely, with Bolingbroke, Henry V, and Octavius Caesar, who subdue the self to win the world, or with the complex case of Lear, using royal power to coerce a pageant of individual will, demanding as king the stroking of the insecure boy beneath the robes. An ending that resonated with so pervasive a Shakespearean theme, and an ending that forced its auditor to consider his own discrepancies between public posture and inner imperative—such an ending might be debatable, but it could not be called wrong.

Miller's ending was as right as that of Don Taylor's less "intellectual" *Measure for Measure* at St. George's in 1977, where the same Duke (Joseph O'Conor) took a different Isabella off to the parish priest. But Anna Carteret's opulent Isabella was not framed for the veil. She had learned how to get herself out of a nunnery and into a ducal palace. She had needed someone to give direction to the "prone and speechless dialect" of her latent sexuality. Production is interpretation, and a director of so ambiguous a script as *Measure for Measure* should be given some scope about what "clarity" he wishes his production to reveal.

Recent productions of *Measure for Measure* hardly suggest that a conventional sense of its ending has grown up around the script. "When the Duke offered his hand to Isabella, she first looked at Francesca the nun, then at the Duke, and then smiled . . . a 'Mona Lisa smile' as the lights came down and the play ended."[8] Isabella "hesitated before turning around to face the Duke and extended her hand to him, giving a tentativeness to her decision and an enigmatic ending to the play."[9] "Before speaking [the Duke] took off his ducal robe and scepter, thus suggesting that he wanted her to become his partner simply as a human being. Isabella thought she had again become the mere object of man's sexual desire and fainted. Soon she recovered, however, and silently followed the Duke."[10] "Highly enthroned upon a scaffolding that was completely enveloped by his gown, the Duke asked Isabella to marry him. Isabella, who had already taken off her nun's dress, slowly disappeared within the scaffolding. It seemed as if—resigned—she entered a prison."[11] It is precisely the ambiguous zone that Shakespeare leaves open for exploration that has made *Measure for Measure* suddenly such a popular play. The script has, of course, created a continuum that has pulled modern theory, particularly feminism, toward it.

II

The counterpart of the aberrant criticism that Levin brings to correction is, in the theater, "the bright idea," the concept, born of the fairy's midwife, that springs full-blown from the directional skull and becomes the "concept of the production." Has the "director's theater" of the sixties and seventies begun to surrender to a theater in which the actor is given greater freedom and focus?[12] Michael Goldman and John Russell Brown advocate a theater more like Shakespeare's,[13] in which, if "Pyramus and Thisby" is any example, the director serves to organize production, perhaps combatting the actor who wants all the good parts for himself, perhaps forcing the maturing boy actor once more out of the breeches, and perhaps telling his less astute brethren that they must observe but not speak their cues. But Peter Quince, perhaps Shakespeare's parody of himself, as Bertrand Evans suggests,[14] does not impose an overall concept upon his company— although we might agree to the impossibility of such a process in this instance. Quince does *not* say, however, We'll have the French ladies ride in on Hondas, or We'll play the Trojan War as the Battle of Gettysburg, or We'll set *Much Ado* in nineteenth-century India or 1910 America, or We'll have the Weird Sisters descend from a space ship hovering over a predictably blasted heath. Whatever their merits, the visions of modern directors like Kahn, Barton, Papp, and Brustein typify tendencies in the director's theater and seem to me to be as invalid as much of the criticism Levin refutes, though erring on the preferable side of the bizarre rather than the banal. The quest for contemporaneity spurred by Freud and pricked on by Jan Kott has wrenched some productions so out of context that meanings still available to modern audiences, given skillful directing and acting, have been obliterated. My argument from and for tradition is based on my belief that the Shakespearean world has an amplitude and depth that can incorporate but need not be restricted to the psychoanalytic and/or existential vision of the Twentieth Century. That our *weltanschauung*, even our transitory *zeitgeist*, may be anticipated in a *Hamlet* or *King Lear* does not dictate that we narrow or hollow out these texts to the dimension of their "modern" content.

While some will claim that the pernicious "Director's Theater" has been dismissed, it has not. I cite three recent productions.

In 1986, in the District of Columbia—that never-never land that then still believed in "freedom fighters," "star wars," and the heroic murder of women and children in Tripoli, Shakespearean comedy must have seemed like some version of the real world.

Douglas Wager at the Arena Theater had no respect for the script of *Shrew*. He casually tossed the Induction away and brought his audience into a world located somewhere between *The Godfather* and "Miami Vice." Wager is apparently innocent of the god-awful Bogdanov version for RSC in the late 1970s that imposed the same puerile "conception" upon a hapless company. Wager's version did appeal to the person to my left, who was, after all, watching television and who laughed loudly at external nonsense. He found it very funny that Bianca should interrupt her soft-porn play with Lucentio to watch a soap-opera on the tube that Wager brought onto his insulting set. He also enjoyed Casey Briggs's conception of Petruchio as a flyweight contender with zipper at the ready.

Perhaps Wager's worst scene was the celebrated road to Padua sequence. As semis roared by, via stereo feed, Richard Bauer's Vincentio appeared, a fortyish sports car aficionado. This modernization made ravioli out of a potentially very funny scene. Randy Danson's Kate attempted to prove her superiority to Petruchio (which should have been easy!), but the badly blocked final scene had Petruchio seated. He was not permitted to demonstrate his awareness of her virtuosity. He just sat there.

It was an embarrassing production, playing to some conception of "what the audience wants." It smothered the vibrant comedy under the silliest of modern metaphors.[15]

The Stratford audience adored Bill Alexander's *Twelfth Night*. I did not. The stage was dominated by a huge white blob of a set, ostensibly the seacoast of Illyria (or, less romantically, Yugoslavia). While this concept (almost as uncomfortable for us theatergoers as was Hall's sandbox *Coriolanus* of 1985) avoided the "English manor house" approach that worked so well in the BBC-TV rendition, it introduced a host of extraneous issues that called for a guidebook instead of a program. But a program for this one was a waste of spirit and the expense of a pound.

We spectators learned that we were exploring the problems of a young and gifted and unfortunately alcoholic Belch (Roger Allam) who, from a sociological perspective, had nothing to do but bilk David Bradley's woebegone Sir Andrew. The Chekhovian pace meant that this *Twelfth Night* dragged its slow length along for three lugubrious hours. Those moments when some relaxation of rhythm might have been tolerated ("I left no ring with her. What means this lady?") were just swallowed into the digestive tract of the whale of a set.

The production seemed compelled to cue us to its meanings. After Anthony Sher's badly overplayed Malvolio exited pumped up by Maria's letter, Toby, Andrew, and Maria staggered in with mimed laughter that lasted, literally, for minutes. (Alexander has no sense of the relationship between stage time and real time). Either the Malvolio bit is funny or it is not. A silent film sequence does not compensate for what has not worked on stage. This did not—and perhaps a delighted audience of tourists, laughing for the wrong reasons, proved the point. Let Alexander direct old segments of "I Love Lucy." Monty Python is beyond his grasp.

One problem with *Twelfth Night*, of course, is that the male company has thinned by the time the director realizes that he has yet to cast Orsino. Donald Sumpter, an effectively understated Marcus amid the tumult of Deborah Warner's *Titus*, was a wizened, sensecent Duke. What could Viola see in him? He looked like a homeless trader trying to sell a few pieces of used pottery on the streets of Dubrovnik. The casting created an incomprehensible vacuum of what can be a poignant love story.

Since director Alexander could make nothing of the scene in which Feste/Sir Tophas encounters Malvolio in the madhouse (4.2), he chose to upstage the scene with venereal games played between Belch and Maria. Alexander's Feste was lost in this haphazard production, having been told, it seems, to keep out of the way of the other actors. But if Feste "must observe their mood on whom he jests," he finds no sense of humor in the incarcerated Malvolio. That the scene might depict the limits of "fooling" (as *King Lear* does, more profoundly) did not occur to Alexander.

This production "educated" its audience away from the values and complexities of the script and fulfilled the expectations of a generation of television viewers, even including a built-in laugh track. Theater was once considered an alternative to television. Not any more.[16]

Michael Kahn's 1989 *Twelfth Night,* at the Folger, "achieved a consistency of performance that cannot be bettered by any Shakespeare company I've seen this year," said Frank Rich, crediting Kahn's "unerring direction."[17] Joe Brown called the *Twelfth Night* "triumphant," and says that Kahn is "re-establishing Shakespeare's reputation as a hot playwright."[18]

Kahn's *Twelfth Night* had some very good aspects: convincing identical twins in Kelly McGillis and Mark Philpot, both charmingly winsome, splendid ensemble work between David Sabin's Toby, Franchelle Steward-Dorn's Maria, and Floyd King's wonderfully vague Andrew, already sliding away from the life he glimpsed when he was "ador'd," and a fine *tour de force* by Yusef Bulos's Feste in the excellent prison scene (4.2).

The problem here was Kahn's fatal attraction to the "bright idea." Provincial District of Columbia may believe that Raj India sparkles with originality, but those of us who saw RSC's *Much Ado* flounder against an identical concept over a decade ago know otherwise. Here, Malvolio was a cleric, not a steward, leading his ladies in Hymn 542 ("Jesus Shall Reign": Duke Street). Why did everyone call this obvious curate a "steward"? Yusef Bulos's Chaplinesque Feste was a skillful stage tactician, but he couldn't sing. The "Indian" settings for his songs were part of the problem. "O, Mistress Mine" did not translate, and the Final Song was excruciating. It can, given its late seventeenth-century setting, create a powerful and conclusive bridge from Globe to "real world."

The bright idea blacked out, however, with Peter Webster's Orsino, whom even Rich called "fatuously romantic."[19] What could this vibrant young woman see in this idiotic rajah, except his money? Not a damned thing. Now had Malvolio been an ambitious native, tricked into believing that Olivia loved him, the play might have made a point about the viciousness of colonialism. I do not believe, though, that Washington is ready for much more than the basic sappiness of Kahn's conception and rendition.

I believe that we watch any production filled with our own perhaps unperceived "subtext" and that that energy participates in the dictation of our "conscious" response to the production. I saw the film *Mash* twice. When I watched it the first time, with a civilian friend, it was very funny. When I saw it again with a wounded Vietnam veteran and felt *him* responding, I found it very *un*funny.

Peter Coe's *Othello* (New York City, 1982) did not produce *any* energy field for me. In this instance I could not indict the "bright idea."

Many aspects of the production were excellent. The Winter Garden itself is a magnificent space, filled many years ago by the voice of the great Al Jolson. The set was created by filmy curtains that swirled as scenes changed, like clouds melting and reshaping in time-exposure film. On the flat behind these images of transition, the blue of the Mediterranean sky and the ominous bloom of sunset showed time passing swiftly into Othello's night of error. I had minor objections: Brabantio's palace overlooked a bistro and was therefore inappropriately located in Venice's red-light district. The final scene was badly staged. Desdemona's bed, downstage center, forced the actors on the increasingly crowded stage into increasingly awkward blocking. Basically, however, the sweep and rhythm of spectacle filled the large stage and projected a Shakespearean grandeur to the audience. Director Peter Coe employed an effective "freeze frame" for Iago's asides, allowing Christopher Plummer alone to talk and move, and showing us that Iago controls the sequences in which the other characters are trapped.

The lines were beautifully read—the actors ringing each syllable from the tongue to the ear of the spectator. In an age when song lyrics are merely part of the noise made by "recording artists" and when that pernicious tendency is reflected all too often in performance, I enjoyed hearing the language again. I was startled when James Earl Jones "clarified" the "Indian/Judean" crux in Othello's final speech by telling us that the Moor perceives himself to be "like the base Judas." That reading destroys the rhythm, and it was a surprising imposition in a production that kept reasonable faith with the inherited text.

While I have some minor objections, then, one might ask why I found the production curious. Is it not enough that Shakespeare be well-mounted and that the language be clearly articulated? No.

Jones brought no subtext to his conception of Othello. We heard the words. We could not know what they meant to Othello. Jones stepped into the clearing air above Cyprus, clad in a splendid suit of ceremonial armor, but his spectacular moment was hollow. Jones gave Othello's great speech no sense of the tragic shadow gathering beneath the Olympian music. Here is the play's climax: the tragic hero rides his rhetoric to a height that insists upon a psychic law of gravity. We watched and listened, but the fatal posture of man insisting on his own platonic conception of himself, the dark power behind the magnificent facade simply was not expressed.

Given Jones's externalized Othello, Plummer was left to caper about like a character in a situation comedy. While Iago is self-amused, and chillingly amusing to us, as we are dragged into his scheme via his soliloquies, Iago is also evil. But not Plummer's Iago.

We received, then, an *Othello* that nicely reflected its *commedia dell'arte* origins and that looked ahead to plays like *A Trick to Catch the Old One* and *The Country Wife*. But this production did not explore the issues of Shakespeare's play—misdirected passions, sexual jealousy, the murder of an innocent, and the mystery of human iniquity. We received something akin to what Rymer called *Othello* some three hundred years ago—"a bloody farce." Jones tossed Othello's great final speech away, as if his Moor were simply exhausted.

Yet, on the Sunday afternoon I attended, the production received a standing ovation. Why? Broadway has had little Shakespeare in the past thirty years, and only Richard Burton's 1964 *Hamlet* could be called a great production. Joseph Papp, while popularizing Shakespeare in Central Park, has tended to play to the groundlings. Jones's Othello might have worked on television, which would probably erase whatever subtext *was* there. Television, at best, is a verbal medium. As I glanced at my program, I noticed that this *Othello* was produced "in association with CBS Video Enterprises." Thus, we got an *Othello* scaled down to the diminished expectations of television, where real emotion would be disturbingly out of place. This audience remained blessedly undisturbed. We got no evil, no tragedy, no catharsis. We got a diverting way to fill the space between brunch and dinner. And, as New York City goes, I suppose that thirty dollars a ticket becomes a cheap way to fill out that gap of time.

These productions suggest, obviously, that their directors know their audience—it expects to see television when it comes to the theater. When such an expectation is met, theater dies, even as the box office thrives.

The line between "fallacy" and the "possible" interpretation that the script offers can be drawn between three recent productions of *Hamlet*. In the 1988 Ingmar Bergman production, Fortinbras had Horatio killed at the end. Such a decision may reflect some Swedish antipathy toward Norway, but it deviated from even possibility and represented, for me, an imposition as unwarranted as the Polanski *Macbeth* ending.[20] In Ragnar Lyth's 1984 film, also from Sweden, Horatio attempts to read Hamlet's justification from the documents that Hamlet had brought back from his sea adventure. The documents crumble in his hands as the simpering dowagers of Claudius's court turn to bestow their flabby favors upon Fortinbras. Horatio is ignored. That rhythm captures the Gertrude of this production perfectly—she had bought into power and had concerned herself only with what maintained her position as queen, even if that position depended upon a weak and queasy Claudius. It is an ending that reilluminates Lyth's interpretation of the script. At the end of the 1985 RSC production, Fortinbras suddenly remembered that he *was* King. He held his arms above him and insisted that all the survivors of the throne room massacre abase themselves around his phallic centrality. Like that of the Lyth production, the RSC ending did not seem imposed, but appropriate, even if extratextual. It is precisely through such extratextuality that we learn what the script may be saying. I do not believe that it suggests that Horatio adds to the feast being prepared in death's eternal cell.

Another example of the imposed directorial vision, and of its possible advantages and probably greater disadvantages, was Liviu Ciulei's extravagantly praised *Hamlet*,[21] at the Arena Theater in Washington in 1978. In an effort to bring the play forward in time for a modern audience, Ciulei set *Hamlet* in Bismarckian Germany. Such a placement struck me as far less appropriate than Jonathan Miller's Victorian mounting of the Olivier-Plowright *Merchant of Venice*. The conflict between old money and the alien entrepreneur emerged in Miller's version, assisted by performances that overcame the potential straitjacketing of the script into a post-Shakespearean setting. Miller's setting provided Christian piety with a visual irony that worked very well for me, partly, I admit, because of my view of Portia, more negative than what I take to be the consensus. While watching the Arena production, I kept asking why these suave politicians and militarists were crossing themselves all the time. Since much of the religious activity was not for public consumption, I could not rationalize it into the uses that Henry V may find for "God"—which seems at times to be Machiavelli's pious facade or Marx's "opiate of the masses." I

finally ascribed such activity in this setting to a compulsive effort
to stave off rampant Darwinism. The anachronistic clash between
directorial vision and the premises of the text, at times overtly
Catholic, created a schizoid effect, as the imposed vision often
does in production. *Hamlet* poses problems enough for the director. Too often, his "solution" makes of the script a forlorn subtext
struggling to be recognized but smothering beneath the imposed
format. The first half of the graveyard scene was cut from the
Arena production (although Polonius-Renaldo remained intact!),
apparently because Elizabethan burial practices—or malprac-
tices—could not translate into the late Nineteenth Century. The
rest of the scene translated poorly, too, and the vexed question of
Ophelia's death was left to confuse the spectator, robbed as he or
she was of the insight that, as the gravediggers "make clear,"
Ophelia's death confuses the world of the play as well.

But this production's concept of "fatherland" gave the Ghost's
injunctions a Prussian pointedness. And the Players emerged for
"Gonzago" in Elizabethan costumes, their contrast with the attire
of the courtly audience creating the most effective visualization of
the play scene I have ever experienced. A sense of depth—an
audience watching another audience watching a play—was brilliantly achieved.

A similar effect is achieved through very different means in the
BBC-TV version of *Hamlet,* as described by director Rodney Bennett. "We wanted it like Rembrandt . . . the figures lit, the background mysterious. Then I had the idea, with the players, of
reversing the usual process, so the only time we have scenery is in
the theatre and then we make it look real, three-dimensional, like
the Italian renaissance theatre. So we built a little renaissance
theatre with a street scene. The scenery for the main play looks
unreal, the architecture for the theatre looks real."[22]

Ophelia's madness in the Ciulei production broke out amid the
decorous setting of a state dinner party, perhaps a borrowing
from *Macbeth.* Many of Claudius's and Gertrude's lines were
voiced over Ophelia's songs. Thus the scene neatly avoided the
pauses for songs that can be painful for an audience while at the
same time dramatizing the awkwardness of characters trying to
deal with such an extreme breach of etiquette. I felt, however, that
the director, however inventive here, created his own version of
broken ritual within a text that provides its own better examples.
The play's concern with Christian ritual and with the ultimate
question of salvation and damnation was rendered incomprehensible in this modernization.

Modernizations are not to be condemned out of hand. If the director allows his or her script to emerge from one of the play's central metaphors, a modernization may work. Director Ciulei could respond that the adventures of Fortinbras, Claudius's policies on Norway and England, and the military careers of both King Hamlet and King Claudius (who had, he claims, "serv'd against . . . the French"—4.3.82) create the Clausewitzian-Moltkean imagery of this production. Perhaps. The political and dynastic elements of the text emerged from Ciulei's conception but at the expense, I believe, of more central concerns. *Hamlet* as history play is not *Hamlet* as tragedy. Perhaps Ciulei suggests that, since tragedy seems no longer available to the modern playwright, it can no longer be apprehended by the modern audience. I would assert, however, that a modern audience can be "educated" over the course of a performance. If the production cuts the spectator off from traditional elements of the text, from a worldview, for example, that incorporates Heaven and Hell, the production confirms an unfortunate divorce between the spectator and his or her cultural heritage. Even today, Shakespeare allows us to feel a cosmos very different from our own. Good production can recreate that world for us—without ignoring more "modern" meanings.

A modern *Hamlet* that worked—for me—was Gielgud's controversial version, starring Richard Burton. The play was produced in rehearsal clothes, an amply endowed Gertrude luxuriating in a cashmere sweater, Hume Cronyn's Polonius natty in a hand-tailored vested suit accented by an obviously brand-new and expensive cravat. The actor, facing the end of his career, the role of Hamlet never having been his, tries to exude confidence and success but denies both in the effort. The apparel proclaims the man, but not as he wishes it to. And, of course, the failing counselor, no longer sniffing the trail of policy with the sure scent of younger years, strives to regain what will never be his again. Modern dress suggested the oedipal possibilities embodied in Gertrude and captured the career of Polonius—but what of the play that tells us that *it* is the thing? Did not rehearsal clothes call attention away from Renaissance Denmark or England? No doubt they did.[23]

But the use of a theatrical metaphor as a key to costuming did not represent so much an imposition upon the text as a visualization of one of its prime metaphors. From Hamlet's disquisition on the so-called tragic flaw and his scorn of "actions that a man might play" to the coming of the Players, the delivery of the Pyrrhus audition piece, Hamlet's plan for "guilty creatures sitting at a play," the internal performance of a portion of "Gonzago," Hamlet's wild wish for a share in a cry of players, and his confusion of the "comedy" he claims to have presented with the tragedy he has made inevitable by interrupting "Gonzago," *Hamlet* resonates with variations of the theatrical theme.[24] To see *Hamlet* as occurring within and emerging from a literal theater as opposed to some version of Elsinore or England, was to bring the script into contact with the source of much of its power. Whatever *Hamlet* may be "about," Shakespeare here, as elsewhere, employs his profound knowledge of his own craft to pose questions about the problematical nature of reality.

The decision for rehearsal clothes may have called attention to itself at first. I found it gradually dropping away from my focus— as did the more obtrusive Victorianism of Miller's *Merchant of Venice*—so that I could concentrate on performance. I do not recall that, in 1964, a rehearsal of *Hamlet* blocked my response to the play's exploration of the ultimate issues of its world. "Rehearsal" surrendered gradually to a more profound imitation of action. Perhaps the best thing that can be said for Miller's and Gielgud's conceptions is that they allowed performance to emerge. Of course, it helps to have Olivier in the cast. And Burton brought an ineffable sadness to the Hamlet of act 5, uttering homilies about the fall of sparrows from a heart hollowed out by an existential awareness that undercut the spoken words. The irony of Burton's Hamlet, the poise between continuing hope and undermining nihilism, the balancing of the opposites that have created such wildly diverse opinions among critics of the Hamlet of act 5, made this a Hamlet that others—Paul Scofield, Alan Bates, David Warner, Nicol Williamson, Albert Finney, superb as many of them were—have not come close to touching.

Of course, it depends upon who Hamlet is to you. When asked what *Hamlet* was about, the Canadian actor, Richard Monette, said, "It's about *me!*" echoing Coleridge, who confessed to having a "smack of Hamlet" in himself. For me, the brilliant failure Richard Burton, drawing on the vivid subtext of his own disaster, gave the brilliant failure Hamlet a depth and resonance not likely to be duplicated. But those who do not see Hamlet as a failure— and they are the "consensus"— will accuse me (validly) of surrendering to the vice of imposition. My only defense is that I am aware of such subjectivity, and that I believe that Shakespeare intended that his play evoke individual response. Burbage and Shakespeare would, I think, have said of *Hamlet*, "It's about me!"

Perhaps one of the reasons why Shakespeare made Hamlet an explicit thirty was to account for the thirty-four year old actor playing the part. The original audience must have savored Burbage-Hamlet's response to the Gravedigger's precise chronology. If Bradley Pearson, the eccentric protagonist of Iris Murdoch's *The Black Prince*, is correct, then "Shakespeare [in *Hamlet*] makes the crisis of his own identity into the very central stuff of his art."[25] If so, the art of *Hamlet* is designed to capture the ongoing crises of our own ongoing identities. So successful is Shakespeare in transmuting what was intensely personal into a dramatic dialectic that interrogates its spectator profoundly that very little of what is said of the play and its chief character is ever completely false, and nothing that is said about *Hamlet* or Hamlet is every completely true. But so deep is the working of play and character upon us that we must say something.

One recent modernization of *Hamlet* that I found effective was Ron Daniels's production at Stratford, England, in 1989. Daniels's was actually an anachronistic concept combining two times—a time when armor was a regulation item of military equipment and a time between the two world wars. This approach was appropriate to a script that blends Norse mythology with the language and culture of High Renaissance Europe. This production redefined the script and then presented it in a version that forced us to redefine it for ourselves. It was a vivid and exciting experience.

The interior of Elsinore was in the 1930s. The full effects of the Crash had yet to be felt, in fact were ignored as Claudius ushered in a new era of peace and happy days. However, a huge window slanted downward, as if looking out from the first class salon of the Lusitania, and revealed a boiling green sea of troubles beyond. The Ghost was in armor, as were the guards on the great ramps that pistoned up and down on the front of the stage. Fortinbras and his soldiers also wore armor. The complacent inner world was being invaded by the past. Prince Hamlet was ambassador to the future. Finally, of course, the past, represented by Fortinbras, would enter a room become a battlefield and take over. The specters of outmoded systems flooded over the parapets because no new value had been introduced to an Elsinore therefore rendered defenseless. It was Hamlet's tragedy that he could not bring a new and human order to his world.

The pace, wit, and intelligence of this production were irresistible. Among many good things were the fact that Claudius seemed to break a promise to let Hamlet return to Wittenberg, Hamlet having made good on his deal to appear at the coronation as crown prince; Patrick Godfrey's stiff Polonius, Claudius's man and chief factor in Claudius's elevation and a father who forced his children to seek an affection that bordered on incest; Claire Higgins's Gertrude, a foreign princess who has spent much more time with Young Hamlet than with old, again with a tremor of incest apparent; the Players who had been banished to the provinces, it seemed, for producing a subversive play, and who would soon be interrupted for producing, unconsciously, another one; the anger of the Players at Hamlet's advice to them; and Horatio's anger at Hamlet when the latter interrupted "Gonzago." It was, as Mark Rylance (Hamlet) explained to me, "as if Ron Daniels had come down from the stalls during a performance to tell us what we should be doing." But while Hamlet could not sit still for his production, neither could Claudius. At first offended for Gertrude's sake, Peter Wight finally rushed toward the Player King, recoiled in horror, and fled the room. He had seen his own brother. The recognition was achieved by the doubling of Ghost and Player (Russell Enoch). The profound moment within which "Gonzago" collapsed back into the outer fiction of *Hamlet* made "the invisible become real" for inner and outer audiences. We shared simultaneously Hamlet's fatal impatience with mimesis, Claudius's terrifying shock of recognition, and even the Player's annoyance at having his space so impertinently invaded by both prince and king.

Within this richly subtextual production, Hamlet was superb. Daniels, clearly, trusted Mark Rylance's inventiveness but just as clearly trusted himself to keep Rylance from producing a *tour de force* that would have erased a frame of intentions larger than that of the title character. This Hamlet was a young man in whom his father had been disappointed *before* the latter's death. The Ghost and Hamlet touched each other in 1.5, with Hamlet, in effect, promising to make it up to his father. Hamlet wore striped pajamas throughout much of the production, beginning with "To be," which was given its early Q1 placement. Denmark was "a prison," an institution in which Hamlet could retain sanity only in anticness. To play Elsinore's game was to be really insane (cf. R. D. Laing). Michael Billington, the *Guardian* critic, told me that he found Rylance's Hamlet "unequivocally mad" and that his madness "animated long stretches of the play." The problem, Billington felt, was that Hamlet's soliloquies, in which he "reflects upon his moral dilemma were inconsistent with his madness."

The same Hamlet, clearly, can evoke different responses. I found Hamlet adopting a quite conscious antic disposition. When he mooned Polonius he knew to whom he was offering his ass to kiss. He used his position as protection for behavior he knew was outrageous. The soliloquies were an escape to a rational faculty he could not exercise in Elsinore. He began his first soliloquy with his back to the audience and maintained his position for eight lines, until "But two months dead!" He made us aware of him, pulled us in, and permitted us to become the listeners he could not find within the script. We, "but mutes or audience to this act," could do no more for him, however, up there on the stage than he could do for himself in his perceived Elsinore. As Michael Pennington, who played Hamlet for John Barton in 1980, says, "Hamlet's purest and most distinctive encounters [are] those with his audience. These form the character's most confidential relationship; and in practice it meant preparing to meet the audience on terms as open and mutual as possible."[26]

Rylance found his "inner friend" not in Horatio, who was by turns puzzled or upset by Hamlet's bizarre behavior, but in Yorick. "Antic" is also a death's-head. Yorick whispered the joke about being "chopfallen" to Hamlet, listening with the skull at his ear like a seashell. Hamlet repeated it with a chuckle. He carried the skull from graveyard to throne room, placed it on a shelf, then paused to turn it so that it could watch the duel. Never have I seen a prop so superbly energized. Yorick became, then, one of the play's few survivors, casting his bony gaze across the graveyard of Elsinore as ghosts rose to claim it.[27]

III

Harry Berger in "Text Against Performance" suggests that Shakespeare's own "textual antitheatrical" tendency argues "against the stage centered approach."[28] It is certainly true, as Berger says, that the "time bound sequence of performance must be respected and the reader's page-flipping freedom disallowed as a mode that falsifies theatrical experience."[29] It is *not* true, however, that the page "gives us a control over meaning which performance in the theatrical space and time denies us."

Immediately, before Berger moves into his argument, problems appear. His example of "anti-theatricalism which targets specific conventions of the theatrical traditions Shakespeare inherited" is, via Sheldon Zitner, the Aumerle subplot in *Richard II*, which shows Shakespeare's "disaffection from the mode of historical tragedy."[30] Berger quotes Alvin Kernan on "the reduction of the morality-play conventions, and their inability to reveal the full human truth."[31] No doubt the silly and over-written Aumerle subplot does parody an inherited version of dramatized history. The parody, however, works *within* the drama to suggest the more complex and ambiguous mode in which Shakespeare is working, one in which history is hardly allegory.[32] The subplot is to *Richard II* as "Pyramus and Thisbe" is to *A Midsummer Night's Dream*, and is, in another way, to the romantic tragedy, *Romeo and Juliet*. Generic contrast serves overall dramatic design and cannot be adduced as "antitheatrical" per se. In *Dream*, indeed, Shakespeare explicates the nature of his dramaturgy by having Quince and company so radically misunderstand it. Even Bolingbroke reconcizes what Shakespeare is doing in *Richard II*. He will recognize at the end that he has been a player: "All my reign hath been but as a scene / Acting that argument" (4.5.197–98). At the beginning of his reign—as he confronts Aumerle, the Duchess, and York—he says, "Our scene is alter'd from a serious thing, / And now chang'd to 'The Beggar and the King' " (5.3.79–80). Bolingbroke likens the scene to melodrama, in this case raising issues to be resolved by the dictates of politics. But Bolingbroke's policies will not erase the problem of which Aumerle is only one manifestation. Even as parody, the inner play tells us what the outer play is all about and tells us further that the issues raised in the outer play have no solution. They are genre-less.

The "inner play" sets "the word itself against the word" (5.3.122) as does Richard in his soliloquy (5.5.1–66) and reiterates the outer play's pattern of a family divided against itself (cf. Carlisle: 4.1.145–46). Bolingbroke may "win [Aumerle's] after-love" (5.3.35), but Bolingbroke will not solder up the deeper divisions that Aumerle represents. Shakespeare's alleged "anti-theatricality" serves theater here and not some page flipper. Shakespeare's audience was being educated about many things, including even outmoded theatrical conventions, *by* theater.

No need exists in theater for anyone to "jump from his seat, cry 'cut,' and ask the players to do that take again two or three times, and then shriek out 'Aha!' "[33] In fact, the play Mr. Berger adduces as his antitheatrical example demands the pressure of an ongoing theatrical experience. To test that thesis, have an intelligent person read the first scene of *Richard II* and explain what it means. He or she will be baffled. The second scene explains the first. It is then that we say "Aha!" and all the page flipping in the world would not have helped us. If we are reading, we can then flip back to 1.1. In the theater, however, we recognize that Shakespeare has given us a private scene in which people speak the truth. The truth is that the opening scene has been a cover-up devised by the improvisational politics of a desperate king. In the theater we will be eager to find out what happens next, and we will learn that the event that triggered the first scene—the murder of Gloucester—has yet to explore its ramifications in the world of the play. The "public" versus "private" rhythm is characteristic of some of Shakespeare's first acts (in *Hamlet* and *Lear*, for example) and, in the Second Henriad, of a vision of history that reveals "the truth" only as an action discovers its consequences, which are negative in these plays. At the end of *Richard II*, Bolingbroke assigns to Exton the guilt he had assigned to Gloucester's murderer—the mark of Cain (1.1.104 and 5.6.43). We know, however, as does Bolingbroke, who the guilty man is.[34]

The Aumerle subplot may be a parody of the theatrical tradition that Shakespeare inherited. Berger, however, sees the Aumerle sequence as typical of Shakespeare in performance. For Berger, "plays as proclamations of Morality" are challenged only "by the legislative authority of the parliament of readers."[35] Performance, for Berger, ritually reinscribes what Montrose calls "the dominant social institutions and cultural forms" of Shakespeare's and, it seems, our times.[36] Drama *can* do that, of course, as Olivier proved with his *Henry V.* Berger goes on to make a point that seems confusing on the surface. "The image of the community," he says, "is clearly inscribed and developed only in the text; it is blurred and subordinated by the conditions of performance."[37] What Berger means by "community" is not the imagery and imposed allegory of a particular power elite, but "a group of speakers placed in relation to each other by differences of gender and generation, of social rank and political stations, and of position in households, families, and extended families."[38] So community is what is created and lives partly because of and partly in spite of the dominant institutions and forms. What the reading text, provides, then, is "a conflict within the poetry, between the individual character's struggle to appropriate the common rhetoric and make it mean what he says, and its resistance to that effort, its ability to make him say what it means."[39] What *it* means is also what dominant institutions and forms would say it means. And those are the meanings, it seems, that performance imposes upon us.

Berger suggests, then, that reading is the only subversive activity, the only means of discerning what lies beneath the ostensible allegory that the play-in-performance invariably depicts. Certainly performance *can* allegorize, *can* reinforce a perceived consensus, as in the instance of the BBC *Henry V*. A Henry we *must* like may be the product of an establishment BBC and of the multinational nature of its American sponsorship, Exxon and Morgan Guarantee.[40] But even such a "standard" version must depict precisely the values and structures that Berger claims can be distinguished only in reading the text. Here even a bland performer makes his point, since one of the things that David Gwillim does well as an actor is to mimic aristocratic behavior.

A performance of *Coriolanus* at the National Theatre in London in August of 1987 made the point that Berger claims exclusively for reading. Certainly the script balances on the seesaw of aristocratic arrogance and effective leadership. It is an issue that troubles those of us who must suffer the ineffectuality *and* arrogance of our administrative incompetents. Peter Hall, in an apparent birding of the Arts Council, impounded civilians to serve as onstage crowds, witnesses to the turmoil swirling around the streets and alleyways of old Rome. On the night I attended, an American family had been recruited for front row, stage left: a father in a blue business suit with red tie, a mother just unwrapped from Laura Ashley, and two early-teen daughters clad in the expensive raffishness that bespeaks Larchmont or Darien. The Tribunes really got to Daddy. They were spewing subversive stuff! Daddy was *not* acting. This was the last place in the world where he would have assembled his clan, much less permitted them to return after the interval! They had come to see London, perhaps even to glimpse a harmless Hyde Park as an example of the democratic ideal, but primarily for Harrod's and that version of Liberty found on Bond Street. It was fun to watch Daddy's discomfort, Mumsie's stupification, and the enjoyment of the girls as a transitory chord of adolescent subversiveness was strummed by the production.

This performance, quite by accident in one sense but by design in another, produced precisely the "exposure" of community that Berger claims can only occur via the act of reading.

Performance can also explore intentionally the issues that Berger claims only reading can discover. Some of the issues that Berger explores in *Macbeth* had already been produced. Berger defines a male world terribly afraid of feminine power, afraid of becoming, as Madelon Gohlke says, "the plaything of powerful feminine forces."[41] The script, of course, shows that it is the subversion of "the feminine" (what Jung calls the "anima") in

Macbeth that results in the loss of true masculine power. He exchanges a "nature . . . full of the milk of human kindness" (1.5.18) for a "mind . . . full of scorpions" (3.2.36). That transaction makes the external feminine become a threat indeed, as does Macbeth's own androgyny, which can confront him only from the stance of "horrible shadow[s]" (3.4.106) and "terrible dreams" (3.2.18).[42]

Berger's second and secondary point about *Macbeth* is that betrayal is hardly the exclusive property of the Macbeths: "The 'good' Scots are complicit both in the murder itself and in the subsequent acts of violence by which Macbeth maintains his shaky hold on the throne. . . . Banquo contributes to the betrayal by carefully keeping the prophecy secret."[43]

Berger's points are made and reiterated in Polanski's film of 1970, although Berger chooses to ignore the film for obvious reasons. Berger's thesis coalesces in Polanski's ending, in which Donalbain limps through a highland storm toward the foul coven of the Weird Sisters to enlist their terrifying but very powerful feminine resources for his own act of betrayal. Berger's insights could work themselves out within a more successful production. Not all of the flaws of the Polanski version were the function of directorial insight into the script, but the film, if limited to Berger's thesis, as it tended to be, was for me a diminution of the possibilities of the script. I thought the acting was terrible, but there is one of those old-fashioned and unfashionable criteria creeping in!

Performance, Berger claims, "diverts us with perceptible embodiments that conceal their true nature by their very form and existence as embodiments."[44] Thus Berger, like Levin, emerges from a sense of Ur-performance or Ur-text—a platonic context which must condemn any manifestation as imperfect. But productions do not strive to be "perfect" or "definitive"—they freely admit that they are partial and transitory manifestations of an ongoing energy known as a script. The script is not sitting there in its perfection. It is awaiting a new interpretation, one that may be assisted by the act of reading but which must emerge in production, which, in turn, can be enhanced by reading. The conflicts that emerge confusingly in *Richard II*, for example, for characters and spectators, can be grasped with some clarity if one understands the concept of "the king's two bodies." The grasping of that concept can occur before or after a performance of *Richard II*, but the act of reading is subordinate to the action of the spectator.

A film is less a mimesis than a stage production, but it does not necessarily follow that a film must be a "naturalistic" rendition of a Shakespeare script. As I shall argue, television has little choice but to reproduce a "naturalistic" or "realistic" version of a script. It was Polanski's choice to suppress the Christian content of *Macbeth* in his film. Berger claims that the play's "Christian ideology of restoration . . . conceal[s] the ongoing dialectic of gender conflict and role reversal."[45] Why? While I do not believe that *Macbeth* reflects a Manichaean universe, no reason exists for a production not to emphasize the subversion of "the good," in the two principal characters, indeed the strong hints of their damnation. Even Macbeth, as he contemplates his murders, must express them within the frame of an inherited dispensation: "Hear it not, Duncan, for it is a knell / That summons thee to heaven, or to hell" (2.1.62–63). "Banquo, thy soul's flight, / If it find heaven, must find it out tonight" (3.1.141–42). These scene-ending couplets are indisputably in the *text*. While they certainly reflect "Christian ideology," they are nicely undercut by their speaker and the deeds he contemplates. His own ultimate destination is clear to him (cf. 3.1.64–69). I feel that Polanski might have made more of the play's ostensible "Christian world picture." As good as the purely filmic aspects may be, I feel that Polanski pulled the narrative down to a literal level that lost suggestiveness in its search for sheer violence. What would Polanski have done with the syncretic *Titus Andronicus?* Trevor Nunn's television version of *Macbeth* had liturgical music behind Macbeth as he simultaneously passed the loving cup and questioned the Murderer. Nunn's was admittedly a "ceremonial" version of the script, but by the time of the Banquet Scene, Nunn was playing ceremonial aspects against Macbeth's loss of the positive aspects of nature and supernature. Ian McKellen and Judi Dench brilliantly charted the fears that Berger claims must be erased by the play's overt allegory. I am suggesting, of course, that Berger's thesis can find its way powerfully into production.

Berger quotes Stephen Greenblatt, who says that "one of the highest achievements of power is to impose fictions on the world, and one of its supreme pleasures is to enforce the acceptance of fictions known to be fictions."[46] In theater, Berger suggests, we become "more fully complicit in our submission" to fiction (to simplistic allegory) than we do, I assume, when we can stop, go back, and reread.[47] But this is to ignore the ways in which performance can force us to respond on more than one level—that is, to see beyond the simple one to one equations of allegory—and, crucially, to *evaluate* our response in the after-moments that are part of the experience of going-to-theater. Berger may or may not have seen Alan Howard's Henry V for RSC in the mid-1970s. Howard shared with his audience his own enjoyment of his imposition of fictions upon his "community." He could not, of course, share that level of insight, the simultaneous making of fiction and evaluation of it, with his onstage audience. *They* accepted the allegory. *We* were given a stance from which to see it as allegory. The onstage audience took mimesis for "reality." Howard's performance and Terry Hand's direction gave the theater audience precisely the "examined text" that Berger claims can emerge only from reading. Admittedly, it was Hand's and Howard's version of the text, but so is the reading of any single reader. The latter can hardly claim definitiveness for his reading, no matter how many pages he flips. Certainly a careful reading and a lot of questioning precede any modern performance, and that process should help in achieving the goal that William Worthen enunciates: "to displace the enervating polarization of 'criticism against performance.' "[48] I reassert, however, that criticism that does not help us understand the text as play—that is, as script—is irrelevant, or relevant only to the careers of its practitioners.

The book that emerges from Berger's explorations as I complete my own modifies his sense of a master narrative resulting from the fusion of all the possibilities that "decelerating and reaccelerating reading"[49] permit in theory for what Berger calls "complex acts of imaginary audition."[50] In his book, Berger graciously acknowledges "the simplistic and tendentious privileging of reading over audition,"[51] and his failure to observe "an important distinction between the psychological constraints that playgoing imposes on interpretation and the theatrical circumstances (the 'structure of theatrical relationships') that reading must attend to. Reading can ignore the constraints while attending to the circumstances."[52] If Berger is correct to assert that "Those who operate the theatrical model do not seem aware of the literary model,"[53] my book is an effort to place separate awarenesses into useful juxtaposition. Berger's modification grants him more flexibility than Barbara Hodgdon attributed to him when she said that "the critical reading seeks to stabilize the text."[54] The performance, Hodgdon says, "acknowledges, in its every aspect, its ephemeral nature. Such an acknowledgement is truer to history—both critical history and performance history—than attempting to create a text that will not be disturbed by time. For disturbance—one might also call it transformation—is just what Shakespeare's texts are all about."[55]

Hodgdon anticipates and, of course, helps to formulate Berger's new synthesis.

The words on the page wait in their print for the interception of critical ingenuity and imagination. Performance, however, is an act of ingenuity and imagination demanding the fulfillment of a spectator and an audience. Both critic and director are free to engage in the activity described by Nina Auerbach to find "cultural patterns that [give] new contexts, letting . . . texts tell new stories,"[56] but "imaginary auditions" cannot provide anything definitive in production. Too many decisions in actual production lead to further decisions, so that by the time of, for example, the graveyard scene in *Hamlet*, we encounter choices that are stylistically consistent with their productions but irreconcilable with the choices made in other productions. In other words, one unstated corollary of Berger's earlier thesis—that we could splice together the best moments of a variety of productions and achieve a master production—will not work. In an "imaginary audition" we must be permitted to select, recognizing that our selection *excludes* other possibilities, as any production must. It is at the point where imagination encounters the script *as* script that the first and enabling decision is made.

In the Lyth *Hamlet*, the Gravedigger (Aaje Fridell) thinks he should know who Hamlet is but can't quite come up with the name. This Gravedigger is offended by Hamlet's antics with the skull. The puppet-skull dances in a puddle as Hamlet sings "Julius Caesar, dead and turned to clay." Branagh holds the skull aloft as he speaks of Caesar, an ironic elevation for what becomes Hamlet's apostrophe. In the Lyth, Horatio obviously cares for Hamlet and would spare him as Ophelia's maimed rites approach via a two-wheeled cart. Horatio knows whose funeral is slogging down the muddy hillside but can only watch helplessly as Hamlet learns. Julian Curry, McKellen's Horatio, is offended by Hamlet's preoccupation with death and its artifacts. McKellen, recognizing Horatio's discomfort, shoves the skull in Horatio's face on "look'd i' th' earth," causing the latter to jump back. Plummer's Gravedigger (Ray Kinear) shows us that digging a grave is hard work, as opposed to that done by the Gravedigger of whom Partridge complains. Kinear manages to hit Hamlet with a shovelful of dirt. Schell's Gravedigger (Paul Verhoevan) affects anger at Yorick's pouring a flagon of Rhenish on his head. The Gravedigger's ploy neatly motivates Hamlet's laughter. The Kozintsev Gravedigger (Vidal Kolpakov) finds Yorick's fool's cap in the dirt and gives its bells a jingle as he sets it aside. Jacobi's Hamlet, unhappy at being outwitted by the Gravedigger, glaces to a distant Horatio for help. Chamberlain repeats Olivier's gesture—as if applying facecream—on "let her paint an inch thick." Smokhtunovski repeats—unknowingly—as he stares at the skull the earlier posture of Gertrude, primping in a mirror as she says "All that lives must die." The skull sends back the ultimately antinarcissistic image. Burton points at the Gravedigger (George Rose) on "whose flashes of merriment . . ." as if to say, "We share the same memory of Yorick." Burton reminds us that the speech is not the soliloquy that film and television tend to make of it.* Williamson, for example, looks at the skull in a tight two-shot, having accepted it from a dying Roger Livesay as Gravedigger. Horatio (Gordon Jackson) is apostrophized, but not included in the frame. John Gielgud delivers an elegant lecture to the skull, as if scolding it. His Hamlet is decorously detached from the experience of Yorick and of the death for which Yorick has become emissary, metonomy, and synecdoche. The Gielgud approach (1944) may show us something of the shift in acting style and in conceptions of Prince Hamlet that has occurred in the past fifty years.[57] The text is inevitably "disturbed by time."

My point, however, is the multiplicity of choices that actor and director make at every instant of production. My emphasis is not on imaginary auditions but on actual faces, bodies, and voices. We have productions whereby to observe, describe, and evaluate the choices. Obviously, we need more productions, another *Measure for Measure*, for example, to place against the excellent BBC version of a decade ago, the only extant production of that splendid and very "modern" play.

While I grant the inadequacy of cassette as a medium for Shakespeare, it is now possible to do what Berger claims cannot be done within the inexorable flow of production—to rewind, re-watch,

---

*Television can work well with speeches that are not soliloquies. In the BBC *Richard II* (1979), for example, Derek Jacobi begins his "Of comfort no man speak" upstage center of Aumerle and Carlisle, comes down between them, kneels as he says "sit upon the ground" and gives the rest of the speech in a single-shot close-up. At the end, he glances to each side to see what effect his self-pity has had on his few followers. In that the speech is intended for a passive onstage audience it is a kind of soliloquy. In this instance, television is as effective as stage. On stage, Richard's followers have to stand stiffly around as the panegyric rolls on and on. While the close-up is probably too long on television, it gives us the chance to respond to (and I think reject) Richard's self-pity.

and re-view the ways in which productions evoke, or fail to evoke, our own imaginative response. This book will provide a few examples of that process. The possibilities are manifold and increase as new productions become available and as older productions finally make it to the marketplace.

2

Kate and Consensus

I

Richard Levin continues to confront different critical approaches to Shakespeare, including the feminist analysis:

> It is hard to see how these plays [Shakespeare's tragedies] could be blaming the patriarchal society for the tragic outcome. It is even hard to see how they could be conducting an inquiry into patriarchy, when the actions they focus on are clearly meant to be atypical.
>
> This attempt to blame the catastrophes on patriarchy is illogical in another sense as well, for while it is true that they would not have occurred in a non-patriarchal society, it is also true that they would not have occurred in a society that was even *more* patriarchal than the one we are shown—a society, for instance, where Juliet and Desdemona could not be married, or Ophelia be courted, without the consent of their fathers, or where Goneril and Lady Macbeth were completely subservient to their husbands (which is just another way of saying that each tragedy could only take place in the specific "world" depicted in that play). Moreover, if patriarchy is held responsible for the unhappy endings of the tragedies, then it must be equally responsible for the happy endings of the comedies and romances, which are also brought about in patriarchal worlds. Some of the critics try to account for the happy endings by claiming that women have more active roles in these other genres, which is true (with a few notable exceptions), but that does not alter the nature of the society. In fact, in their final scenes all these "strong" heroines reinsert themselves into the patriarchal structure, which presides over the marriages and reconciliations. It seems evident, then, that patriarchy cannot have any necessary causal connection to misery, when it is just as capable of producing happiness.[1]

Levin's effort to reduce feminist criticism to a variation of the thematic approach he has devastated in the past is only partly persuasive. Male versus female may be "theme," but it deals with the fictive flesh and blood—and psyche—of *character*, not with thematics like appearance versus reality and reason versus passion, which often seem like the products of critical ingenuity and which are remarkably unhelpful in dealing with the plays as plays.

As Berger suggests, however, the feminist/psychological mode wedges open a "community" of relationships inherently dramatic because involving inevitable psychic misunderstanding and conflict. Productions have begun to reflect the insights made available by the feminist perspective. I will deal with the Ragnar Lyth *Hamlet* later. In 1985, Juliet Stevenson created a Cressida for RSC who was a function of "the male gaze," not the slut that Ulysses insists she is. In 1989, the Stratford RSC Hippolyta (Claire Higgins) used her silence to insist that Theseus (John Carlisle) overrule Egeus in the matter of Hermia. The line was clearer at Regent's Park in 1989, where Brigitte Kahn became enraged at Theseus (David Henry) for providing Hermia such ominous alternatives in 1.1. Thus Theseus's "What cheer, my love?" (1.1.122) responded to her anger. She was later happy and willing to be reconciled with Theseus when he countermanded Egeus. In the 1989 production at the Arena Theater in Washington, Petronia Paley's militant Hippolyta accepted Theseus only when he finally did something right and permitted Hermia to marry Lysander. Such instances of a "feminist point of view" permit the Theseus-Hippolyta plot to parallel and reinforce the comedy of Oberon and Titania and to enrich our experience of the script.*

It is unfair, then, to label the feminist viewpoint(s) as thematic, just as it would be misleading to say that this approach represents "character criticism." Feminist criticism, often using Freudian formulations, is *psychological* criticism. Many of the plays, comedies and tragedies, do shape their conflicts out of the unexamined assumptions of male characters—Baptista Minola, Egeus and Theseus, Orlando, Polonius and Laertes, King Lear, Posthumus, and Leontes, for example. In various ways they press their agendas upon Katharina, Hermia, Rosalind, Ophelia, Cordelia (and Goneril and Regan), Imogen, and Hermione. The vantage point that feminism provides permits us to see these plays, and others,

---

*On the uses of silence in Shakespeare, see Philip C. McGuire, *Speechless Dialect: Shakespeare's Open Silences* (Berkeley: University of California Press, 1985). Hippolyta's silence can create "meanings and effects that differ, sometimes profoundly, yet remain compatible with the words that Shakespeare did pen" (17).

as plays—drama crafted out of conflict between older values and the new insights that youth often claims for itself (yuppiedom being a distressing exception that tolerates no scratching at the impervious surface of its unexamined assumptions). The feminist approach helps us to evaluate our response to the psychic continuum that drama creates and can force us to sense our own shortsightedness and so to "see better." In pigeonholing feminist criticism under the thematic category, Levin denies this dynamic attitude toward the plays much of its vitality and potentiality. Who among us wishes to be an old-fashioned thematic critic?

Some feminist approaches—those too narrowly focused on patriarchy—are limited and self-defeating, as Levin points out.*

---

*Feminism can, of course, be merely a label for narrow political or merely personal agendas. Shirley Nelson Garner, for example, says that "Petruchio's stringent mode is just that used to tame hawks; it might well come from a manual on falconry. The notion behind this central metaphor of the play is that a shrewish woman is less than human, even less than a woman, so may be treated like an animal. Only the audience's acceptance of this premise allows them to feel the play as comic" ("*The Taming of the Shrew:* Inside or Outside of the Joke?" in *"Bad" Shakespeare,* ed., Maurice Charney [Cranbury, N.J.: Associated University Presses, 1988], 109). An examination of the woman-falcon equation, however, suggests that it need not be read as a degradation of Kate and of women. As Margaret Loftus Ranald suggests, "The falcon must be taught obedience to her master, but at the same time her wild and soaring nature must be preserved. This is a cardinal principle of hawk-taming. The bird must retain her hunting instinct: otherwise she is useless" ("The Manning of the Haggard: or *The Taming of the Shrew,*" Essays in Literature, 1, no. 2, (1974): 149). I would go further and suggest that Petruchio's soliloquy (4.2.191–214) represents the taming of Petruchio. In falconry he discerns his metaphor for his relationship with Kate, for the transformation he is achieving in her and in himself, and for their relationship. Indeed, it is precisely the "manual on falconry" at which Garner sneers that would make the case. In Edmund Bert's *An Approved Treatise of Hawkes and Hawking* (London Reprint, 1891) we find a sense of relationship between tamer and bird that might be reserved for the relationship between man and woman in a society that tolerated or encouraged such relationships. The book, according to Gerald Lascelles, is one of "the standard works of the seventeenth century, and embod[ies] the best hawking experience of Shakespeare's era" ("Falconry," *Shakespeare's England,* vol. 2 [1916]: 352). Bert says, for example, something that Petruchio cannot say: "I assure you in all my proceedings, from the first to the last with my Hawke, I never found it painefull, but the comforts I had of a goode conclusion fedde mee with sweete contentment and plesure" (41–42). Furthermore, as Bert says, "I could never be too frequent with my hawke, nor she with me" (22). If the falconer gives his bird this kind of attention, he says, "shee will pay you for it in her flying" (23). Bert calls his process a "loving dealing" (39). The process is similar to that conducted by Rosalind with Orlando in *As You Like It.* Here the man seems to learn at least as much as the falcon. Petruchio merely

Regardless of the world in which the characters find themselves, the failure of male and female to achieve an androgynous balance can contribute to tragic catastrophe, just as the achievement of a positive dynamic *within* a male or female character—an Orlando *or* a Katharine—can be basic to the comic ending. That balance or imbalance interacts with the cosmic givens or not-givens of the play to seem to produce a generic result—even if the genre is actually a priori. When Macbeth's "milk of human kindness" sours, he becomes the stereotypic male his wife would insist he be. If Hamlet cannot contact his "anima" (or feminine self), he must scorn himself as the worst of female stereotypes—"a very drab, a scullion," and must sneer at his own intuitions as misgivings that "would perhaps trouble a woman." While Lear comes to recognize Cordelia in 4.7, it can be argued that he reasserts control over her in 5.3 and so dooms her. I cite *Macbeth* and *Lear* since they occur in very different worlds, one in which the cosmic facts are absolute, the other in which the cosmic facts are one issue the script explores, without finding an answer. Yet the conflicts within those worlds are driven by the issue of gender, not just what exists *between* male and female, but the competing archetypes of male and female *within* the individual psyche.

Feminist critiques tend to employ the Freudian model. Jung, of course, posits a deeper, inclusive metaphor in which stereotypes lose themselves in the fusion of humanity. Some feminist critics commit the "gender fallacy," as Levin rightly demonstrates. The argument often merely involves the substitution of one stereotypic attitude for another. The feminist viewpoint should not be threatened by a theory that suggests that the ultimate reaches of the psyche are genderless, or, to put it another way, that permits

---

utters a commonplace of falconry when he says, "Another way I have to man my haggard, / To make her come and know my keeper's call . . . ." (4.2.196–97). The echo of George Turbervile is exact: "to knowe the call of hir keeper" (*The Booke of Faulconrie of Hauking* [Amsterdam: Theatrum Orbis Terrarum Reprint, 1969], 146). The emphasis on a singular voice suggests the uniqueness of the relationship. "Call," of course, can glance at emotional pull, an attraction toward a specific person. The rigor of Petruchio's "taming," suggested in his use of the word "haggard," might be explained by Bert's statement that a haggard "hath lived long at liberty, having many things at her command, and she is therefore the harder to be brought to subjection and obedience" (3). The feminist, of course, would respond by saying that falconry is observed from the male point of view and practiced for male benefit. I stress the affection and reciprocity in the transaction. I owe many of these insights to research done by Jill Seymour for an honors project at Bowdoin College in the spring of 1990.

each individual to participate positively in the energy of the orientation which is only stereotypically an opposite.

While it is true, as Levin says, that at the end of the comedies, heroines tend to rejoin the established society—there being little, if any, alternative—it is *not* true that it is patriarchy that "produc[es] happiness." (Levin's prose here slips from refutation to conclusion with artful ease!) The "new society" that opens out at the end of comedy is sometimes partly attributable to the woman's rebellion against her father's choice of husband (Hermia) or her father's manipulation of the marriage market (Katharina). Rosalind educates Orlando out of his silly Petrarchan model and does indeed rejoin her father's restored patriarchy. But this is an aristocratic society that the play questions only through its couple of bad-men. Regardless of "the harmonies of *The Merchant of Venice*," Portia does not seem to surrender her control at the end. If anything, her working of the rings reestablishes her domination as a living daughter finally able to dictate the terms of *her* will once she has escaped the trap set by her father's will.

It is the complexity of the scripts and the variety of responses to them—from directors, actors, and spectators—that Levin's critique tends to ignore. Indeed, he would pull us all into the numbness of consensus, as if a BBC promoter:

> Shakespeare wrote to please an audience that was neither particularly sophisticated nor literary. He wrote for people, not coteries. It is our intention to bring his plays on the same plain terms to a mass audience. . . . There has been no attempt at stylisation; there are no gimmics; no embellishments to confuse the student.[2]

When this goal *was* reached—as unfortunately it was from time to time—students were not confused, they were numbed. That numbness is the goal of those who promote "consensus."

II

The issue of Katharina in *The Taming of the Shrew*, particularly the question of *how* she "rejoins" society at the end, will suggest that no consensus exists. If consensus ever did exist—and Levin's assertion is intended to proclaim a *fait accompli* similar to that "touch of nature here" that the eighteenth-century "critick" would discover in a line that confirmed the confident biases of an age—

consensus has been challenged consistently by directors of recent versions of *Shrew*. I suggest that it is in such versions and there alone that the script exists—there being no essential version of this splendid play.

Coppélia Kahn suggests that *Shrew* "satirizes not woman herself in the person of the shrew, but the male urge to control women."[3] Kahn says that "part of the myth of female power . . . assigns to women the crucial responsibility for creating a mature and socially respectable man."[4] I question norms of "social acceptability," since the society that sets the norms does so according to its own interests and therefore to some brainless conception of status quo or of "progress" only for "party members." But Kahn is right to argue "the dependency that underlies mastery, the strength behind submission."[5] By the same token, the weakness that lies behind bluster and bullying permits insecurity, when unchallenged, to come to power. Comedy issues that challenge and permits the paradox of male and female to resolve itself in a zone somewhere below the stereotypic surface. Kate and Petruchio achieve a mutuality that accepts differences—including the possibility that she may be better at the game than the Petruchio who has taught it to her. The paradox of loving and still retaining one's identity can be resolved in production, as Berners Jackson suggests. *Shrew*, he says, is "Shakespeare's burlesqued projection of male chauvinism fantasy concluding with the richest send up of all, Kate's submission speech."[6] When produced "with careful attention to the insights of the text [the production can show] the tamer also tamed, and . . . a resolution [in which] Kate and Petruchio find equality in their respect and admiration for each other."[7]

That is another "consensus" point of view, perhaps, but it links itself with the play as play, and not with the out-of-context assumptions on which Levin's case rests. The latter would deny directors and actors the use of their own imaginations within a script that, like any Shakespearean script, asks for the interception of another imagination or more.

In a 1974 Theater at Monmouth production, for example, director Richard Sewell included the induction—that frame that can show the inner play to be a projection of male fantasy. Sly was conditioned by opulence to believe a falsehood. In 4.1, a bewildered Sly was dragged into the line of servants greeting Petruchio and his new wife. Sly thus participated in the conditioning-by-deprivation of Kate, as Petruchio held a mirror of her former behavior up to her and insisted that she accept the truth of a deeper identity, one in which she must beg the principle of patience she had rubbed raw in all others earlier. Sly's own omnipotence ended even as Kate's effort at controlling her world began to crumble before Petruchio's power, which in the production was only temporarily coercive. The parallel between Kate and Sly was nicely drawn as was the distinction between the illusion Sly had accepted and the reality that Kate would embrace.

If Kate and Petruchio continue in Padua the game they have begun on the road (4.5) they are conducting an extemporaneous play with a Paduan audience at hand, a play that reverses Petruchio's previous announcement that " 'Tis bargain'd 'twixt us twain, being alone, / That she shall still be curst in company" (2.1.298–99). The other frame has been pulled (and was, literally, in the Monmouth production) *into* a play. A fictive level is at once erased and regenerated. Paduan society, with its conventional values, where patriarchy lacks men and can only be challenged by sheer frowardness, and its willingness—eagerness—to accept the surface of things is mocked by Kate in a speech that may radically overstate the conventional case for submissiveness but that assigns a role to the husband for which Lucentio and Hortensio would not qualify. Kate satirizes a group of numb consumers who do not realize that they are "but mutes and audience to this act." The Monmouth production permitted Kate and Petruchio to achieve identities *through* their game, identities separate from but dependent upon the manifest content of the roles they played. They had been two actors in search of the authorship of love. Within the economy of the production, Sly had found employment as a supporting player in an ongoing play-within-a-play.

As D'Orsay Pearson says of the ending,

Homer once defined the ideal marriage as a state in which "a man and woman live together, pleasing their friends and confounding their enemies." Kate and Petruchio in the final scene are surrounded by "enemies" who have baited them, pitied them, reviled them; we as "audience" are the "friends" who have earlier seen the growth of the two in concord, culminating in Kate's new fear of making a spectacle of herself with a public kiss which she nevertheless gives as well as takes. Petruchio orchestrates a scene which allows Kate to confound their enemies and please their friends as she performs to the point of absurdity the role of meek, docile wife, confirming in action his public image as Kate's "sovereign" head. But it goes further; we must, I think, accept a mutual understanding of shared purpose—otherwise, Petruchio lays his "public" image on the line when he orders Kate to tell her sister and the widow what their duty to their husbands is. Kate goes *beyond* his command, creating through her copious words a husband so superior, so protective, so self-sacrificing that one imagines Petruchio "becoming" that image as she creates it, just as her words create herself as that wife who returns "love, fair looks, and true obedience." Her speech, then, is full of stage directions, both for Petruchio and herself. It confirms two "ideal" images; that she recognizes the disparity between what she finally creates and reality, between the ideal and the real, is suggested by the earlier scene in which she "creates" a young, budding virgin with words, even as the reality confronts sight to deny her creation. The mutuality at the end of the play is achieved in a social context, but in a situation where man and wife set out to confound the other inhabitants of the play world and in the process create each other. Kate's speech "creates" two ideal figures, but she could not create them without Petruchio's help. They play to each other, in the metadramatic sense, exhibiting a mutuality the audience has already accepted. It's Homer's ideal relationship; we as audience are delighted that all those nasty people have been put down, just as we are delighted with the sense of shared purpose Kate and Petruchio have demonstrated at length. The coming physical consummation of the relationship, announced as the play ends, ratifies the relationship.[8]

Another response to the play's seeming lack of "formal" closure is that of Joel Fineman, who also delineates the "linguistics of gender stereotypes" as central to Kate's apparent domestication at the end:

Speaking very generally—and recalling, on the one hand, the Petrarchan idealism of the wooing story and, on the other the parodic Petrarchanism, the Petruchioism, of the taming story—we can say that the two subplots of *The Taming of the Shrew* together present what in the western literary tradition is the master plot of the relation between language and desire. Sly, however, to whom this story is presented, wishes that his entertainment soon were over, for only when the play is over will Sly get to go to bed with new-found wife. "Would 'twere done!" (I.i.254), says Sly (these being the last words we hear from him), of a play which, as far as Sly is concerned, is nothing but foreplay. The joke here is surely on Sly, for the audience knows full well that the consummation Sly so devoutly desires will never be achieved; if ever it happens that Sly sleeps with his wife, he will soon enough discover that she is a he in drag disguise. This defines, perhaps, the ultimate perversity of the kinky lord who "long[s] to hear" his pageboy "call the drunkard husband" (Ind.i.133), and who arranges for Sly to be subjected in this tantalizing way to what for Sly is nothing but the tedious unfolding of the play within the play. But it is not only Sly's desire that is thus seductively frustrated; and this suggests the presence, behind the play, of an even kinkier lord. I refer here to the ongoing editorial question regarding the absence of a final frame; for this response to the play's apparent omission of a formal conclusion to the Sly story is evidence enough that the audience for the entirety of the play is left at its conclusion with a desire for closure that the play calls forth *in order* to postpone. To say that this is a desire that leaves something to be desired—a desire, therefore, that will go on and on forever—goes a good way towards explaining the abiding popularity of *The Taming of the Shrew.*[9]

For all of Fineman's treatment of the play as *text,* he makes a strong case for not "re-framing" the inner play at the end. A valid deconstructionist critique must attend to the play as play—as Levin's consensus does not and cannot.

Jeanne Roberts offers another description of the ending: "The end of the play is not the social celebration characteristic of festive comedy. . . . The lonely lovers create a private sanctuary for themselves, but the surrounding world continues to be paralyzed by its illusions."[10] I would argue, however, that the lovers create not a sanctuary, but theater, and are hardly lonely as they improvise their play-within-a-Padua.

Jonathan Miller, producer and director of the BBC *Shrew* (1980) sees things very differently: "Shakespeare is extolling the virtues of the obedient wife. . . . If we wish to make all plays from the past conform to our ideals and what we think the state or the family ought to be like, then we're simply rewriting all plays and turning them into modern ones."[11] It is not that we are rewriting the plays according to narrow modern metaphors—although that did happen all too often in the 1970s. We are discovering in the plays an exploration of issues, sexual and ideological, that are as alive to us as they were to the Elizabethans. And we are discovering that the scripts are susceptible to different interpretations in performance that *cannot* distort the "meaning" of the play. Meaning is generated, at least partly, by response to what the stage depicts. That we are capable of responding to *Shrew* in light of the insights of feminism does not mean that we are rewriting the play in our own image. It means that the play's exploration of the issue of patriarchy and gender continues to communicate to us and communicates more accurately, perhaps, because of discoveries that we believed to be recent and our own—until we took another look at Shakespeare.

But talk of rewriting! Miller's assumptions are those of the late-sixteenth-century commonplaces that form the conflict in many of

the plays, commonplaces that are *explored*, not presented as doctrine: "We've taken one of the Psalms which talks about the
orderliness and grace and beauty of the family. It's one of the
Psalms that would have been sung in a household after a meal in a
Puritan household, and it somehow reconciles all the conflicts of
the previous two hours. All these characters have been working at
odds with one another, working against one another, trying to get
their own ends. Now they are suddenly brought together in what
the Sixteenth Century regarded as *communitas*, which is the bringing together, the unifying and harmonizing of all individual desires so that they actually work together."[12] It might be argued
that television demands a "Father Knows Best" closure, where
Psalm 128 can tell us males that "Thy wife shall be as the fruiteful
vine on the sides of thine house" (Genevan), but here we end up
with a Petruchio and a Kate pulled *into* Padua. Whatever searching out of patriarchal and bourgeois assumptions the script has
conducted, those assumptions are validated here. Miller "domes-
ticates" the script. As Kenneth Rothwell says of Sarah Badel's
Kate, "This healthy aggressive woman ultimately supports traditional values as set forth in the Anglican wedding vows, which in
turn reflect St. Paul's opinions on the authority of the husband."[13]
The application of the historical fallacy gives us a Kate who is not
so much a victim *in* the play but a victim of the male behind the
camera, as Irene Dash suggests: "Miller describes Petruchio's actions as 'bringing a spirited steed under control' (!) This inability
to see Kate as a whole person informs and mars the work. . . .
Thus Miller joins a long line of misogynistic producers who could
not accept a strong, attractive Kate."[14]

Dash's response to Miller's production recalls Shaw's assertion
that *Shrew* is "altogether disgusting to modern sensibility." Mary
Pickford may have eclipsed Shaw with a wink in the 1929 Don
Taylor version, but Miller returns all the way to 1595 to affront the
"sensibility" of yet another generation.

The Miller production is available and is, presumably, being
shown to students. Modernizations usually reduce Shakespeare
to our own narrow metaphors. We may think we know more than
Shakespeare could have known; we usually prove that we know
less. Shakespeare, for example, depicts the modern problem of
sexual harassment in *Measure for Measure*, prefigures Darrow's
defense of Loeb and Leopold in Hamlet's "apology" to Laertes,
displays an eerie knowledge of neurology in inventing Caesar's
deaf left ear, suggests in *Othello* that slavery is an inevitable part of
the black man's past, and, in *The Tempest*, demonstrates in the

opening scene that he had apparently read Conrad, and later, that he knew that "fire-water" was a necessary ingredient in the subduing of an aborigine, and that to educate a beast might be to leave the beast "between two worlds—one dead, the other powerless to be born," like Penny Patterson's Koko in San Diego.

Miller grants Shakespeare no genius, and, instead of reducing Shakespeare to the meretriciousness of our times, clenches him into the narrowness of his own, as Miller conceives of the late Sixteenth Century. Miller sees *Shrew* as mere reflection of a normative "Elizabethan world picture," where king is to kingdom as husband is to wife. "Taming" is taken literally in this production—as subordination. Thus Shakespeare's exploration of the issues of marriage and his probable transcendence of the commonplaces of his own age is ruled out of this production at the outset. Indeed, Miller appears before his production to tell us so. His opening comments are as gratuitous and as intrusive as is the modern director's misbegotten "bright idea." Miller tells us what *his* play means, thus conditioning our response, even removing our ability *to* respond, denying us the opportunity to evolve our own continuum of energy between the production and our own unique psychology of perception. The issue is not what Shakespeare might be communicating, but what Miller decrees Shakespeare *has* communicated. While any production is an interpretation, Miller immediately robs Shakespeare of his potential largeness of vision—"negative capability"—and does what Shakespeare seldom if ever does: tells us collectively how to interpret the production that is to follow. The "Shakespearean moment" has been denied before the play begins! Miller's elimination of the frame does not "liberate" the script. Miller imprisons it within his own concept of "how things were back in the 1590s."

Things quickly go from bad to worse. Without any establishing shot, like the beautiful drawing of Renaissance Vienna that Desmond Davis employs in his production of *Measure for Measure,* Lucentio and Tranio pop in front of the camera to deliver a virtually inaudible "exposition." We realize, suddenly, that Miller's interpretation of a play we have yet to see has substituted for the Induction. We did not realize that Miller would betray his misunderstanding of the medium (to say nothing of the play!) by using the same static camera for all of the scenes on the streets of Padua. Even situation comedies played before live audiences— "Barney Miller" and "All in the Family," for example—employ a three camera format. Miller's direction for these scenes must have consisted in his saying to his actors, "Come up to the camera and read your lines." While the lines are usually poorly read, at best, and while Miller allows non-speaking actors to upstage those who have lines, and while Grumio's series of asides in 1.2 are all alike inaudible, the camera never moves. It never zooms in. It never shifts its angle to catch the edge of a building. It presupposes a wholly passive viewer locked into a straight-on closed-up confrontation with terrible acting. The scenes are dull, so bad that the foreground grouping can be—again—upstaged by a stilt walker in the background. The static camera calls our attention to the remorseless nature of "studio production" and induces in the spectator a restlessness akin to the cabin fever that most of us employ the tube to escape. The Padua camera squats relentlessly over the town well. The Padua scenes have the effect of a taped play, and a bad play at that.

That the scenes inside the Minola household have an airiness and a Vermeerian suffusion of light, that they employ a mirror with some effect, and that they contrast with the Rembrandtian shadows of Petruchio's grubby hideaway proves merely frustrating. We dread our return to that static camera, knowing that we will look at the church door from a precisely defined twenty yards, and that we would never get inside that church, as Zeffirelli allows us to do in his film version. We can predict that we will get mere narration delivered in front of that damned camera. Even the very funny scene on the road back to Padua is delivered in front of a single camera. We do not know whether Vincentio can hear Kate's salutation: "Young budding virgin, fair and fresh and sweet," or the rest of her speech. He stands upstage. The scene is destroyed by blocking that no high school director would have permitted. And the scene is further destroyed by Kate's cracking up at the material Petruchio has handed her. It is as if Miller felt that he had to introduce a laugh track to his production. Unfortunately, the scene cheats us out of our own laughter.

John Cleese delivers a sensitive Petruchio, but one who lacks an ability to reach that Shakespearean "upper range" that some of Petruchio's speeches either require or invite. Cleese loses some lines by yawning them away or by rubbing his hand over them. Gestures can work, particularly on television, but never, never at the expense of the line, which is inevitably the *bottom* line in Shakespeare. Cleese is the only actor, however, able to work an effective pause or two into the helter-skelter of this dismal production. But Cleese's primary problem is the absolute lack of direction that Sarah Badel receives. What is this sensitive Petruchio responding to?—an adolescent girl having temper tantrums because her father takes Bianca at face value. While an

oldest daughter might well react unfavorably to rejection even at
the hands of as simpering an idiot as this Baptista, Badel's heaving
bosom and hysterics give us Kate *already* broken. That she is a
proud and spirited woman, veiling her inner nature behind a
facade of shrewishness, and that it is that inner woman to whom
Petruchio—even to his own surprise and delight—begins to respond, ah well! I think that Miss Badel could have brought it off.
As it is, her crucial scene with Bianca is a misdirected, or un-
directed mess. I suppose, however, that the early "uncontrolled"
Kate is intended to set up Petruchio's imposition of absolute
domination. It can be argued that Petruchio's game is to show
Kate that she is "immature." I believe, however, that Petruchio's
"loving perversity" is designed to suggest to Kate that her *role* as
shrew represents a version of self-punishment alien to her innate
maturity. Petruchio teaches her a more satisfying game. She masters it to the point that, by the time of her final speech, she shares
a huge and loving joke with Petruchio, a joke that has become
process, that has become the progress of a love that can "be-
dazzle" the eyes of a world conditioned only to stereotypes like
"shrewishness" and "wifely obedience."[15] Miller tends to accept
what the world says about Kate and to add a foolish admixture of
"psychoanalytic theory," and thus confuses the role of Kate, the
central relationship of the play, and the potential meanings of the
play itself. Miss Badel reads the submission speech as Miller's
conception dictated it—with all the fire and passion of an audition
piece. Kate may have said it, but she doesn't believe it, and the
play ends with a communal song to cover the closing credits. But
the song does not mask what Kate and Petruchio learn together in
the inherited script but are not allowed to share in this stillborn
production. Petruchio's final lift of eyebrows might show us that
he knows that he has more than merely a subdued "haggard" in
hand. He might show us that he is happy to be engaged at last in
the warm give-and-take that he sought when he first claimed to
"come to wive it wealthily in Padua" (1.2.73). He has accomplished that, within a qualitative dimension that transcends his
initial conception of rich marriage.

Having recognized that Miller had excluded the Sly Induction
from his production, I ascribed it to Miller's belief that Shakespeare's framing device would not translate effectively to television. I tried to accept that directorial decision. Even as bad as the
production per se is, however, it might have been enhanced by
the framing device, even including the probably non-Shake-
spearean ending, in which Sly moves again to the "real world,"
thinking he has learned how to tame his froward wife but headed,

we surmise, into a flying frying pan. The frame, perhaps depicted with some of the greasy grubbiness of Petruchio's castle, would have suggested to us that *Shrew* itself is a play-within-a-play, a play concerned with simplistic assumptions about male dominance—an illusion. Miller's simpleminded *Shrew* can find no complexity within the script. The frame would have given this production a compensatory irony that would have allowed us to question Miller's interpretation of the "inner drama." We are robbed of that opportunity, within a sequence of robberies that went well beyond what happens at Gad's Hill.

If we exclude the silly chit-chat between Miller and Cleese at the end about "bringing a spirited steed under control" (Badel had been tamed by fiat in advance), Miller's final "frame" is an abject complying with the dug. Graham Holderness, writing about the BBC-Time-Life series as a manifestation of "an oppressive agency of cultural hegemony," describes the ending: "Miller covered the end credits of his production with a Puritan psalm celebrating 'the orderliness and beauty of the family,' thus curtailing any potential liberty of the drama to arouse the play of meanings, by imposing the sovereign authority of *scripture*, the written word."[16] That anything might *continue* to happen between Kate and Petruchio, that they might keep on with their game against Padua is not possible here. They had been absorbed into the very bourgeois conventions they had been holding up to ridicule and into the necessities of television's sense of closure.

Another version of "domesticated" Kate is that described by Ralph Berry in his review of the 1981 Stratford, Canada, production, in which Len Cariou

> offered a Petruchio in the current social worker mode . . . he imparts to [Kate] the correct role model. To see the *Shrew* assimilated into homiletic drama is hard for those of us who regard its vital essences as brutality and sexuality . . . the great final speech came over with entire conviction, as why should it not? . . . The key is that Petruchio has won a bet, and Katharina knows it. The glance that Sharry Flett shot at her groom registered the point fully ("Did you? Good for you! And now you can buy me another gown!"). I see no reason why Katharina, alone in Padua, should be untouched by the economic drives sustaining the community. So Kate sings for her supper, and very prettily too.[17]

I believe that Berry rejects the interpretation the production did present for his own economically determined imposition. Kate does congratulate Petruchio when she learns of his winnings, but *she* has paid for the supper. If Kate reverts to the woman who merely wants fashionable clothes—for herself *and* her husband, if she merely reembraces the economic advantages of her status, then Petruchio has failed. It is unto his ability to buy her clothes that she is married. Petruchio has himself abandoned his initial motive—to wive it wealthily—for this thing called love. Does he then gain a wife whose wit is subordinate to what she can get by it? I doubt it. It is Kate who is the winner—"too little payment for so great a debt," Flett emphasizes. She speaks as a woman whose body has been discovered by someone else, thus rediscovered by herself. She speaks from her secure stance as wife of the best man in the house. Petruchio interrupts her move to place her hand beneath his foot. That action brings her up to his level. Flett does stop to hug Baptista before her exit with Petruchio, but I take that as simple good nature with a suggestion of "Kate knows best" thrown in. Suffice it that two critics who saw the same production can fail to achieve consensus.

The crux, of course, is Kate's speech. Much depends on what the actors have learned from the script and about each other, a point amusingly made by Streep and Julia in the backstage segments of *"Kiss me, Petruchio."* No consensus will ever emerge from the variables that begin to generate with the casting of each role in each new production.

The final speech can show that "The doctrine of woman's subservience [is] subordinate to the triumph of Eros."[18] It can show that "the game of obedience is more fun than the game of shrewishness . . . and the fringe benefits are more satisfying."[19] It can be "only a speech designed to please the Slys of the world"[20] (assuming that Sly is an observer). If the Padua play is Sly's dream, the final speech is "part of the play's point that a man's achievement of absolute dominance over his wife can only happen in a dream."[21] It can represent, simply, "an Elizabethan woman's wise restraint,"[22] and therefore the wisdom of restraint that Kate has learned within a society of patriarchs. The speech can show that "Petruchio can turn a hateful Kate into a plucky, fun-loving helpmate."[23] "Kate's aversion to men had [resulted from] their inability to match wits with her, to perceive the real worth of her personality and of women generally, and to muster the psychic energy necessary to elicit her admiration."[24] The speech can be "a private understanding, like the sun/moon, young virgin/old man game they had played on the road, rather than a demonstration of Petruchio's macho prowess for the company. His refusal to take the money he had won made the point nicely."[25] In the latter instance, the collecting of the wager was not the goal. The wager was merely a way of continuing a game that had become no longer a gamble.

Much depends on how the scene is staged. One Kate sang quite consciously for her supper: "Her self-abasing final speech was cunningly explained by allowing her to linger on stage . . . long enough to overhear the terms of the bet."[26] Even a single line can elicit a different action. Kate claims that her "hand is ready [to] do him ease." "After some hesitation, the lord and master buckled under by taking that hand in his own, acknowledging that he had been tamed by love itself."[27] "By the time Kate offered her hand, which Petruchio kissed instead of permitting her to put it under his foot, male sexual conquest had been transformed into female seduction. It worked to defuse the potentially sexist bomb."[28] That review, by a female reviewer, suggests the replacement of one negative stereotype with another. It tends to validate negative male assumptions. Something is to be said, however, for the rhythm of the dance that gets both partners what they mutually desire. As this reviewer goes on to say, "the audience [was left with] a genuine sense of *con*-summation."[29] Petruchio's "gesture of kneeling beside Kate," says another reviewer of another production, "placed the two lovers at last on an equal footing"—or at least on an equal kneeing.[30]

A more violent reading is possible, however. "As she spoke the words 'may it do him ease,' she suddenly tossed his feet upwards, turning him topsy-turvy off the bench."[31] The latter action was, the reviewer claims, in keeping with "her whole tongue-in-cheek attitude during the scene"[32]—as opposed, one assumes, to the half-a-tongue or tongue-in-tail approach. But the hand as catapult tends to support the contention that "contemporary sexual politics, if undigested, can vitiate the play,"[33] even if the staging challenges the assertion that "The speech will not play as anything other than what most obviously it is: an eloquent exhortation to wifely submission."[34] The topsy-turvy flip of Petruchio does support Charles Frey's countercontention that "*Shrew*, like the rest of Shakespearean comedy, is reduced to farce at the peril of its deeper life."[35]

Balz Engler suggests that "Katherine's submission may be acted as full of irony; or Katherine may be depicted as a human being wantonly destroyed by Petruchio . . . or the play may be acted as farce, its significance as a model for behavior therefore denied."[36] We discover in a production that Engler describes the scenario that Berry denies the script: "Petruchio was less a tyrant taming a shrewish Kate than a sympathetic and perceptive—if secret— lover painfully instructing a defensive Kate to discover that attractive self he has seen earlier."[37] The middle ground that Engler tends to ignore is described by W. L. Godshalk: "she had learned how to live in a basically nonrational world . . . changing from a selfish shrew to a woman who could transcend her own preconceptions about her importance."[38] The Artaudian aspects of the script that Engler indicates are evinced in a production that "depicted the ironic imprisonment of both men and women in their respective sexual roles. . . . When [Katharina] was fully defeated, her speech of capitulation was delivered as if she meant every word. There was no facile irony in it. [She had become a] docile, suppressed, and vapid creature. [Petruchio] had himself destroyed what [had] attracted him to Katharina."[39]

Much as I disagree with that bleak finale, it may capture that segment of "modern love" that captured some of us—precisely because we fell into the trap of our own stereotypic assumptions of ourselves and the opposite gender. But against that negation is the production described by James Lusardi and June Schlueter:

> Indeed, the encounter with Vincentio prefigures the climactic banquet scene. Kate and Petruchio once again become performing partners, their audience now expanded. Kate speaks her submissive monologue with confidence and with calculated effect. As she walks around the table, reproaching the other women, she registers Petruchio's approving look and notes his obvious pride. Knowing she has passed his test, she then administers hers: approaching her husband, she slowly begins to bow, allowing her extended hand to proceed slowly toward his foot. Looking sober now and perplexed, Petruchio suddenly grasps her hand to prevent any further descent; then, in full appreciation of the gesture, he declares, "Why, there's a wench!" Their big clinch makes everyone else look small. On "lets' to bed," it is Kate who leads her husband up the stairs, running.[40]

The play shows us that Kate's speech is a culmination, even if it be "Peggy Ashcroft's tongue-in-cheek mistress learning how to speak through her master's voice"[41]—Petruchio having mastered Kate's tongue earlier.

And closure can occur *before* that final speech, as Lusardi and Schlueter suggest, and as other critics attest: "we do not see her fully transformed until the journey home. . . . All is ready for the settlement and for Kate's last full-dress speech which can say a lot between the lines . . . Petruchio and Kate have a rewarding theatrical game"[42] in which we can participate olfactorily: "The smell of onions floated through the theatre and through the audience, making Katherine's hunger-pangs more immediately sympathetic"[43]—particularly for an audience arriving at Petruchio's country house in 4.1. "When Kate finally passed her identification tests so that she could tell the sun from the moon, Petruchio quietly picked up the bundle she was taking back to Padua and added it to his load."[44]

The final speech is the culmination of what a specific company has discovered in the script as it has worked with it and worked it out in front of the response of a live audience.

Kate "jumped on the table to deliver her speech from the middle of it . . . and thereby took her turn as the spider ruling her web . . . or was it the last fly caught in the deadly marriage trap?"[45] Even an individual reviewer will have conflicting opinions about what he or she saw in the final stage image.

In 1978, I felt that my objections to the Bogdanov *Shrew* were based solely on the imposition of a metaphor that drew attention away from whatever the script might have been offering for exploration and forced us and the production to concentrate on the fidelity to Mafioso detail and "style." The production tried to say something about the Mafia, as Papp's *Much Ado* tried to say something about pre-World War I America. All energies go into someone's concept of historical fidelity, and the consequence is that the productions say nothing about the *zeitgeist* they imitate and nothing to the moment that encapsulates the audience.

That is not to say that the scripts will not accept settings other than doublet and hose. A 1982 Monmouth *Dream* succeeded largely because its Victorian setting had been nicely calculated to make distinctions within a very anachronistic play text. Lysander became a young Tennyson, jotting some of his better phrases in the notebook he kept ready in the pocket of his frockcoat. Demetrius was a stiff young officer in a very good cavalry regiment. The 1988 Stratford, Canada, *Shrew* employed an Italian *mise en scène* as a festival within which the "kind of history" could develop. We did not need Marlon Brando to say, "See that she gets a good dowry. That boy thinks all Italian girls go barefoot." This *Shrew* provided the comfortable upper-bourgeoisie as a "given," not as a structure trying to look "legitimate" on foundations of bootlegging, drug dealing, protection and numbers rackets, and tommy-gun assassinations of rival "families."

The conception of the 1978 RSC *Shrew* crushed my own sense of the play. I do believe that Kate and Petruchio win at the end. They win themselves. They triumph over Padua and its stereotypic expectations and results. While that interpretation is questionable, as all totalizing myths are, the RSC *Shrew* was bound to defeat any sense of the victory of Kate and Petruchio. If it left something in place of victory, the final impression could only be a negative note about timing. I base my reinterpretation of my dissatisfaction on remarks that Paola Dionisotti—the Kate of that production—makes. Dionsotti suggests that the production had to be a letdown since it had built expectations. Of 4.5—the road back to Padua scene—she says, "Kate picks up all those images of sun and moon and intensifies them. She *dances* with it. The beauty of the speech becomes like an escape from the situation. The images are warm and the meshing of the lines gives the feeling that they're writing a love poem together, or playing a game. She has finally discovered that it *is* a game, and that they can play it together."[46] The ending, however, destroyed the rapport that Kate, at least, thought she had achieved. "But the game he is playing," says Dionisotti of Petruchio's wager, "is just a traditional macho power game. What I find impossible is, having been through all that stuff over Bianca's elopement, having watched all that rubbish, that 'ado' in the previous scene, I then discover that Petruchio *still* has a need to prove me—just one more test—in front of them all."[47] In other words, Petruchio asks one time too many. "My Kate," Dioniscotti says, "was kneeling and I reached over to kiss his foot and he gasped, recoiled, jumped back, because somehow he's completely blown it. He's as trapped now by society as she was in the beginning. Somewhere he's an okay guy, but *it's too late*. The last image was of two very lonely people."[48]

Dionisotti tells me, then, why my response was as it was. I had rationalized my dislike of the production through my attack on its concept. I had wanted the comic ending regardless of concept, and did not get it. I had wanted the ending Fiona Shaw describes: "When Petruchio lays a bet on Kate, maybe that's where he renders himself up: he takes a chance on her. She took a chance on him, she rendered herself up in the sun/moon scene. Now *he* takes a chance on her."[49] It is precisely that reciprocity that I sense at the end of *Shrew,* but my own expectations merely prove that I am bound by generic expectations, no doubt by establishment and even patriarchal strictures, and that I deny my own Marxist notion that the script itself contains the countertext that subverts the manifest content. Such reappraisals of our responses are an inevitable function of our experience with production. I would not "like" the Bogdanov *Shrew* in 1990, but I now understand more of the why. Criticism is, often, an analysis of response, that is, the articulation, possibly the rationalization of the feeling function that does the evaluating.

III

I wish to end this chapter with a few notes on "framing" and its variations. Certainly our aesthetic distance from a script is not a constant. The script offers too many options for its "camera shots"—emotional linkages or alienations—options like the stage, always different from theater to theater and invariably angled at each spectator in a different way even in the same theater, the media in which the script attempts to discover itself, themselves subject to our unconscious or half-conscious expectations of what can happen within that frame and, invariably, our own subjective and half-perceived or unconscious responses to the experience of theater.

The artisans of *A Midsummer Night's Dream* misunderstand—as they misunderstand so much else—the nature of aesthetic distance. Afraid that their play will be taken for reality, they make sure that their play won't be taken for drama. They deny their audience any opportunity for the suspension of disbelief through which the imagination can flow. Even if that leap between artistic and spectator synapse might occur, Bottom batters it down, anticipating his play as Hamlet does later on. The spectator is the "local habitation," or "final cause" of drama. We name the experience we have received from the signifiers. "Pyramus and Thisbe" will not permit the transaction, but *Dream* insists on it. As does *Shrew.*

A frame gives us space within which to evaluate our response, to determine our reality as we sort out various levels of fiction. The frame reminds us that we are not observing reality except insofar as mimesis activates something within us into recognition. The proscenium arch or the plastic around the tube make a pretense of creating a window into reality. Television, with its instant endings and readily interchangeable stations, erases our "zone of response."

Shrew probably offers the most variations in framing of any Shakespeare script.

Famous frames for *Shrew* include Jonathan Pryce's drunkard in the auditorium, whom Paola Dioniscotti's usherette tried to subdue, in the Bogdanov 1978 RSC version. (She told me that she often got offers of help, always from Americans, and had to tell them in a whisper that it was part of the show.) Pryce then went on to trash a pretentious set. The Pickford-Fairbanks film opens with a Punch and Judy that anticipates the violence between Petruchio and Kate. The Zeffirelli film provides a brief glimpse of a drunkard in a cage as Lucentio rides through the streets of Padua.

I assume that Shakespeare's stage kept Sly in view, probably on the upper stage. The frame around the fiction is always there, even when the action and our attention are elsewhere. In the 1982 Stratford, Canada, production, the Pedant opened a window *above* Sly so that the latter was momentarily physically inside the play-within-a-play. When does Sly disappear? Earlier, I mentioned the Monmouth, Maine, production in which Sly was yanked into the line of Petruchio's servants. Is Sly at the end part of an applauding audience? At the end of the 1982 Stratford, Canada, production, the real Lord throws a purse to the actor who had played Baptista in the inner play, even as Sly is being removed so that the "A Shrew" ending can be retained, and the inner play can become Sly's dream of male superiority. The joke, we infer, is on Sly as he repeats Hortensio's belief (4.5.77–79) that lesser men can learn the taming process from Petruchio.

The entertaining 1988 version at Stratford, Canada, is set in modern Italy, but it does not press the "Godfather" theme as did the Bogdanov production at Stratford, England, in 1978. Here Sly doubles as Petruchio (Colm Feore) and Hostess as Katherina (Goldie Semple). The Induction is a pastiche of the Sly frame. I am not sure what sense it makes for Sly to say "I am Christophero Sly, call not me 'honour' nor 'lordship,' " when no one is doing so. Sly's line "go to thy cold bed and warm thee," becomes an invitation to Hostess: "come to my cold bed and warm thee." It is an invitation that sets up the Petruchio-Kate relationship in the "play-within," which is Sly's dream. He passes out. A clown-magician creates "Padua" in neon lights and a festival begins in high Italian style. At the end, after Petruchio and Kate have exited triumphantly and expectantly from the upper stage, the extras sing a final celebratory song. As they exit, Sly is discovered, in shirt and leather vest. He awakens and exits through the audience without a word. His did not seem like a fantasy of male power and domination but rather a dream of wealth and happiness similar to Caliban's. Sly, sober now, seems aware that any plea to dream again would be in vain. This framing makes us believe the fiction—here modern dress and Italianate mannerisms are helpful.

And the final moment makes us believe with Sly that it has all been a fiction woven out of his brief, half-conscious invitation to the hostess of a Stratfordshire pub.[50]

If the Sly induction is retained but the *Shrew* ending left intact, then we discover, perhaps, that Kate and Petruchio are playing stereotypic roles for a Padua that operates on the principle of the numbness of consensus. Kate and Petruchio have become the play-within, with Padua as audience. That format is predicted by Kate and Petruchio on the road to Padua, where they define reality and their audience, the Vincentio who is soon to arrive at a Padua already taken in by the Pedant. That is—all except Gremio (V.1.89–91).

Some editors see Sly as merely introducing the story (or "history": 1.139 of the Induction). "Sly's main function," says G. R. Hibbard, "is to lead the spectator into the imaginary world of the play; and once he has done that, he is no longer required."[51] H. J. Oliver suggests that *Shrew* is "a play in which the enclosed story is the longer and the enclosing story is apparently no more than a way of introducing it."[52] Oliver argues for the erasure of Sly by saying that "One does not improve a farce with the reminder that it may have been only a farce; far better to let the audience make that judgment . . . [Shakespeare] had very good reasons . . . to get Sly out of view of the audience early in the play and let them forget him—until perhaps they have left the theatre and have time to wonder what happened to him and even, perhaps, what has happened to them."[53]

Shrew without a frame can become a wild slapstick farce—like the American Conservatory Theater version, which has the benefit of a live audience—or it can become the somber Puritan rendition that BBC provided. In the latter, we were meant to take Kate's submission at face value. She (Sarah Badel) sat soberly at the communal table. Then copies of music were handed out and all sang Psalm 128. The psalm is both Puritan and patriarchal. The heading for it in the Calvinist Geneva Bible says, "He sheweth that blessedness apperteineth not to all universally, but to them onely that feare the Lord, and walke in his wayes." It is subtitled "A Song of degrees" and promises the *man* that "Thy wife shalbe as the fruteful vine on the sides of thine house." The Geneva gloss says that "God approveth not our life, except it be reformed, according to his worde." I believe that Petruchio's "He that knows better how to tame a shrew, / Now let him speak; 'tis charity to show" (4.1.213–14) is a secular glance at the *Book of Common Prayer*'s "Therefore if any man can shew any just cause, why they may not lawfully be joined together, let him now speak or else hereafter forever hold his peace" (1558 PB). One of the few moments where that injunction has been engaged is in *The Philadelphia Story*. The allusion to the *Book of Common Prayer*, if it be one, does not insist that *Shrew's* vibrancy be straitjacketed into a Puritan mode.

A variation in the framing of *Shrew* is "Kiss Me, Petruchio," a documentary based on Joseph Papp's production with Meryl Streep and Raul Julia. "Kiss Me, Petruchio" appeared on ARTS Cable Network in April 1982.

It begins with Petruchio getting booed as he lists the ways in which Kate is his possession at the bridal dinner scene (3.2.232–34). Julia tells us that he loves it when they boo him. "They haven't seen the agreement of forces between the man and the woman," he says.

Papp, sitting in a snow-filled amphitheater, then introduces the show. We cut to summer, with picnickers waiting in line for tickets in Central Park. Streep is getting made-up as a voice cries, "Half an hour, please!" Streep speaks of a society that "constricts" Katherine just as one of her dressers pulls a corset stay too tight: "*constricts* her." Julia talks of being allowed to express his own "rhythms, feelings, and Spanish culture" through Petruchio, without having to speak in what he takes to be the received British manner.

While Sly is absent, we get plenty of shots from upstage, incorporating the Delacorte audience along with closer shots of two or three people laughing.

On stage, Kate ebbs and flows away from and toward Petruchio, resisting even as she begins to understand the game he is teaching her. Her ambivalence creates a series of small moments that predict the completed action of her final speech. Streep reads the speech with joy and conviction. This mobile Kate is telling the world that she has discovered who she is. The effect is so powerful that Petruchio's "Why, there's a wench!" doesn't get a laugh. Everyone agrees, and the word "wench" is one of praise.

Backstage, Streep and Julia discuss their roles and the relationship they depict:

JULIA: He's here to make money. He doesn't think he's going to meet the girl of his dreams. That [shrewishness] is just an act. That's not what she's really like.
STREEP: She is unhappy. They smash into each other.
JULIA: Petruchio says, "I'm going to show you how to get off [her

shrewish behavior] , to give her the opportunity to find that she has
a choice not to be a victim."
STREEP: Nobody's ever denied her anything because . . .
JULIA: She's a spoiled person.

Streep reads the Tailor's correction about making a puppet of
Katherine (4.3.105) as the Tailor's wanting Kate "to conform to
society's idea of fashion . . . to be a conventional woman." Petruchio, then, wants Kate's unconventionality to find its positive
purpose. Streep says that Petruchio promises "to make [Kate] as
great as [she] can be. Passion and love provide the sources of
[Kate's] change." Streep says that Kate "is mad about him—but
doesn't tell him that!" Kate watches Petruchio's tantrum on the
road to Padua with sudden recognition. "He's being me," Streep
says. "Or what I was." Julia says that Kate must "accept someone
else's way." Then he can clasp her hand and kiss the palm that
would have been placed under his foot.

The interplay between stage personalities and the insights of
the actors is enjoyable. This is a documentary about Julia and
Streep.

Also entertaining are the comments of the audience. The
women are aware, rightly, that the emphasis of this production is
on taming, even if the goal finally reached is one of mutual love
and respect. During the interval, a woman complains about Petruchio's treatment of Kate as he drags her away from the wedding
feast. Her companion, a man, says (tongue-in-cheek, perhaps),
"that scene is a representation of what our relationship strives to
be." She gives him a withering glance. "We have met Mr. and
Mrs. Sly."[54]

At the end a woman says that she knows she shouldn't like the
play intellectually: "I feel very ambiguous. I also feel—isn't she a
lucky woman!" Another woman suggests that the play represents
"a fantasy that is very dangerous for men. How many men are as
appealing, sexy, wonderful and strong as Petruchio?" Few, if any,
of course, but these women are willing to leave Kate to her fate,
even if they resent Petruchio's sexism and wish there were more
men like him in the "real" world.

In the "Moonlighting" version, the inner play becomes the
projection of the teenage boy forced to do his homework. This
version comes close to Garrick's "Catherine and Petruchio," in
which "Bianca lost her lovers and the play its drunkard." This
Shrew becomes a function of zeitgeist—as it always does, but
overtly in this instance. The zeitgeist is partly that of the boy,

reading *Atomic Shakespeare* and finding "music" and kung fu therein, and partly that of the script's enunciation of a feminist manifesto ("I have learned from a woman, one with much to teach," says Willis-Petruchio) and partly from a sense of "Moon-lighting's" characters, as already established in the series. As Jack Oruch says, "the writers, by hitting upon *Shrew* as the basis for a fantasy segment, allowed the antagonists to share a bed without ending their 'real' opposition."[55] The inner play announces its meaning to both the Paduan and the "Moonlighting" audience: "For Kate never needed to be tamed. She merely needed to be loved." A subsequent secondary message already manifest is delivered when Shepherd and Willis interrupt their final smooch to announce, "We hate iambic pentameter." The boy comes down-stairs again to learn from Mom that it wasn't very good tonight and that he hasn't missed anything.

In *Kiss Me, Kate, Shrew* becomes the play-within. The movie deals with the "offstage" conflict of Fred and Lilli, a conflict resolved within *Shrew*, as Lilli appears as Kate, late and unexpec-tedly, and signals to Fred that all is well. The "frame" collapses into and is resolved by the inner play. We respond to Lilli and Fred via cameras placed "upstage." The film ends as *Shrew* ends in front of an enthusiastic "audience" staring at the proscenium but unaware of the "real" drama worked out behind the fictive arch. We were also the audience in the stage version (I saw the produc-tion, with Patricia Morison, Alfred Drake, and Lisa Kirk, in Janu-ary 1950 at the Century Theater), but we knew of the subtext that Lilli and Fred were working out as Kate and Petruchio. The cardboard film "audience" responds only to the resolution of the Kate and Petruchio story. The stage version forced us to sort out the analogy between "Kate" and *Shrew*. The stage version also insisted that we respond at the end via curtain calls to actors playing characters in a musical by Cole Porter playing characters in an old play by Shakespeare.

I suggest that the matter of framing and distance goes to the heart of the experience of drama. The question is not envisioned in Berger's concept of flipping pages back and forth or in Levin's insistence upon consensus.[56]

3

Hermia's Dream

Help me, Lysander, help me! Do thy best
To pluck this crawling serpent from my breast!
Ay me, for pity! What a dream was here!
Lysander, look how I do quake with fear.
Methought a serpent eat my heart away,
And you sat smiling at his cruel prey.
Lysander! What, remov'd? Lysander! Lord!
What, out of hearing? Speak, an if you hear.
Speak, of all loves! I swoon almost with fear.
No? Then I well perceive you are not nigh.
Either death, or you, I'll find immediately.

(2.2.145–57)

Hermia, briefly, but profoundly, reflects the central comic experience of *A Midsummer's Night's Dream*—that of Titania. Titania actually has intercourse with a beast, even if within a drug-induced vision. She has rejected her lover, experienced a vicarious pregnancy through her vot'ress, and has transferred her affections to the child. Her punishment is to explore the bestial undernature—the "bottom" she has created by repressing her natural instincts. Or—if conception is not possible for a fairy demigoddess—the punishment results from her hubris in becoming emotionally mortal. Titania's awakening represents a transition from monstrosity to "my Oberon"—a reestablishment of proper relationship and a restoration of order to a cosmos whose deep disturbance she has described at length.*

This essay owes much to a shrewd paper written by my student Gregory Merrill of Bowdoin College in the Fall of 1987.

*Cf. Marjorie Garber: "Titania's apparently secure world is actually in the process of a fall—a fortunate fall, as it turns out, since the fantasy experience in the wood helps to reunite her with Oberon and to restore order to the fairy world" (*Dream in Shakespeare* [New Haven: Yale University Press, 1974], 72). Garber calls Hermia's dream "an equivalent structure" to Titania's experience (72).

Hermia's nightmare at the end of 2.2 is a précis of Titania's more extended experience. Hermia resists a necessary progression. Titania makes a useful regression—useful because it presses her toward a reintegration with her psyche and a recognition of a conscious intention toward which she gropes even while seeking favors for Bottom. She explores the underworld—unwillingly— and emerges from it calmly, if with a shudder at her memory of being "enamor'd of an ass." The underworld explores Hermia for the millisecond of an eyeblink. It is that exploration that I wish to examine here.

Three versions of Hermia's dream are available in cassette form—the 1935 Reinhardt film, the 1982 Joseph Papp production in Central Park, and the 1982 BBC-TV production.

In the BBC version, Robert Lindsay's Lysander obviously loses ground with Pippa Guard's Hermia by admitting that he is lost. He attempts to compensate with an overardent advance but is shoved to the ground. Hermia is a bit surprised and embarrassed by her violence and is almost seduced by Lysander's subsequent rationalization—platonization—of his intentions. She evades him, however, and delivers a chaste kiss on the mouth. "There. Be content with that." Lysander's "Amen" is reluctant. He can scarcely resist touching Hermia after she has rolled away to go to sleep. As he settles down "further off," he slides his sword aside.

Demetrius draws his sword on Helena on "thy peril," threatening more than her modesty. Lysander, awakening and paddling toward Helena, discovers that he has left his sword back at his campsite. He retrieves it and kisses the hilt as he vows to become Helena's knight.

Hermia has been lying on her back in a white gown, looking like Juliet in the Capulet tomb. The scene's affinities with *Romeo and Juliet* (and "Pyramus and Thisby") are thus delicately implied. Hermia cries aloud and recounts her dream, turning on "cruel prey" toward the place she thinks Lysander lies. She moves down to that empty space, kneels on "all loves,' " and places her hands across her lap.

The BBC version captures the phallic intentions of the two young men and the sexual, indeed the physical, vulnerability of the two women—particularly that of abandoned Hermia. She has rejected Lysander and his lust. The dream—and his smiling within it—is his revenge, the vengeance of the male world upon her.

In the Benjamin Britten-Peter Pears opera version (directed by Peter Hall in 1981 and subsequently televised), Hermia, virtually asleep after Puck has anointed Lysander's eyes, is given the line,

"Amen, amen to that sweet prayer say I." She sings it drowsily as a version of a child's "now I lay me down to sleep," tumbling from maiden piety into the phallic zone her repression has opened in her unconscious. In a sense, then, "the lord" does "take her soul" as she sleeps.

The Papp version is overacted—partly because it is a live outdoor production captured by the confining and intimate television camera and partly because the actors are mostly amateurs.

Deborah Rush's bosomy and petulant Hermia is angry at Lysander for ripping the sleeve of her gown. Kevin Conroy makes no bones about his intentions—concupiscent. After pretending to accept a space downrange of Hermia, he slithers serpentlike uphill and is mounting Hermia when she pushes him off. He rolls downhill again. Hermia lies on her back—very vulnerable—between Lysander and Helena, who struggle in the foreground. Lysander rips Helena's purple belt from her waist and drops it on Hermia as he exits. It becomes the physical manifestation of the serpent with which she struggles. Her awakening is superimposed upon Lysander's exit—as if she were dreaming of his desertion.* His smiling, then, means that he doesn't give a damn what happens to her. That bit of editing links Lysander with Oberon, who approves of Titania's coupling with Bottom.

The scene, however, fails—except for the concept of the scarf. As Hermia handles it, she looks as if she is having a fight with her knitting. When she realizes that Lysander is gone, she feigns unconcern—as if she will have to find another ride home. Her reading may have meant something to a big-city ear, but it hollows out a promising set of possibilities. This Hermia does not realize that she is alone in the woods, suddenly prey to forces more dangerous than Lysander's lust. The scene trivializes its issues, dropping us back into Central Park when it should take us far away.

The Reinhardt Hermia, Olivia de Haviland, seems willing, even before her escape to the woods, to accept anything Dick Powell's sappy Lysander has to offer. Her "tomorrow, deep midnight" emerges from a deep, anticipating sigh. The lovers are not lost in the forest. Hermia accepts Lysander's suggestion that they rest and he hers that he find himself a bed. No debate, no wrestling, no sexual over- or undertones. Hermia's absolute acceptance of Lysander sets up her reaction to his rejection of her later, in a film that seems to concentrate more on Hermia than on Helena.

---

*Cf. Garber: "Her dream is monitory and predictive, describing in metaphorical terms the estrangement which is actually taking place" (73).

Hermia sleeps in a fetal position. She cries out and then awakens. She grasps her single strand of pearls—a "choker"—but feels the serpent under the pearls.* While the serpent is deeper—about her heart—the pearls themselves are interesting. Had they been a present from her father? An heirloom inherited from her mother? They embody the previous generation and its control over her—as exemplified by Egeus.

Hermia wipes her eyes on "dream"—what a relief! She then smiles at her description of the serpent and at Lysander's seeming approval. That had been a dream! Hermia is no longer in the hold of those terrifying images. De Haviland, however, gives much more to her Hermia than an "it was only a dream" response. Her sleep has been refreshing. In it she has faced a fear and awakened to discover that she has made a transition that permits her to smile at the *images* of her dream, not just at its having *been* a dream.

She is, however, alone in the woods. She lifts the hem of her elegant and revealing ball-gown (she has dressed for her destination, perhaps, but like most Hermias, not for her journey) and takes off through the underbrush after Lysander.

De Haviland's Hermia confirms her love for Lysander via the dream. As soon as its ominous symbols are dismissed, the dream emblemizes their mutual satisfaction at the consummation of their relationship. Hermia shares Lysander's smile.† The dream fulfills, in a psychic way, her earlier anticipation. Hermia's vulnerability is captured in the aura of old money she brings to this desert place. While she has a comeuppance to come, however, her dream seems to resolve psychic issues for her. The question of her physical height will cast only a momentary shadow across a resolution already achieved.

For Pippa Guard, Hermia's dream makes the issue of sexuality and vulnerability stark within consciousness. Her last line—"Yea, and my father"—is delivered to Helena. Egeus has accepted Theseus's overbearing of parental will and has, somewhat stiffly, accepted his daughter's hug. Egeus has given his blessing to her match with Lysander, however reluctantly. Guard reads Hermia's last line to suggest merely recognition. She conveys no fear of

---

*Cf. Jack Jorgen's comment: "The snakes adorning Hippolyta's dresses and the undulating pillars of Theseus's palace reappear in Hermia's erotic nightmare in which she grasps the pearl necklace and dreams a serpent ate her heart away" (*Shakespeare on Film* [Bloomington: Indiana University Press, 1977], 49).

†This reading of the lines is in contrast to Garber's subtle Freudian interpretation: "The splitting of the menacing figure into two, Lysander and the snake, may thus be considered as a compensatory action on the part of the subconscious" (73).

further blocking actions. The generational conflict has been resolved. Guard's emphasis is on her battle with Egeus for her
independent will, as opposed to her insistence on a love that
transcends or eradicates parental prohibition.

Other readings of the line could suggest that Hermia still fears
her father's power—in spite of Theseus's edict. Egeus's reaction to
Theseus and Hermia is, of course, crucial to the comic closure. In
a graceful Regent's Park production of the mid-1970s, Egeus met
Hermia and Lysander outside the temple, shook the latter's hand,
and took his daughter's arm. He intended, obviously, to give her
away during the ensuing ceremony. Egeus can, of course, be
excluded from the comic closure, an exclusion that can then send
Hermia uncertainly into her marriage.

Hermia's dream can signal a problem to be addressed or one
that has been resolved within the dream. The dream does signal
that, of the young lovers, Hermia's problem is the deepest. Guard
and de Haviland capture the range of possibilities within which
the "meaning" of the dream and of Hermia's experience in the
play is to be discovered.

The scripted world of Shakespeare's play shows that the immediate issue Hermia confronts—or that confronts her via the serpent—is that of her sexuality. She has rejected Lysander's
premature advances (correctly, of course), but her nature, the
energy riding beneath propriety and awaiting the confirmation
that ritual will confer, is ready for the next step. Her running away
from Egeus argues her readiness. But it cannot be all until after
the wedding service.

The dream represents fear and, possibly, the way beyond fear—
the growth and individuation that is at the center of the comic
experience.

We have no problem in fitting Hermia's dream into the Freudian frame, as "a psychological structure, full of significance, and
one which may be assigned a specific place in the psychic activities of the waking activities."[1] The dream seems an obvious
product of repression and at the same time an emblemization of
wish fulfillment, or, as Freud says, the "dream [is] a form of
expression for impulses to which a resistance was attached during
the day, whilst at night they were able to draw reinforcements
from deep-lying sources of excitation."[2] The dream would seem to
insist upon what Hermia wants but cannot consciously express.
The snake, says Freud, is "the most important symbol of the male
member."[3] Norman Holland is even more explicit about the content of Hermia's dream: "the male genital is represented by elongated objects. . . . the sexual act appears metaphorically as

climbing, eating . . . or violent action."[4] Hermia has been raped within her dream, if we accept the Freudian reading, even if the violence has been a function of wish fulfillment. She has been the victim of precisely the activity she has rejected just before she fell asleep. I hasten to add that this is *her* dream and therefore a product of her psyche, as opposed to an actual action imposed upon her by an actual male.

Freud tends to see the unconscious as an epiphenomenon of consciousness. While meaning is disguised, it is clear. Hermia's dream is sexual, pure and simple. The problem bounces back into consciousness. If understood, it is still a problem but one that can be coped with and that is unlikely to produce the condition that psychoanalysts used to call neurosis. If *not* understood, the problem will create further problems and awaits resolution later on.

Freud, of course, argues for a kind of repression even in dreams, a veiling of reality beneath *fin de siècle* Viennese cloakings. The analyst must decode the censor's metaphors. "Further," says Freud, "it might be expected that the sensory intensity (vividness) of single dream-images is in proportion to the psychic intensity of the elements corresponding to them in the dream-thoughts. In the latter, intensity is identical with psychic value; the most intense elements are in fact the most significant, and these constitute the central point of the dream-thoughts. We know, however, that it is precisely these elements which are usually not admitted to the dream-content, owing to the vigilance of the censorship."[5] A "control" intrudes from consciousness—that repository of consensus and social conformity—and conditions the content of the dream, turning male members into narrow fellows in the grass, for example.

Norman Holland employs psychoanalysis to read the dream toward the play's thematics. He sees the dream as evidence of Hermia's ambivalence—a half-dream in which she can reject content: "In the dream [a] sexual union of hearts becomes a snake eating her heart away. . . . [Lysander is] a double person. . . . Hermia's free association for falseness is a snake, and her free association to the snake is the doubleness of its tongue [cf. 'Lysander riddles very prettily.']. She deals with the nightmare by saying she is both in the dream and out of it. . . . She is working out a theme of love within her characteristic way of dealing with inner and outer reality, namely, by finding alternatives. Union in love is one possibility, but she dreams about her fear of it as a deadly possession that could prey upon and eat away her very being." The issue "permeating the play," Holland says, is captured in Hermia's dream: "separation and fusion."[6]

As she dreams, Hermia lies separate by choice, at a moment just before a promised fusion in marriage. She is both outside and inside the experience, the former actually and the latter potentially. Her dream, from a Freudian perspective, captures this undefined "in-betweenness" and must reflect confusion and fear.

The BBC production tends to portray the Freudian approach. Pippa Guard is disturbed by the dream. This is a healthy enough reaction. Hermia's disturbance emerges from the dream and is greatly augmented by her discovery of Lysander's disappearance. Guard carries the "dream anxiety" with her into Hermia's further experience, which involves humiliation and rejection on the personal plane and the rather grudging acceptance that her father finally gives to her determination to be free of his will.

For Jung, what Freud calls the unconscious is the "personal unconscious"—a repository of repressions, not all necessarily sexual. For Jung, sexuality itself can be metaphor: "Sexuality in dreams is, in the first instance, a means of expression and by no means the meaning and aim of the dream."[7] For Jung, the dream metaphor is not necessarily the disguise in which the unconscious conceals the object but is itself often independent of conscious sense impression, indeed a product of that deeper zone that Jung calls the collective unconscious.

Jung, however, would hardly deny the Freudian content of Hermia's dream: "most people who are afraid of the sex-instinct are especially likely to dream of the male sex-organ under the disguise of the snake."[8] And again: "sexuality appears as . . . a terrifying serpent that squeezes its victims to death."[9] Jung goes further, of course: "The snake is the representation of the world of instinct, especially of the vital processes which are psychologically the least accessible of all. Snake dreams always indicate a discrepancy between the attitude of the conscious mind and instinct—the snake being a personification of the threatening aspect of the conflict."[10] Indeed, "the snake, because it casts its skin, is a symbol of renewal."[11]* Thus, that which seems to threaten Her-

---

*Cf. Oberon's "And there the snake throws her enamel'd skin, / Weed wide enough to wrap a fairy in." The fairy world can express its own powers of transformation by embracing the tangible example of that power as provided by the natural world. No doubt the world of the fairies is the "deepest" of the worlds that *A Midsummer Night's Dream* presents. Since, as Jung says, "the snake is the representative of the world of instinct, especially of those vital processes which are psychologically the least accessible of all" (*Symbols of Transformation*, 396), Oberon's couplet supports the analogy between the fairy world and that of the "unconscious."

mia—sexuality—represents a necessary step for her, a step away from the parental control she already resists and away from Egeus's proxy, Demetrius, whom she has already rejected in explicit sexual terms:

> So will I grow, so live, so die, my lord,
> Ere I will yield my virgin patent up
> Unto his lordship, whose unwished yoke
> My soul consents not to give sovereignty.
>
> (1.1.79–82)

While Hermia can reject what she does not want, she cannot yet accept what she does. Indeed, it is tempting to see her choice of the poetic Lysander as opposed to the militant Demetrius as the selection of a less threateningly sexual male. Her ultimate fear, however, is not sexual. "The tendency to stand still," says Jung, "can easily be seen from the special emphasis laid on the inviolateness of the body as well as from the wish to preserve it from the corruptions of the grave. She wants to stop the turning wheel that rolls the years along with it—wants to hang on to childhood and eternal youth rather than die and rot in the earth. But although we can forget, in the dreamy recollection of memories stubbornly held onto, the wheel rolls onward. . . . the poison of the stealthily creeping serpent of time consumes our bodies nonetheless."[12] Hermia's dream encompasses a fear of death itself, not just of that "dying" of a woman's submission to the sexual act. The scene of which Hermia's dream is the finale deals with apparent death, "on the dank and dirty ground" (2.2.75).

In describing the myth of Gilgamesh, Jung says that Gilgamesh "had won the herb of immortality [when] a serpent stole the elixir of life from him while he slept."[13] The herb of immortality is not for mortals to keep. The awakening from sleep to find it gone—stolen by a serpent—is the awakening to the responsibilities of being human, of accepting the death that will come and the love that may. The serpent is an enemy only if we submit passively to his imposition of time upon us.

For Jung, of course, symbols ultimately have positive meanings, regardless of the terror they may impart to the unconscious mind as represented by the dreamer or the conscious mind as it absorbs a dream's impact in that vulnerable zone before full wakefulness occurs. The dream-symbol represents, for Jung, "an analogy [whereby] a change is to be brought about."[14] The serpent "signif[ies] healing. . . . [It] is not only the god of healing; it also has the quality of wisdom and prophecy."[15] It is "an instrument of regeneration."[16]

Indeed, the ultimate myth of human growth—that of Eden—encompasses the serpent not just as Milton's "arch fiend" but as a bringer of wisdom. The myth represents the coming of man to consciousness—a necessary process, regardless of the loss involved. As Edward Edinger says, the myth of Eden "symbolizes the birth of ego."[17] Ego here means consciousness rising free of symbiosis, both phylogenic and ontogenic. "At some point," says Edinger, "unless the forbidden fruit is eaten, unless one dares steal fire from the gods, he will remain stuck in a dependent transference and development will not proceed."[18] We notice in Hermia's dream a glance at Prometheus's punishment, but perhaps primarily the importance of her breaking free of Egeus: "The acquisition of consciousness is a crime," says Edinger, "an act of *hubris* against the powers that be; but it is a necessary crime, leading to a necessary alienation from the natural unconscious state of wholeness."[19]

Hermia—or something in her—knows that this alienation must occur. We watch its progress, one that incorporates even her rejection by the community of youth that has lurched out into the forest. Olivia de Haviland's Hermia does not need her father's blessing, as Pippa Guard's does. De Haviland already approves of Lysander (a considerable feat for the actress!). While the threat in her dream is real, so is de Haviland's relief in discovering that it *was* a dream. De Haviland combines that comfort with an insight *into* the dream. If it signals sexuality—fine! She approves. And so does her partner, Lysander. The editing of the script, of course, shows that she does not reject him at the beginning of the scene. Nor does this Hermia require any consent from her staff-stamping father. Egeues is overruled by a Theseus who has somehow recognized the resolution of the quarrel of Oberon and Titania. Theseus can now wave away a law that had been immutable in the first scene.

It is also, however, the resolution of the conflict within Hermia that permits the decision for comedy. That resolution can be validated by the father figure, Egeus, before the other father figure, Theseus, delivers his judgment, or after. If Hermia, however, has already made up her mind—or psyche—Egeus's blessing is unnecessary. If Egeus's blessing is requested but not forthcoming, then Hermia's comedy is shadowed. Her dream either presents a problem to be resolved within the play—or not resolved—or permits Hermia to resolve the issue in her immediate response to the dream. The former, I suggest, represents the Freudian reading, the latter the Jungian.

That the two approaches, while different, are not mutually exclusive can be suggested by quoting Garber's equation between Hermia's dream and Titania's experience, an equation that emerges from Freudian premises:

> Hermia's experience in the woods . . . is a first step toward a heightened awareness, a necessary incident in the pursuit of self-knowledge. Both specifically Edenic moments in the play [the other being Titania asleep in her bower] thus utilize a fundamentally comic form: the fortunate fall leads ultimately to regeneration, and the apparently innocent unfallen state is seen to be fraught with danger and concomitant with an interior disorder. Experience and change are clearly necessary if the persons of the play are to progress toward a fuller understanding of themselves.[20]

I would go further to suggest that Titania's "understanding" facilitates the restoration of cosmic harmony, thereby permitting other rites of passage—like the multiple marriages of the comic ending—to occur. The "season of matrimony" cannot arrive until the seasons themselves are restored to their sequence.

Obviously, no "right" reading of Hermia's lines exists. Each reading has its power and validity. Just as obviously, no actress could convey a fraction of the theory the serpent summons. Guard and de Haviland, in their very different responses to the material, demonstrate the richness of the moment and the depth of possibilities that resonate within it.*

---

*Since writing this essay, I have seen Peter Hall's made-for-television film (1969), now available commercially. Helen Mirren's dream is pure nightmare, her "Help me!" coming from within the dream. She awakens into similar helplessness. She pushes a branch aside and stares down the path along which Diana Rigg's Helena has loped, with David Warner's Lysander in pursuit. Hermia cowers against a tree, waiting for death, not seeking Lysander. Her appearance in 3.2 is inexplicable, her vigorous rebuff of Demetrius a reflex of her concern for Lysander. While Mirren is out played by Rigg's consciously melodramatic "rejected lover," Hermia is permitted no independent identity here. Gray Athens and muddy woods are variations on a trap: "to be Athenian in the forest is to be ridiculous," says Jack Jorgens (*Shakespeare on Film* [Bloomington: Indiana University Press, 1977], 61.). To be Hermia in the woods is to remain dependent on male decisions and to be victimized by Lysander's passivity in dream and by his absence in wakefulness. On her second awakening (4.1) she gives Lysander a kiss before recognizing the ducal party, as if wishing she had done so earlier, rather than demanding that he "lie further off." Her "Yea, and my father" (4.1.195) emerges from her rediscovered security with Lysander. She seems to choose, as Kathleen McLuskie says, to be "seen *vis-à-vis* men" ("The Patriarchal Bard," in *Political Shakespeare*, ed. Jonathan Dollimore and Alan Sinfield [Manchester: University of Manchester Press, 1985], 95).

The Hall version is notable for the jump cuts and changing landscapes suggestive of the way dreams appear as projected to the awareness of the dreamer. The camera seems at times to have a will of its own, free of what the words seem to dictate. The camera seems intent upon "fracturing . . . naturalistic surfaces," as Jorgens observes (*Shakespeare on Film*, 58), but the effect can "puzzle . . . audiences" (Jorgens, 65). It may be that the effort to simulate "dream" steps at moments over the borders of imitation and denies us appropriate "distance" from the art form. Reinhardt's camera is more languid, as if Mendelsohn were dictating the montage. But Reinhardt does evoke the borderland between human and ethereal—the Indian boy pauses as the fairies launch over a pool, realizing that he cannot fly—and the human and the bestial—Cagney's face transmogrifies to donkeyhood. Cagney sees his new face in a pool—a reversal of Narcissus's experience— is stricken with grief, and takes several crawling steps in his translated status before he stands. Hall attempts to make us experience "dream." Reinhardt attempts to share with us the experience of the humans entangled in the world behind our human assumptions.

In Joan Kemp-Welch's 1968 BBC-TV version, which has just been made commercially available, Maureen Beck's Hermia extends her anger from "cruel prey" to "Lysander!" Her call, then, is a recognition of his violation of his vows of "innocence" (II.ii.45) and of conventional morality within the dream. Lysander, or part of him, is the serpent. The call is also an accusation-in-advance of his desertion. "What remov'd?" seems to have an immediate sexual connotation here, pointing back to the coitus interruptus of the dream and to the bent grasses from which Lysander has arisen to chase Helena.

4

"Must There No More Be Done?": Images of Ophelia

In a brilliant essay, Elaine Showalter describes the difficulties of treating Ophelia as more than "a metaphor for male experience."[1] Lee Edwards claims, after all, that "We can imagine Hamlet's story without Ophelia, but Ophelia literally has no story without Hamlet."[2] Yet Carol Neely asserts that "As a feminist critic, I must 'tell' Ophelia's story."[3]

One teller of Ophelia's story is Rebecca West, who claims that "there is no more bizarre aspect of the misreading of Hamlet's character than the assumption that his relations with Ophelia were innocent and that Ophelia was a correct and timid virgin of exquisite sensibilities."[4] West puts the blame on Millais's model— "the correct, timid, sensitive, virginal, and tubercular Miss Siddal [who was] especially wan during the painting of the picture, for she was immersed in a tin bath full of water kept warm by a lamp placed underneath, like an old-fashioned hot-water dish."[5] By using an objective correlative to indict the Victorian era and its distortion of Ophelia, West at least frees Ophelia from Hamlet, but not from male domination:

> The truth is that Ophelia was a disreputable young woman: not scandalously so, but still disreputable. She was foredoomed to it by her father, whom it is a mistake to regard as a simple platitudinarian. [Ophelia] is not to be kept out of harm's way. She is a card that can be played to take several sorts of tricks. She might be Hamlet's mistress; but she might be more honored for resistance. And if Hamlet was himself an enemy of the king, and an entanglement with him had ceased to be a means of winning favor, then she can give a spy's report on him to Claudius. Surely Ophelia is one of the few authentic portraits of that army of not virgin martyrs, the poor litle girls who were sacrificed to family ambition in the days when the court was a cat's cradle of conspiracies. Man's persuasion that his honor depends on

the chastity of his womenfolk has always been liable to waste away and perish within sight of a throne. [Ophelia is] treated as a thing because it happens to be female.[6]

I quote West thus at length not merely because I believe her indictment to be true but because she demonstrates some of the problems inherent in "telling Ophelia's story." West's book emerges from some questionable premises about Shakespeare's disgust with sexuality. That attitude, if accurately attributed, conditions West's telling of Ophelia's story. West thesis depends upon an elaboration of textual hintings and an ignoring of aspects in the Elsinore environment that favor Ophelia, like Gertrude's belated hope in the graveyard. (though one could argue that Gertrude's hopes preceded her own abandonment of Ophelia: "I will not speak with her" [4.5.1]).

West's is a kind of "new historicism." She appeals for her Ophelia to Ann Boleyn, Katherine Howard, and Lady Rochford, who had been tortured into madness by the time her head was cut off. Ophelia comes alive in West's context. Ophelia comes alive in the world of Elsinore's hypocrisy: "Shakespeare will not allow anyone in the graveyard scene, even to the priest, to be without sin. Each of them has helped to dig the girl's grave. Hamlet was the most guilty, for he had been her spurious lover and a tyrant prince, giving her no protection as a mistress or as one of his people; but it was the whole court that had destroyed her."[7]

One could extend West's insights by suggesting that Ophelia's "Come my coach!" (4.5.71) signals her conscious acceptance of her brother's and father's arguments about Hamlet being a "prince out of [her] star" (2.2.141). Ophelia becomes a queen in her madness, oblivious to the helplessness of "beauteous majesty" (4.5.21) and to Gertrude's hope that Ophelia should have been "Hamlet's wife" (5.1.244) and therefore Queen Ophelia of Denmark. Gertrude's hope is expressed too late, perhaps even with that hypocrisy that is too deep to be anything but sincerity to its perpetrator. The belated hope, however, signals in several ways the predominance of the male points of view. Ophelia's hidden self, now free to express itself, knows as much:

> Young men will do't, if they come to't.
> By Cock, they are to blame.

> (4.5.60–61)

In *Hamlet*, the effort to defeat the phallic intention is as destructive as the intention itself. As both Laertes and Hamlet leap into her grave, Ophelia becomes Freud's third feminine manifestation—death.

Showalter brings the Millais painting forward in time through the iconography of the Victorian madwoman, often tricked out as an Ophelia, paradigm of feminine weakness (and of feminine vulnerability to such cruel stereotyping and display). "Ophelia *does* have a story," Showalter argues. It is "the *history* of her representation."[8] Showalter concludes that "There is no 'true' Ophelia for whom feminist criticism must unambiguously speak, but perhaps only a Cubist Ophelia of multiple perspectives, more than the sum of all her parts."[9]

As an addendum to the history of Ophelia's representation, I will describe some filmic and televisual versions of Ophelia. My interpretation is conditioned by my own psychology of perception and my awareness that Derrida doesn't "believe that anything like perception exists."[10] I do not attempt to coerce agreement even to the principle of perception but do hope to stimulate discussions of those images of Ophelia that various viewers may perceive as she descends the staircases of a variety of productions.

Olivier's Ophelia, Jean Simmons, is a "timid, innocent"[11] contrast to Eileen Herlie's solidly sensuous Gertrude. Simmons is associated with nature, the out-of-doors, a linkage finally fulfilled in the "cruising down the river" scene. The camera permits Ophelia to float on by then pans to an empty surface of stream—the canvas hanging next to the Millais, a portrait of weeds and bubbles. As Robert A. Duffy says, "Olivier often composes [Ophelia's] scenes to include a glimpse of countryside visible in deep field. A floral pattern decorates her walls. Only she seems to have direct access into the daylight world of generation. . . . Hers is the only apartment with real windows and seemingly the only one accessible to sunlight."[12]

Claudius (Basil Sydney) is reduced to Hamlet's worst assessment of him. Simmons's fragile beauty and her destruction makes her role more than a gracenote in a film focusing upon Hamlet (and Olivier). The "Ophelia moment" comes when the Boy Actor dons a blonde wig and looks just like Ophelia.* Olivier sees the resemblance and disapproves, thereby rejecting the concept of androgyny and the feminine nature within himself, that nature

---

*A similar moment occurred in the undistinguished RSC production of 1985. As a disconsolate Ophelia wandered off after 3.1, the Boy Actor entered and stared at her, as if recognizing another person forced to play a role that proclaimed against identity.

burgeoning beyond the claustrophobic corridors and phallic columns of the castle, the nature into which Ophelia runs early in the film. Hamlet embraces misogyny at that moment, and nature becomes that little plot of ground enclosed to make a graveyard.

This Ophelia is given more than just the status of projection of brother's/father's/lover's expectations/fears/fantasies. Her independent configuration, however, is still imaged out of what Hamlet, like the Boy Actor, her other look-alike, lacks. Simmons's Ophelia is still partially a function of a male point of view, even if that viewpoint be the unconscious and unexpressed position of the anima.[13]

It is probably true of *Hamlet* that, as Kathleen McLuskie says of *Measure for Measure*, "the text . . . denies [the] free-play of a [feminine] character. [It defines] women as sexualized, seen *vis-à-vis* men."[14] Women are, in *Hamlet*, as McLuskie argues, "objects of exchange within [a] system of sexuality."[15] It is to Olivier's credit that he allows Simmon's Ophelia to represent an alternative feminine option to the system that destroys her, however timid and innocent *she* is. She draws on resources deeper than mere personality, even if the Elsinorean norm takes her personality away—or forces it to emerge under the shield of madness. Like Anne Frank, Ophelia never understands what happened to her. Evil can be more real than optimistic theories to the contrary. But Simmon's Ophelia is an individualized embodiment of a point of view other than that of the dominant ideology. As E. Ann Kaplan says of "essentialist feminism," "Female values become a means for critiquing the harsh, competitive and individualistic 'male' values that govern society and offer an alternate way, not only of *seeing* but of *being*, that threatens patriarchy."[16] That thesis, applied to Olivier's *Hamlet*, makes Ophelia's death more than merely pathetic.

Lillian Wilds's description of Dunja Movar's Ophelia in the Wirth/Schell made-for-television film (Austria, 1961) is unexceptional.

Dissonant music is [used] to project the discord that Ophelia sees in Hamlet's mind as he comes to her chamber wearing his antic disposition. The first jagged note sounds when Hamlet's shadow falls across the girl and the flowers she is embroidering—forever blighting her and them. The strange music mounts in intensity as Hamlet himself appears in the shot and mimes the actions . . . Ophelia describe[s] (unspoken . . . in this film). The music growing louder and louder pursues Ophelia and she runs terrified past the rough square columns, coming to an abrupt stop only when she encounters her father and flings herself into his arms.

This approach makes Ophelia not only the victim of Hamlet (and, since she has repelled Hamlet's letters as instructed, of Polonius) but also of the sound man's rheostat. Wilds's description of the nunnery scene, however, reflects a sensitive Hamlet and the purposes mistook and gone awry in Elsinore:

> Hamlet, having overheard the scheme to use Ophelia to trap him, holds her—both of them framed in a close-up two shot—as he whispers in her ear. "Where is your father?" giving her, in this version, the opportunity to whisper back the truth. She starts to tell him, then glances desperately at the concealing arras and lies, "At home, my lord." He flings her roughly onto a stone bench and, holding her down, kisses her brutally twice, while speaking loudly for the benefit of his hidden auditors. He is kneeling behind Ophelia with the concealed Claudius and Polonius behind him. . . . The medium close-up lets us see what even Ophelia cannot, the misery and anguish in his face as he touches his lips—too lightly to be felt—to her hair before he leaves. (One is convinced in this film, as one is not always, that Hamlet really loves Ophelia).[17]

At the court exits from 1.2, Ophelia pauses next to Hamlet, expecting a response. He, however, is involved in the internal monologue of his first soliloquy. As she passes by, the voice-over is saying the lines about the everlasting having fixed his canon against self-slaughter. Movar is given the lines about Hamlet's "noble mind . . . o'erthrown," and speaks "Woe is me . . . to see what I see" to Claudius, identifying him as the source of "overthrow" in Elsinore, in a fleeting moment that presages her own madness. She is "metal *more* attractive" in the play scene. The colloquy about "country matters" is left in, but gently so, in a production that is more "pro-Hamlet" than even Olivier's version. Ophelia has one mad scene here, after Laertes's angry entrance. She has little more than two minutes on screen. Her "flowers" are a clump of wheat—their specific identities her invention—and her songs are mostly humming. Her "rosemary" goes to Laertes. Her line, "Pray, you, love, remember," is delivered to the brother she no longer remembers. Gertrude drops her "rue," but Movar picks it up and hands it to Gertrude again. "You may wear *your* rue with a difference." Movar is like a child insisting on *her* gift and its recipient. While she gets some of the lines about Polonius's death and bare-faced funeral, the emphasis of the scene is on Laertes's revenge. The dominant lines are "by heaven, thy madness shall be paid by weight," "Had thou thy wits and didst persuade revenge, it could not move thus," and "where the offense is, let the great ax fall." The mad Ophelia is primarily someone who helps Claudius turn Laertes's rage against Hamlet.

The Ophelia of the Richardson film (1969), Marianne Faithfull, remains controversial, to say the least. Critics cannot agree on what they take her portrayal to signify.

I take the relationship between Ophelia and Laertes to be obviously incestuous. It makes his return to Paris imperative, lest the scarcely concealed lust become public as well as pubic. Laertes is already "aboard—for shame!" as Polonius interrupts an Ophelia who is not prone to argue. The question of Hamlet's love for her is strangely answered. She has already been appropriated by the young man across the hall. Michael Mullin notes that "Marianne Faithfull chuckles when her dandified brother cautions her to guard her 'chaste treasure,' as if they shared a naughty secret."[18] Jack Jorgens says that "a passionate kiss between Laertes and Ophelia shows how the disease of incest has spread outward in the court from the King and Queen."[19]

Mullin's description of the nunnery scene suggests that Ophelia is willing to accept Hamlet as a stand-in for Laertes:

> She lies back in a plush hammock, posed for seduction, her dress in dishabille, waiting for Hamlet. He comes to her, needing solace and ready to take it. As he speaks, he bends over to kiss her. Suddenly, we are in the darkness behind the arras with Claudius and Polonius. Unseen we watch, like voyeurs, as she leads him on. A flicker of movement behind the arras catches Hamlet's eyes, he checks, sees the trap, and, looking now at the confused Ophelia, now at the dark opening in the arras, his fury mounts, fed by hatred of his enemies and a sexual frustration which makes every word he speaks a bawdy insult.[20]

Give this reading of this Ophelia, those insults seem overdue.

Glenn Litton, however, discerns a very different Ophelia within the identical performance: she represents a "languid love-in-idleness. . . At one moment she seems pitifully vulnerable, especially when Hamlet turns against her after spotting Polonius in hiding. Here her prone position in the hammock makes her all the more defenseless."[21] One could argue, however, that Ophelia has placed herself in a specifically vulnerable position by making herself an obvious object of male desire with a format of male-dictated politics. The frame may be beyond her control, but her position within it is not.

Litton goes on to say that "at other times her unself-consciousness, innocent sexuality seems almost perverse."[22] He describes her departure from Laertes as

> exchanges which [begin] to look like intimate love play [and] end in a long, ardent farewell kiss. The embrace seems indulged in not only as an expression of brotherly and sisterly affection but also for sensual pleasure. Yet Ophelia's unashamed and quite composed reactions upon Polonius's interruption of the kiss show that at least she has no incestuous intentions. She naturally indulges in pleasure without knowledge of its potential dangers and without the consequent guilt. She is as Eve before the fall.[23]

This subtle reading of a Faithfull's performance puts Ophelia into that category of qualified innocence where the precocity of her body trembles on the verge of articulation. One could argue as well that she sees nothing at all shameful in incest, particularly as Elsinore, where the practice has been royally condoned. Litton's reading, however, allows him to go on to suggest that, in her madness,

> separated from the painful meanings of what she has experienced, Ophelia can attempt to share her experience with Claudius and Gertrude. [Claudius] must pretend, in defense of his own sanity and for political reasons, not to understand the tragic intuition Ophelia presses upon him. . . . for Claudius, Ophelia's songs, chatter and mime are as threatening as The Mousetrap and his own efforts, under the crucifix, to come to terms with his sins. . . . Gertrude . . . perhaps wholeheartedly seeking salvation, is more receptive to Ophelia's opaque communications. [Getrude's] report of Ophelia's death is a poetic reworking of the same vision, of perverse beauty, of love-in-death, even of chaste innocence mixed with coarse sexuality.[24]

This Ophelia is a conveyor of knowledge that cannot be brought to consciousness. Insight is contradicted by language, and intuition is canceled by that construct of rationality we call consciousness. Litton, then, refutes the grosser name that I and other auditors of the film have given Faithfull's interpretation. I leave it to others to determine which area of the spectrum of possibilities this Ophelia inhabits. Perhaps she is in a "pre-Gertrudian" state, that is, precisely in that zone where meaning resides before naming begins. Flowers and their specific equivalencies only italicize Ophelia's sense that "You may wear your rue with a difference."

A reviewing of the film convinces me that brother and sister are also lovers. Faithfull resents Laertes's sermon at first. She smiles on "chaste treasure," then begins to laugh as he talks of Hamlet's "unmastered importunity," Oh, so that's what you are trying to tell me! Well, you had better heed your own advice! This is a priggish Laertes couching his jealous fears in apparent concern for his sister. The incestuous subtext gives the scene and the stilted homilies an exciting energy.

Ciaran Madden, in the 1970 Peter Wood television production (Hallmark Hall of Fame), is excellent, except in the scenes she shares with a Richard Chamberlain who has rehearsed only the soliloquies. Madden, a pale blonde, is a victim of a male world dressed in dark George Thirdian garb. While Madden is a younger version of Margaret Leighton's maturely glamorous and sombergowned Gertrude, Madden's spiritual alter ego is John Gielgud's wispy Ghost.

This version is greatly condensed for television. Left in, however, is most of Polonius's lecture on the true cause of Hamlet's madness and Hamlet's question of Polonius: "Have you a daughter?" Ophelia is shattered by Laertes's dismissal of Hamlet's love. "No more but so?" she says, deferring helplessly to her brother's expertise in these matters. After Laertes rattles off in an elegant barouche, Michael Redgrave's Polonius draws Ophelia to a calm and sunlit area of the courtyard. She is reluctant to discuss her private life with her pompous father and responds to his contempt with an effort at dignity. Trying to grow up, she is pooh-poohed by this self-serving father. He forbids her to see Hamlet and strides off, commanding, "Come your ways!" "I shall obey, my lord," she says, then closes her eyes against her anguish.

Madden's mad scenes, which consume a bit more than four minutes, are splendid. She sweeps in with a "Where is the beauteous majesty of Denmark?" that is triumphant—almost as if *she* is that person. The moment nicely anticipates Laertes's later break-in. She covers the eyes of a startled Gertrude ("How should I your true love know?") as if to hint that Gertrude has come between her and Hamlet. She knows she has said a bad thing with "the owl was a baker's daughter," covers her mouth and hides behind a chair. She hops cross-legged to a table to confront Claudius with "Then up he rose and donn'd his clothes," as if he had been the seducer of her song. But then, to demonstrate her own freedom from such male game-playing, she spins around to embrace Horatio.

She enters again, wrapped in a sheet, with "He is dead and gone," as if, like the Ghost, bringing news from beyond the grave. On the word "thoughts," she tosses pansies over her head. So much for thoughts. The sheet she wears pinions her elbows à la Millais's floating Ophelia. Laertes unwinds her winding sheet, but she retrieves it and puts it on again, as a shawl. She kneels and crosses herself on "God have mercy," then rises and poses triumphantly, a burlesque bride, beauteous majesty of Denmark, symbol of eros-thanatos, marriage-funeral, the play's beginning and ending.

Madden's Ophelia is considerably enhanced by Redgrave's Polonius, whose absence—far more than Hamlet's—leaves a vacuum in his daughter's life. But this Polonius has built the vacuum. Having submitted to her brother's vision of Hamlet's "trifling" and to her father's insistence that she is but a "green girl," this Ophelia can find maturity only in a delighted madness that plays off the appalled reactions of her mute audience. Asserting her own authority, she reduces that lecturing male world to silence.

Kozintsev's Ophelia, Anastasia Vertinskaya, has a fragile, almost Oriental beauty and wears a dress embroidered with flowers. She wanders through the smoke and tumult of Laertes's rebellion in uncomprehending bliss, her madness an event mirroring psychically Elsinore's politics. Of an earlier Ophelia, Nina Mamaeva, Kozintsev says,

> She must only be convinced that madness is happiness for Ophelia. . . . the happier the madwoman feels in her madness, the more tragic her situation. . . . She has not yet said a word, but everyone already knows what life is for her. Her father and brother instruct her, compel her to renounce love. . . . She is confused and understands nothing. Elsinore chains her to lifeless ceremonial. She is "the minister's daughter," the "first young lady of Denmark." And she is not suited by her spiritual constitution for all of this.[25]

Thus Kozintsev elevates a good and uncomplicated child to the status of "rose and expectancy." She can only escape into madness. Kozintsev's Ophelia is not just a victim of inevitable male insensitivity, but of the politics of the inevitably male world. "Olivier," says Kozintsev, "cut the theme of government which I find very interesting."[26]

This Ophelia, then, even in madness, is more the figure Rebecca West presents than was Olivier's. Kozintsev's Ophelia achieves a madness beyond anything she might have intended, even via the indirection of the unconscious. "Ophelia's madness," Kozintsev says, "is a social event. People listen to her gibberish and look for a secret meaning in its nonsense. The government reels. This madwoman is a sign of disaster. The consciences of Gertrude and Claudius come to life."[27] Ophelia's "gibberish," of course, emerges from a context at which the people can guess. Polonius has not been given a state funeral, but he has not been kept alive, either, by the support systems of state propaganda.

Kozintsev's Ophelia "does not love Hamlet with any sort of exalted abstract emotion, but probably as Juliet loved Romeo. I speak of passion. In the beginning, Polonius's daughter must have all of the nuances of those first feelings towards a man: the sinking of the heart, the expectation, passion, and breathlessness."[28] Here a man, however gifted and sensitive, describes Ophelia's experience of "first love." As Kozintsev emerges from his own androgyny, he provides sensation for his actress, and a stereotype for his Ophelia. Drama, however, and film (and particularly television, which cannot get beyond them) emerge from stereotypical models. Shakespeare explores the normative point of view, holds it up, turns it around, and fires it in the kiln of his curiosity until it emerges as a person whose story we feel compelled to tell. If we can forgive Kozintsev for what some would call a "male view" of Ophelia, we grant him his prerogatives as a maker of films.

Kozintsev assigns the blame accurately: "The people who are driving Ophelia to madness and death love her very much. Both Laertes and Polonius, and Hamlet. In every scene of violence of her feelings and will, it must be perceptible that they demand her rejection of happiness only because they love her. A tender brother, an affectionate father, and an ardent lover drive her to the grave in the name of the finest emotions."[29]

"There is," says Kozintsev, "among the rocks of Elsinore, a strange aerie, the room of a little girl; it is painted with fabulous unicorns and birds, as though it were a copy of the spiritual world of Polonius's daughter."[30] If this were accurate more mythology should emerge via the avenue of Ophelia's madness. As it is, Kozintsev depicts a little girl who can find no doorway into Narnia behind her wardrobe. Whether the background for the psychic portrait is accurate or not, Kozintsev documents the foreground and future: "They force her to be a court lady. She is crammed into finery and smothered with a corset. She is utter naturalness, but they cripple her with a conventional etiquette, mutilate her simple language with artificiality."[31]

Olivier's concept of Ophelia as energy opposite to that of the espionage of Claudius's court is extended here to an Ophelia who characterizes Claudius's court—as do the many reluctants whose identities are denied by some transient "dominant ideology." Kozintsev cages Ophelia in iron that dominates his constant sense that "thoughts of Ophelia recall flowers above all."[32] Beneath the repression drives the demand for regression, as Kozintsev has suggested in limning Ophelia's room: "she tears off the collar, which strangles her, and unfastens a corset. She gets out of the huge unyielding dress as though crawling out of a black shell; she steps out of her high heels—a small, slender girl who was born under a cold northern star. Now it is well, and easy for her. She frisks and plays about in the dark empty halls."[33]

Jorgens expresses Kozintsev's Ophelia nicely: She is "a living paradox—supple and young, yet dancing like a puppet to a tune whose rhythm is out of joint, played on the harpsichord with the hesitant irregular pace of the novice. She is innocent and well-meaning, yet easily manipulated by Hamlet and Hamlet's enemies, angelic and girlish in her madness, a saint among barbarians, yet paradoxically aged, bawdy, and shrunken as she sings ballads, runs stiffly under the stairs like an old woman recalling games of hide-and-seek and distributes dead twigs to hatchet-faced soldiers."[34]

Kozintsev, then, sets in motion more than one plane of the cubist Ophelia—the life-in-death that West, for example, attributes to Millais's model, poor Miss Siddal. Kozintsev's Ophelia withers when her father dies even as she flowers into madness. Finally, however, she merges with the Elsinorean norm, as Jorgens suggests: "In her lyrical madness she seems to escape the restraints and ugliness of the court, but lying dead in the stream she has become once more a solitary, two-dimensional figure."[35] Not guilty by reason of insanity turns out to be no defense for Ophelia.

Henry Fenwick, writing of the BBC-TV production of 1980, claims that "the part of Ophelia [is] underwritten, from an actress's viewpoint."[36] But Lalla Ward, the Ophelia, disagrees: "One thinks wouldn't it be nice if there was a scene where Hamlet and Ophelia were happy together. But . . . you don't actually need it—in the end you find it's all there. To me it's nonsensical to think she could ever have had an affair with Hamlet. . . . * I don't see, if she had, how she could have been as frightened of him as she was in the nunnery scene."[37]

---

*And yet a perceptive observer can see otherwise: Hamlet and Ophelia "have been lovers; this is unmistakable in the intimate gesture he makes to her in the 'nunnery scene'" (Cecil Smith, *Los Angeles Times*, 10 November 1980), vi, 1.

A previous affair, Ward says, would have eliminated the fear she imputes to Ophelia in the nunnery scene. If we grant Ophelia's fear—and it can be there in spite of her awareness of her hidden audience or because of it—we may also claim that a confrontation with a former lover can evoke fear. At some point—and Ophelia has reached it—there will be no more lovers. Perhaps at some point that fact is no longer a fear. But Ophelia has not yet reached that point.

Ward suggests that the actress playing Ophelia must "show her progress from thinking things might go well to knowing damn well they won't. . . . one of the most moving lines in the part is when she says, 'I hope all will be well,' because you realize then how much time she must have spent on her own thinking exactly that. . . . she says to Claudius, in the mad scene, 'I thank you for your good counsel,' [but] *nobody* in the play ever gives Ophelia a *word* of good counsel! She's got no mother and by the time Polonius dies she's neglected—about a month must pass without anybody caring about her or asking where she is or wondering about her. And you have to mull over in your mind what effect that would have. She must have had an awful lot of time to think, an awful lot of time with no one to turn to."[38]

Ward's most effective scenes, as so often with this part, are the mad scenes. They are much more than the balancing of funereal reminiscences and bawdy songs and the distribution of local weeds. Wards plays up to Claudius, discovering in his troubled sexuality a correlative to her repression. She is still a virgin, but her psyche is a strumpet. She gives Laertes a saucy kiss and looks enormously pleased with her newfound ability to express herself as someone other than Gertrude's weak-chinned look-alike. Ward is particularly effective with her frightened "They say the owl was a baker's daughter," which links up with "Lord, we know what we are, but know not what we may be." It is as if Ward's Ophelia is afraid that she, like the baker's daughter, has committed some terrible blasphemy that has resulted in a punishing transformation.

Ward's performance is analogous to that sector of Lear's madness wherein the dissolution of society that Lear has engendered can only be equated to and attributed to the foulness of the female neither regions. Ward implies that Denmark's rot is a function of *male* sexuality gone awry, (that is, assuming it ever goes aright). These scenes balance Hamlet's perhaps equally perverse condemnation of Woman. Hamlet's preoccupation with sexuality, of course, tends to concentrate on foreplay, a fact supporting Ward's denial of an affair. Lear's obsession, and Ophelia's is on the "(no) thing itself."

Ward stresses the time Ophelia has alone. Ragnar Lyth's brilliant (if often gross) Swedish film-for-television (1984) makes much of that time, indeed makes of Pernilla Wallgren's "Ofelia" a powerful focal point of the production.

Since the production is not commercially available, I will give an extended description of an Ophelia apparently conceived within the context of the feminist movement.

Wallgren's dark-haired and stocky Ophelia resembles Mona Malm's porcine Gertrude just enough to lend a shadow of oedipal motivation to Stellan Skarsgaard's Hamlet. The latter seems either sexually ambivalent or so confused about his own adolescent crisis as to confuse and frighten any woman foolish enough to get close. One danger of such fellows as these is that, in an increasingly authoritarian world, they validate the preference of the Danish electors for Claudius (though not necessarily the Swedish Claudius) and force the deletion of Ophelia's eulogy about courtier, soldier, and scholar. If retained, Ophelia's speech would have resembled the eulogy for his father that James Baldwin so brilliantly recapitulates in *Notes of a Native Son*—where the encomiums create a person no one recognizes as ever having lived.

No matter who Hamlet is, however, Wallgren's Ophelia appears before he does. She looks on—although we have not yet identified her—as Laertes practices rapier and dagger in the downtown athletic club that is also Elsinore's room of state. She threads through state business a few moments later with a note for Hamlet. The latter stands with his back to the court, looking out a window. Polonius (Swen Lindberg), a Martin Borman to Frej Lindquist's consistently ingratiating Claudius, notes his daughter's proximity to Hamlet, disapproves, but must attend to his career. He takes a moment off to wave Ophelia peremptorily away from the window. Come here! his gesture says. After he requests that Claudius "give *him* [Laertes] leave," he darts a dirty look at Ophelia, who has arrived behind him. She curtsies. As Hamlet begins a voice-over soliloquy, à la Wirth and Kozintsev, Laertes grabs an Ophelia who would like a private word with Hamlet, now that state business has been concluded, and yanks her out of the room. Lyth makes Ophelia central to a scene in which she is scripted to appear—if at all—as merely an attendant lady.

The "Ophelia music"—the soft, hollow tones of an ocarina (an instrument named after the goose)—sounds as Ophelia lies on her bed, moving her thighs together below her dress as she reads Hamlet's letters. As Laertes enters, she pulls a sheet over the letters. She hums her theme against his lecture and throws "the primrose path" at him as an angry rebuke. She resents his freedom. As Laertes steps into the white light beyond Elsinore's gate, she gives him white violets.

The gate closes, casting father and daughter into shadow. Polonius marches Ophelia under the low stone arches of the cellar, lecturing her on the way. She is angry but helpless.

Hamlet, meanwhile, has been up all night. He drives a dagger into some wooden steps, retrieves it, and breaks in upon Ophelia, who, in a borrowing from Kozintsev, is being strapped into a metal frame. Hamlet sends the servant scuttling away and grabs Ophelia. She slaps him. Polonius appears and orders Hamlet out. Hamlet tosses goose-quills at him, pushes him on the nose, and leaves. Polonius enters Ophelia's room and reads Hamlet's letters. He amends his initial "mad" to "mad—for thy love!": Ah ha!—a plan. Here Ophelia is depicted as total victim—of Hamlet's outrageous behavior and of Polonius's translation of love letters into politics.

The sequence is virtually wordless. The contrast between Laertes's freedom and the restrictions, both verbal and physical, placed on Ophelia is clearly made. Hamlet—a pouty tennis star or a rotten rock idol—shares Ophelia's imprisonment but cannot articulate their common dilemma. His coming to her merely increases the zone of isolation that surrounds each of them. He returns to his chamber and rips apart a flowered headdress we assume to have been hers. Hamlet then smashes the twin Holbein sketches of King and Queen and, like an angry frat-boy, trashes his room, tossing books around and about and out the window, their leaves fluttering down upon a bewildered peasant in the courtyard. Books? Worthless! And so much for love!

Hamlet sees Ophelia summoned to Claudius. As she arrives before the King, her letters from Hamlet spill out, much to Polonius's embarrassment. Untidy girl! She resents his reading the letters aloud but warms to "Doubt that the stars are fire. . . ." The words create status for her even amid the degradation her father is inflicting upon her. Gertrude smiles at Ophelia and, as Polonius and Claudius plot, leads her off in friendly female chatter

Hamlet warns Polonius not to send his daughter to him. As Hamlet trades wit with Rosencrantz and Guildenstern, Hamlet's "about her waist," is delivered to Polonius and Ophelia. His "strumpet" is directed at Ophelia. She is a visible embodiment of fickleness.

Again, before the nunnery scene, Gertrude is friendly with Ophelia. For Gertrude, all of this is an entertaining diversion from official duties. Polonius arranges Ophelia before a fireplace. As Hamlet enters, Ophelia tries to pretend this his gifts mean nothing to her now. But she breaks into tears on "I was the more deceived." Hamlet's "get thee to a nunnery," is tender, delivered from within an embrace. He repeats his "Where is your father?" She weeps again as she lies. He pushes her down, exits, returns with "this plague," tosses apples at her, almost strangles her, then wipes her face roughly. Her "paintings" offend him. She clings to Hamlet's feet. He kicks her away. Polonius adjusts his spectacles.

As Claudius, Gertrude, and Polonius enter, Ophelia lies face down on the floor. She gets up, and Gertrude turns her back. Ophelia, obviously, no longer counts. Gertrude values her own place within the hierarchy and has no time for anyone who cannot contribute to her position. This Gertrude tells us why she married this Claudius—all kings look alike in the dark. She later defends a Claudius with whom she is personally disgusted as Laertes breaks in. As for Ophelia—as West suggests, "If royal approval was withdrawn from . . . the family which had hawked the girl, she was as apt to suffer fatality as any of her kinsmen. The ax has never known chivalry."[39]

Here, Polonius attempts to regain some vestige of authority by ordering Ophelia out with one of his brusque gestures. The "Oh, what a noble mind" speech is cut. This Hamlet could not be the subject for a paean on male perfection, nor does the film depict Hamlet (or anyone else) as skilled in the games that nobles play.

At the play scene, Ophelia is the butt of Hamlet's very public jokes and insults. Polonius, at first pleased by the reestablishment of his thesis, grows uncomfortable but is powerless to do anything for the daughter he has so blatantly exploited.

As "Gonzago" breaks up, Ophelia is jostled in the crowd, no longer able to make her way decisively through it, as she had in the opening scene. Hamlet engages in song-and-dance with the Players as Ophelia returns to her room. She laughs unhappily, looks into the mirror, then wipes compulsively at her mouth, remembering Hamlet's anger about her "paintings." Her compulsive wiping—a slight hint of Lady Macbeth—cannot turn her into what Hamlet wants. She can do nothing about the cosmetic of the flesh itself, now proved to have been unmarketable.

Searching for Hamlet, Rosencrantz and Guildenstern break in

upon a cowering Ophelia, playing her ocarina. They leave, but their shouts of "Prince Hamlet!" voice over her image.

Hamlet exits into a fjord-driven mist. Ophelia sleeps on her single bed. Her theme sounds over an oceanview. Vermeerian light suffuses her room as she twists a braid. She now wears a disheveled frock. She looks at her Holbein sketch of Gertrude and asks, "Where is the beauteous majesty of Denmark?" Trying to get out of her room she opens upon a grossly sexual scene that seems to feature a priest. Denmark is there, perhaps, but no beauty nor any majesty. She is rejected by Horatio, who prefers his book, and runs through the abandoned room of state, still shouting, "Where is the beauteous majesty of Demmark?" She breaks in upon a reception, creating a nasty social problem for Gertrude and causing all the neighboring dogs to bark. Pushed into a room away from the outdoor gathering, Ophelia is that sometime paradox, corrupted beauty vividly imaged in the negative of Gertrude's ugly sanity. Amused at having created her disturbance—the neglected child controlling the grown-ups via the politics of tantrum—Ophelia exits past the faces of the people who have been filling in her blanks and into the same merciless light that has swallowed Laertes and Hamlet. She is out of prison at last.

Burghers look down at something below camera range. A child picks up an ocarina and plays a few notes before her mother angrily plucks the instrument from the child's lips and flings it down into the channel, perhaps an open sewer, where Ophelia lies under an inch or two of water. Gertrude drops Ophelia's soaked cloak into Laertes's lap. He knows. The drowning is not dignified or pastoralized with words about willows or brooks or old lauds. This Gertrude is incapable of even the temporary dignity that West grants her: "the fusion of perception and obtuseness in these lines [4.7.166–83], and the contrast between their distinction and the empty rotundity of all the Queen's other speeches, convince us that just once this dull woman was so moved that her tongue became alive."[40] Here the Queen can only glimpse with resignation the crumbling arch of her own regime. That loss is all that matters to her.

Rain washes clay from a skull. A funeral rushes over a muddy hillside in a Bergmanian dance. The coffin is opened for Gertrude's ministrations—here the necessary rationalizations of politics—and Ophelia, eyes closed, lies there as if alive, her brow luminous. Laertes and Hamlet scuffle and knock the coffin aside. Like a rag doll, Ophelia tumbles down into the mud of her grave. Even in death, she is the victim of the games men play. "I lov'd

Ophelia!" Hamlet cries, as the camera shows the object of this affection curled into muck and shadow.

As Hamlet exits with Horatio over the hill, we hear the sound of nails being hammered down upon the coffin lid. It is a borrowing from Kozintsev, but powerful, as is so much else in this superb graveyard scene. The comic analogues to the off-camera sound are the sawing attendant upon the removal of a stiff horse from the Dean's office in *Animal House,* and the sweetly singing ladies attending a funeral for one of their victims in *Arsenic and Old Lace.*

The Lyth film is to *Hamlet* what Peter Brook's film is to *King Lear*—a suggestion of what the late twentieth century can find in an early-sixteenth-century script.[41]

As Showalter suggests, no *true* Ophelia exists. She is the function of directorial conception and of a script that grants her little, if any, independent identity, except within the self-destructive world she creates out of uprooted flowers.

That world has been created for her, of course, as Anna K. Nardo incisively suggests: "Both her father and her former lover have prepared her for madness by demanding that she be virginal while treating her like a whore, and by discouraging her from thinking for herself, in which case she might perceive the incongruity of their demands"—and might even perceive in Hamlet's "nunnery" a pun that encompasses the contradictory role she is asked to play. As Nardo says, seconding West's suggestions, Polonius "delivers contradictory messages to Ophelia: (1) you are a baby, an innocent, whose virginity must remain undefiled, and therefore you must reject Hamlet's attentions; (2) you are capable of having a baby ('You'll tender me a fool'), of attracting a 30-year-old heir apparent, and perhaps of winning a queenship if you 'Tender yourself more *dearly,*' and 'Set your entreatment at a *higher rate.*' " "Tender" is also a pun, of course, on currency and sexuality. Of the lass in Ophelia's St. Valentine's Day song (4.5.47–66) Nardo says, "If she refuses his sexual encounter, she will jeopardize [the] marriage proposal; but because she accepts the offer, he withdraws the proposal. Like Ophelia, the lass is simultaneously treated like a whore and told to be a virgin. . . . But even though her song verifies and recalls her own situation, Ophelia has lost all clarity of vision, and her mad actions dramatize her paralysis between child-like innocence and adult sexual knowledge."[42]

The Lyth film was shot at the abandoned Nobel dynamite factory. Having invented the means whereby modern war could be conducted, Nobel left his fortune to create prizes for peace.

The world Lyth creates within these abandoned walls suggests that both war and the destruction of women are functions of a male world that existed long before it got its hands on dynamite with which to blow up anyone hapless enough to have been born—male or female.

5

Jacobi and the Players

The BBC *Hamlet* is probably the best version of the play we are likely to see this side of the stage. It is a television production, of course, but one that achieves depth within a medium that tends toward shallowness—its lack of physical depth seeming to dictate a lack of emotional and intellectual depth as well. Part of the problem, of course, is that television has conditioned our expectations to brief episodes between "commercial messages" and to closure in which the issues raised between the commercials are resolved. The conditioning of attention span and the reduction to simplistic problems and solutions means that "Shakespeare on television," unless rendered within a network format, demands a different audience, one conditioned by the experience of the stage. Not much can be done with the scale of television, its feeling of mechanical reproduction, or the fact that Shakespeare scenes are not tailored to television's segmental requirements. Shakespeare is trapped, however, within the conventions of television, as we recognize when we see those conventions ignored, as some of Jonathan Miller's dull static-camera sequences attest.

Although "image" and "thematic" criticism has been replaced by what James Atlas calls "the new canonicity,"[1] no doubt exists that Shakespeare's scripts create interrelationships within themselves, interrelationships that his stage is designed to show us as the script explores that stage but that the shifting point of view of a three camera format often cannot show us. The camera can show us "relationship" but often cannot give us a sense of what Sheldon Zitner calls Shakespeare's "relational stage."[2] In *Hamlet*, for example, we find a repeated motif of a recumbent ruler murdered—as reported by King Hamlet, in the First Player's description of Priam's death, as shown in the death of Gonzago and as Hamlet forces poisoned wine down the throat of the dying Claudius at the end, and it is *almost* depicted as Hamlet stands over a seemingly praying Claudius. Unless a director dictates otherwise, we always have the stage in view. And the stage has no difficulty in linking those moments for us, if a director chooses to do so. The linear movement of television tape makes spatial parallels difficult to achieve—how do we show Hamlet and Ghost and Hamlet and First Player in the same positions as Hamlet hears each narrative, or have Claudius die where Gonzago did? The Jane Howell First Henriad and her *Winter's Tale* create such "visual echoing," since Howell's set is a version of stage. Desmond Davis's *Measure for Measure* creates relationships by using the same set for convent and brothel, the latter getting a lurid paint job. In each instance television imitates, in its way, what I take to be the techniques of Shakespeare's stage, where place was defined by language and where different places, palace and forest, Rome and Egypt, inhabited the same "bare islands." That stage, as Jay Halio suggests, "generate[d] . . . multiple not single perceptions, sometimes occurring simultaneously and often varying from spectator to spectator."[3]

The BBC *Hamlet* creates a metadramatic sense of depth via analogy, for want of a better word. Derek Jacobi dons a skull-mask—one of the Player's props—as the court enters to hear "Gonzago." A first-time auditor, of course, could not know that the skull mask links Hamlet with Yorick, King Hamlet's long-dead jester, whose skull Hamlet will later hold, in the most famous icon that Shakespeare sends forth from his plays. The linkage comes in act 5 and involves what Harry Berger calls "the retrospective mode of structural irony,"[4] in which an imaginative interchange occurs between suddenly related aspects of the script. Shakespeare intended that we retain the entire play in our imaginations (as he did) even as we concentrate on a single instant, and good directors remind us of the "single event" that is the script.

"Structural irony" shows us, retrospectively, how brilliantly the BBC production anticipates the Yorick sequence. Hamlet predicts the mirror of his own biological future that he will later look into. The earlier use of the skull-mask has already been anticipated in the script, however, when Hamlet tells his fellow watchers on the parapets that he may "Put on an antic disposition" (1.5.173). He will, then, "act like a madman."[5]

Other characters in the play refer to Hamlet's "madness" (2.1.210, 3.1.191, and 3.3.2, for example), his being "mad" (4.1.7 and 4.1.19, for example), his "wildness" (3.1.39), and his "dangerous lunacy" (3.1.4)—the "official view," or "containment." Claudius shrewdly perceives that Hamet's speech "was not like madness" (3.1.167), and the "antic disposition" means to Claudius that Hamlet must not be permitted to wander around "unwatch'd" (3.1.191). Whatever Hamlet is up to, Claudius interprets the Prince's actions in political contexts, as Claudius must.

"Antic" also means "grotesque figure,"[6] as in *The Taming of the Shrew* (Introduction: 100), or "buffoon "[7] as in *Much Ado About Nothing* (3.1.63), one who performs "witless antics" (*Troilus and Cressida:* 5.3.86). Polonius picks up on this shading when he talks of Hamlet's "pranks" (3.4.1).

But by the time Hamlet uses the word to define the disposition he may assume, Shakespeare has already associated the word with Death-as-jester. When Talbot learns of the death of his son, John, he speaks of "Thou antic death, which laugh'st us here to scorn" (*I Henry VI:* 4.7.18). David Bevington glosses Talbot's "antic" as "grinning (a personification suggested by grotesque pictorial presentations of the Middle Ages and early Renaissance, such as the dance of death)."[8]

And, in a context closer to *Hamlet*, Richard II says,

> for within the hollow crown
> That rounds the mortal temples of a king
> Keeps Death his court, and there the antic sits,
> Scoffing his state, and grinning at his pomp.
>
> (3.2.160–63)

Bevington glosses "antic" as "grotesque figure, jester."[9]

The skull is the ultimate jester, the memento mori that mocks all earthly pretensions.[10] Jacobi's Hamlet, then, *literally* puts on an "antic disposition."

The skull-mask that Hamlet dons presages the upcoming "Gonzago," designed to insist that Claudius reveal what hides under the rhetoric and facades of power. It is the jester's role to serve as a ruler's compensatory psyche via the jester's entertainments. Some of Yorick's jokes "that were wont to set the table on a roar" (5.1.191) may have been jokes on King Hamlet, secure enough to have his pretensions punctured now and then. We find no jester at the court of Claudius. The "antic" Hamlet has assumed that role, albeit unofficially. "Gonzago" has been planned by Hamlet to expose an already guilt-ridden King. The image of the skull nicely comments on Claudius's guilty aside, delivered before "Gonzago," often cut, but retained by BBC:

> The harlot's cheek, beautied with plast'ring art,
> Is not more ugly to the thing that helps it

Than is my deed to my most painted word.
O heavy burden!

(3.1.50–54)

The BBC production permits Hamlet's skull-mask, with its calculated ugliness, to respond to these lines and allows the lines themselves to echo much later, as Hamlet enjoins the bony jester to "get you to my lady's chamber, and tell her, let her paint an inch thick, to this favor she must come; make her laugh at that" (5.1.192–94). Hamlet's macabre advice is all that is available "to mock [Yorick's] own grinning" (5.1.191).

But before that moment, which is just before "my lady" Ophelia, no longer a living lady of the court, enters unceremoniously, Hamlet has his chance to strip the "plast'ring art" from Claudius:

> I have heard that guilty creatures sitting at a play
> Have by the very cunning of the scene
> Been struck so to the soul that presently
> They have proclaim'd their malefactions.

(2.2.588–92)

Claudius, as the script establishes before "Gonzago," has a conscience to be caught, although his soul eludes him later as he attempts to pray.

I disagree with Meredith Anne Skura's quotation and paraphrase of C. L. Barber: "Hamlet is trying to do what Christ did, even though he did not have Christ's solution available."[11] "The tremendous originality of *Hamlet*," Barber argues, "is that the play poses 'a religious problem without a religious solution,' and that Hamlet finds instead a theatrical answer."[12] But is not the "theatrical answer" also potentially "a religious solution"? As he plans "Gonzago," Hamlet does not use theatrical terminology, but religious—"guilty creatures," "malefactions," "soul," "miraculous organ," and "conscience."

If we put the matter into the religious context, as Barber invites us to do, we can say that Shakespeare, through Hamlet, wedges back to the very beginnings of his dramatic tradition:

> Quem quaeritis in sepulcher, Christiacolae?
> Jesum Nazarenum crucifixum, o caelicolae.

This is also what Hamlet seeks—the Christ buried within Claudius. Claudius, although deeply aware of this guilt, cannot find that Christ by himself. In this case it would take the intermediary of drama to elicit the penitential imperative that the script shows is there and for which Hamlet devises a medium for expression. If *Hamlet*, like *Macbeth*, is grounded on "Augustinian" premises, then Hamlet hopes to catch what *is* there in Claudius, however repressed or distorted: "the image of God," as represented in the psyche by "the magister interior." But as the crucial "guilty creatures" soliloquy also shows, Hamlet is also seeking the biological father, whose alleged ghost claims to have been poisoned. As Hamlet says, he makes things merely "relative." Father, son, and ghost (or "spirit") are bonded in a trinity that captures only consciousness.*

Jacobi's skull-mask links Hamlet with the kind of drama *he* likes, where violence was reported, not depicted: Clytemnestra's account of Agamemnon's death; the descriptions of the deaths of Antigone, Haemon, and Eurydice; of Jocasta's hanging and Oedipus's blinding of himself; and of Hippolytus's disastrous chariot ride.

In those plays the actors wore masks—partly, we assume, to veil the individuality of the actor and to permit the character to achieve the effect of universality. While the mask made the character even more of an abstraction than it already was, it *was* a character with specific problems usually involving that tragic borderland between man and the gods. The mask, however, invited an identification that went beyond a spectator's conscious agenda and into the unconscious from which the character was also masked. This identification with archetypes deeper than consciousness was one factor in the response that Aristotle calls "catharsis."

Before the Gravedigger identifies the specific skull of Yorick, Hamlet uses a skull as a focal point for what could be either a nihilistic or *contemptus mundi* disquisition. Lawyer, courtier, politician, Caesar and Alexander—all must come to dust. The skull tells the story of each profession and each great man who once

---

*Robert A. Johnson suggests the significance of the "Trinitarian trap": "What has been excluded from the Christian trinity is the dark, feminine element in life. So it comes back to plague us as a kind of chthonic devil." Some people, Johnson says, "dream of three turning to four. This suggests we are going through an evolution of consciousness. From the nice, orderly, all-masculine concept of ultimate reality, the Trinitarian view of God, we are moving toward a quaternitarian view that includes the feminine" (*He: Understanding Masculine Psychology* [New York: Harper and Row, 1974], 62–63). I am suggesting, of course, that it is precisely this progression that Hamlet is shown to reject vividly. His external view of woman would seem to contaminate his sense of "the feminine." He reacts with scorn when he discovers the feminine within him (cf. 2.2.586–88, and 5.2.213–14).

masqueraded in the cosmetic flesh. If a mask permits an actor "to assume the other"—the universal inhabiting the character—the undifferentiated skull as Hamlet names and renames it is a physical otherness we will all assume. Jacobi's skull-mask captures the range between mimesis and reality. That a *real* skull lies beneath the prop and that death would seize Hamlet soon enough—indeed, soon after he peers into the grinning mirror of Yorick's skull—are superbly articulated by the visual signifiers of this production, augmented by the inclusion of Claudius's "How smart a lash . . ." aside.*

At the end of his "guilty creatures" soliloquy, Jacobi says, "abuses *me*, to damn *me*," as if to say, "I thought it only happened to *other* people!" Jacobi chuckles snidely as he talks of catching "the conscience of the King," The emphasis is on the return to the merely personal level and away from the larger potentialities of his "entertainment." That play *and* revenge could coincide and could, in Hamlet's religious configuration, set the time right in Denmark are insights that his Hamlet does not pursue. Jacobi's Hamlet moves into the play scene ready to be attacked by his own reaction to his own play—as Hamlet perceives he may be being attacked by demonic forces. Jacobi's Hamlet is ripe for an onslaught from that staging area that Jung calls "the personal unconscious" wherein lurks the "Shadow," that persona composed of what consciousness excludes from "personality."[13]

The script suggests that only Polonius engages Hamlet in the give-and-take of Hamlet's jesting. Claudius says with affronted dignity, "I have nothing with this answer, Hamlet. These words are not mine" (3.3.96–97). The BBC, however, permits Claudius to laugh and point at Polonius as skull-Hamlet says, "It was a brute part of him to kill so capital a calf there." This is a Claudius, then, ready to engage Hamlet on the latter's ground, as the King's attendance at the play signals.

Hamlet doffs his mask before "Gonzago" begins, another sign that he has become "personal" Hamlet again. The mask, however, lies on "Gonzago's" downstage furniture, reminding us that the *play* has become the jester and that Hamlet has transferred *his* role, for the moment, to the play. "*They* do but jest. . . ." The set

---

*An irony inherent in this discussion is that the "real" skull of Yorick would also be a stage prop. Even death is "an imitation of an action." Roger Rees told me of his disgust in using an actual skull during one performance of the 1985 RSC *Hamlet* in London. In a glass case at the Furness Collection at the University of Pennsylvania is an actual skull used in the Nineteenth Century and signed by Irving, Forrest, and Edwin Booth.

for "Gonzago" presents a vivid contrast to Rodney Bennett's set for the outer play. A bright, perspectival Commedia dell'arte set opens out from the dark, Rembrandtian context of the outer play. The vivid contrast makes Hamlet's intrusion *into* "Gonzago" all the more startling. As Bernice Kliman says in a meticulous study of the production: "he breaks up his own 'Mousetrap' by getting right into the play, destroying the distance between audience and stage (a very real raked prosenium-arch stage), spoiling it as a test, because Claudius has a right to be incensed at Hamlet's behaviour. Of course, Hamlet does so because Claudius never gives himself away, an unusual and provocative but not impossible interpretation. Thus, Claudius can only have the court's sympathy as he calmly calls for light and uses it to examine Hamlet closely. Hamlet, in response, covers his face, then laughs."[14]

The reportorial mode—that is, the way in which offstage violence was narrated on stage—comes into English drama via Seneca and *Gorboduc*, the first English play to employ blank verse, in which the death of Porrex is reported. We find a speech similar to such a narrative in the First Player's report of the death of Priam and the grief of Hecuba. The speech is incomplete, interrupted within the larger context of *Hamlet*, as "Gonzago" will be.* At the point of interruption of "Gonzago," Hamlet loses his chance to be an effective jester. He lets fall a further mask—as observer and spectator—and, as Kliman accurately describes, in the Jacobi version literally upstages the players. While "Gonzago" maintains itself within its unities and sententious couplets, it is, like *Hamlet*, "representational"; that is, it purports to imitate an action in action, not just via narrative. Unlike *Hamlet*, however, "Gonzago" is not a metadramatic vehicle. It blocks out the audience via a "fourth wall." Instead of seeing a character come downstage toward us, as Hamlet can do in some of his soliloquies and as Richard III and Iago probably do as they outline their plans directly to us, we have a character going upstage and into a play, destroying a fictive level rather than explaining to us the fiction we are about to witness. Hamlet provides such an explanation, of course, in his "guilty creatures" soliloquy but, as Jacobi depicts its, interferes with the transpersonal depth of his own design even as he later interferes with the potentiality of its production. As Marchette Chute says, "Hamlet the playgoer would not have approved of *Hamlet* the play."[15] Hamlet obviously prefers what

---

*The Ghost's earlier narrative (1.5) is not interrupted but is hastened into brevity by a "scent" of the "morning air."

was "cavaire to the general"—the reportorial mode of the Hecuba speech. He leaps into "Gonzago" to tell the rest of the story, substituting the reportorial mode for the representational. Furious earlier at Polonius for interrupting the narrative of Troy, Jacobi's Hamlet turns with a quick glance and helpless shrug toward the "Gonzago" set, recognizing that he has destroyed the play he had commissioned. The First Player— Emrys James— cannot quite hide his anger at his patron's disruption of mimesis.

Hamlet has attempted with "Gonzago" something like what Barbara Mowat describes in her analysis of the Romances: he "creates for the audience a distinctive kind of dramatic experience, [one] parallel to the experience of the characters on stage."[16] The difference, of course, is that in *Hamlet* the characters on stage are paralleling the lives of the outer stage audience, including Hamlet's, if we accept the unconscious oedipal drama being re-enacted before him. Lionel Abel suggests, in theatrical terms consonant with Barber's religious usages, that "Hamlet, with his gifted playwright's consciousness, has the problem of rewriting the melodrama he has been placed in, but with no alternative form in view."[17] I suggest, however, that it is Hamlet's overreaction to the melodrama he presents that turns the outer play from melodrama to tragedy. The alternative, again, lay within the melodrama-within. If, as Mowat suggests, Claudius is "the 'underdistanced' audience" for "Gonzago,"[18] Hamlet is *also* "underdistanced," so much so that, in a variation on the inevitable ending of the revenge genre, Hamlet falls into his own trap. No matter what Claudius *might* have done, Hamlet erases the possible threat of the play vis à vis Claudius's soul by becoming a quite obvious external threat, as the BBC production shows,* by having Jacobi break in upon "representation," that is, a play "based on creating the illusion that it represents a world entirely different from that in which the audience is while in the theatre."[19] The only production I have seen that created that difference as distinctly as did the BBC was the Cuilei version at the Arena Theater in Washington in 1978, where the actors in Elizabethan dress contrasted vividly with the Prussian costumes of the court.

The question, of course, is why does Hamlet interfere with his own production (as I believe that the script irrefutably shows that

---

*In the Birmingham Rep *Hamlet* of 1988 (directed by Derek Jacobi), Kenneth Branagh came up behind Lucianus and pointed the latter's arm at Claudius. Michael Easton's Claudius had ample warrant to stop the performance as *King*, refusing to let himself and his office be further insulted.

he does)? Hamlet's interference must be more than merely an objection to dramatic style. Skura's paraphrase of Barber is helpful on this point: "Hamlet . . . tries to achieve manhood by making himself the passive childlike worshipper of his father's manhood—which would work if his father were divine, but otherwise infantilizes him."[20] But this "passive" Hamlet, as Jacobi says, "swings into suddenly intensely traumatic states."[21] Those states are also, no doubt, "infantile." "Christ's solution," which would permit representation to appeal to the archetypes that Claudius has already brought fleetingly to consciousness as a "heavy burden," is replaced in Hamlet by a psychological response in which his own repressed content leaps forth to proclaim itself. If the oedipal resonance is a determinant, it can be argued that Hamlet interrupts "Gonzago" after Lucianus-Claudius-Hamlet (fiction-consciousness-unconsciouness) has killed Gonzago–King Hamlet–Claudius (fiction–"something like the murder of my father," as reported by the Ghost-unconscious wish), but *before* "the murderer gets the love of Gonzago's wife" (Baptista-Gertrude). (The conflation of roles that occurs as the poison is administered is remarkable!) Hamlet instead puts *"poison* in jest," using his play for "murder on the mental plane."[22] The point is not that "there is no religious solution to the religious problems posed by Hamlet's world."[23] Hamlet's own words point at precisely such a solution. Hamlet, however, cannot tolerate a solution in which Claudius would be eternally forgiven if temporally punished, as Hamet's "Now might I do it pat" soliloquy makes clear. Hamlet would have to sublimate what he cannot control and bring to consciousness that which he has repressed. But those processes are not available to *him.* He makes them unavailable to his world and thus qualifies as the central character in a tragedy. The voice that is silenced by Hamlet at "Gonzago" and driven into unrepentant self-laceration is that of Claudius's conscience.

The play-within represents a slight advance over Hamlet's interruption of his own recitation of the Player's speech. The play, at least, advances to the killing of the recumbent father figure—Gonzago—and the achievement of the oedipal goal of killing the father in revenge for his invasion of the motherland. Hecuba's "bisson rheum" (2.2.506) makes her "like Niobe, all tears" (1.2.149) and is therefore to be scorned—as are the Player's tears "for Hecuba" (2.2.558). Her reported grief can pull from Hamlet only a sneer. Depicted mourning conflicts with its reality in Elsinore. Hamet's interruption of "Gonzago" is the fulfillment of a sweet Freudian dream—the father is killed, but the murderer does not get the love of Gonzago's wife. Hamlet can render that possibility in narrative form—it is a story he has lived with for years—but he will not permit the actors to represent it. That they have mimed it in the dumb show may account for Hamlet's loss of control as "Gonzago" careens toward the conclusion that Hamlet unfortunately gives it.

In the script, the Pyrrhus-Hamlet equation is clear. As Eleanor Prosser suggests, "If Pyrrhus has any counterpart in the play at all, it must be Hamlet."[24] And, as Arthur Johnston says, "What is significant about the episode chosen to mirror the act that Hamlet is called to do is the reversal of emotional sympathy; the deed is one of terror, its perpetrator inhuman and brutalized. 'Roasted in wrath and fire' the 'hellish Pyrrhus' is damned."[25] The parallel Hamlet draws between himself and the player is, as Johnston says "less immediately obvious"[26] than is the equation between Hamlet and Pyrrhus. Indeed, Hamlet's metaphor is both personal *and* dramatic. He talks of the possibilities of his own overacting: he might "drown the general stage with tears" (2.2.562). This overacting, as Hamlet makes clear, would be a product of repression. Drama would find Hamlet as actor indulging in a wild excess of inundating salt. That may be what he wants for Claudius—as he suggests later in the speech—but it is also what he predicts for himself. Hamlet warns us of the possible effects of drama on his own psychology of perception. If the reportorial mode and a player's response to it can evoke this response from Prince Hamlet, representation may pull even more violence from him. As Andrew Gurr suggests, "Hamlet's motive and cue are not for passion but for 'action,' the word that meant both the acting of a stage role and the action of revenge. An Elizabethan audience would have noted the change and understood the evasion when Hamlet goes on to condemn himself for the fact that he, unlike the player, peaks like John-a-dreams, 'And can *say* nothing.' "[27]

At the end of the Player's speech—a story ended prematurely by the Player's response to his own material—James covers his face, then smiles with what I take to be embarrassment as Hamlet gently pulls the hands away. At the end of "Gonzago," a play ended prematurely by Hamlet's reaction to and interference with its imitation of action—Hamlet covers his face. Patrick Stewart's Claudius holds a torch close to the concealing hands, in an allusion to the Olivier film, in which *Olivier* holds a torch to Basil Sydney's scared-out-of-his-wits Claudius. Jacobi's Hamlet uncovers his face and giggles as if he were the only person who found his practical joke amusing. But the joke has fallen flat, and only Hamlet's immaturity, or "infantilism," has been caught by

"Gonzago." If a personal attack on Claudius, it succeeds only in evoking a response in which dignity overweighs anger. Jacobi's Hamlet permits Claudius's frail body politic to survive intact. In the BBC production at least, the election of Claudius looks to be a wise decision.

The BBC production makes little of the oedipal energy as "Gonzago" breaks up. That is reserved for the violence in Gertrude's closet, where Jacobi plays out the sexual act with a few vivid thrusts above a pinioned Claire Bloom. During "Gonzago" we see more of Lalla Ward, Blooms's weak-chinned look-alike, than we do of Bloom. As BBC depicts it, we cannot read Oedipus into the moment of "Gonzago's" breakup.

The BBC version depicts a regression in which Hamlet fails to find the symbol that would lead to *progression*. He would press Claudius back to that awful moment of his murder of King Hamlet, a moment that has already surfaced in the King's consciousness merely on the basis of Polonius's sententious comment about sugaring "o'er / The devil himself" (3.1.47–48). Jacobi's excited substitution of narration for representation, however, suggests that *he* had regressed to his school days. His giggle—as if at a childish prank—substantiates this inference. This Hamlet, then, denies the positive results of regression to Claudius.

Hamlet's meeting with the Players seems to represent a "progression," which, as Ira Progoff suggests, manifests itself "in an exhilarated sense of well-being; the world seems good and pleasant."[28] As Jacobi depicts the scene, it seems perhaps more like the manic sine wave of depression. Regardless of the interpretation of Hamlet's greeting of the Players and of his commissioning a speech straight, the movement is temporary. Before "Gonzago," regression sets in. The reversal of libidinal energy means, as Jung says, that "the vital feeling that was there before disappears and in its place the psychic value of certain conscious contents increases in an unpleasant way; subjective contents and reactions press to the fore and the situation becomes full of affect and favorable for explosions."[29] The regressive phase pulls its participant down into the psyche and need not be negative, regardless of how consciousness "feels" about it, because regression "activates the images, raises them out of the unconscious, and makes possible an enrichment of consciousness."[30] Regression can "bring up those images and symbols which, when functioning as 'energy transformers,' are capable of changing the direction of the psychic process again into a progressive one."[31]

The question, of course, is whether regressive energy can scour down to the right symbol, the image of Selfhood. Hamlet's introspective movement away from the Player's speech gives him the right symbol—drama that imitates life and that imposes upon the spectator the imperative to "proclaim [his] malefactions," as did the Townswoman of Lynn, of whom Hamlet has "heard," who confessed to murdering her husband during a performance of *Fair Francis*. As O. B. Hardison says, in relating the Townswoman of Lynn to Claudius, "the psychology underlying [such instances] is plain enough. The perpetrator of an undiscovered crime is troubled by a guilty conscience. He is in torment. Confession, the only way to relieve the pain, is prevented by his fear of the consequences. Seeing the crime enacted on the stage can make the pangs of conscience so intense that the need for relief via confession becomes stronger than the fear of exposure. The confession has two beneficial results. First, a crime is solved and a criminal punished. Society is strengthened, if only minutely, by the clearing up on an injustice."[32] Since, in *Hamlet,* the society is Denmark and since the world of the play has clear cosmic intersections, the "strengthening" in the case of Claudius's confession would be more than "minute."

Even Hamlet's identification with the First Player, perhaps a repression of his more obvious identification with Pyrrhus, is not negative, *if* Hamlet would take his own advice: "And let those that play your clowns speaks no more than is set down for them; for there be of them that will themselves laugh, to set on some quantity of barren spectators to laugh too, though in the meantime some necessary question of the play be then to be consider'd" (3.2.38–43). At the ultimate moment, Hamlet moves from impresario to "chorus" (3.2.245) to an interloper who describes only what *he* sees in his play, a transition that Shakespeare consistently avoids. If Hamlet goes back positively to a time when he was happy at university, indeed a patron of players, a time before his father's sudden death and his mother's perceived infidelity, the latter autobiography contaminates the value of his regression, which becomes "a one-sided adaptation to the outer world while the inner one is neglected [thus increasing] the value of the inner world [and resulting] in the irruption of personal elements into the sphere of outer adaptation."[33] The imbalance can result in the "I don't know what came over me" syndrome, as Hamlet later expresses it:

> But I am very sorry, good Horatio,
> That to Laertes I forgot myself. . .

(5.2.75–76)

If Hamlet from himself be ta'en away,
And when he's not himself does wrong Laertes,
Then Hamlet does it not, Hamlet denies it.
Who does it then? His madness. If't be so,
Hamlet is of the faction that is wrong'd;
His madness is poor Hamlet's enemy.

(5.2.234–39)

"Hamlet's enemy" takes over at both the climactic moment of "Gonzago" and *Hamlet*. But it is, of course, an enmity that resides within him. Hamlet "forgets himself" as elements of the personal unconscious (which Hamlet has repressed via his dominant orientation: "Let me not think on't": 1.2.146) break through and destroy Hamlet's conscious plan for "Gonzago"—that it catch Claudius's psyche, not his own.

With himself and his world at stake, Hamlet has merely engaged in what Jung calls "a regressive restoration of the persona. . . . He will as a result of his fright have slipped back to an earlier phase of his personality; he will have demeaned himself, pretending that he is as he was *before* the crucial experience, though utterly unable ever to think of repeating such a risk. Formerly perhaps he wanted more than he would accomplish; now he does not even dare to attempt what he has it in him to do."[34] Hamlet's "fright" is the trauma attendant upon a father's death and a mother's remarriage. As the Player's come, he can for a few moments pretend that he is as he was. The tragic irony is that he does dare to do what he has within himself to do—to design a solution in art that seems unavailable in "life." But life destroys art, as Jacobi so vividly depicts Hamlet's break up of "Gonzago." In the simplist terms, what Hamlet cannot "dare to attempt" should be familiar to those who have been rejected once too often. He dare not love—unless it be to love the ashes that can no longer interfere with his idealization. Orlando can progress toward the flesh-and-blood Rosalind. Hamlet can regress only to the ideal of his liberal arts education and to the painted tyranny of an idealized madonna-father-child. His experience in Elsinore, once the play begins, merely insists upon the "male bonding" of university days (as evinced by his love of Horatio) and upon the infantile fixation of his own biological past, which he cannot go beyond. His father as authority figure merely stands in for the authority that Hamlet assigns to his own betrayal. The dishonesty of women is a paradox only in that Hamlet's thinking makes it one. "Gonzago" proves the point. It is a moment of potential solution to Hamlet's inner and outer problems, but he cannot allow it to succeed.

Why? Because his regression has left him on the plane of his own immature self. His manic response to "Gonzago" calls his play a "comedy" (3.2.293), when, in fact, his response has made the outer play a tragedy. As Jung says, "Regarded causally, regression is determined . . . by a 'mother fixation.' But from the final standpoint the libido regresses to the *imago* of the mother in order to find there the memory associations [whereby] further development can take place, for instance, from a sexual system into an intellectual or spiritual system."[35]

Hamlet keeps "Gonzago" from becoming a "spiritual system." His very choice of material argues his imprisonment in the ideal of marriage, which his biological mother, as he sees it, has violated (cf. his indictment in 3.4). The maternal archetype that regression might energize is that of the anima—the "mothering," or creative potentiality, residing in the male psyche. Hatred and a conscious need for a revenge that sends his victim's soul to hell blocks Hamlet from the dynamic symbol. He does not permit the reversal of libido to communicate to his own deeper need, which is for wholeness. In denying it to himself, Hamlet denies it to Claudius, as on the conscious level he must. The symbol is "of woman," but Hecuba's reported grief is refuted by Gertrude's only *seeming* "like Niobe." Her tears live in an onion, as Hamlet interprets them. Woman, as embodied by Gertrude and by Ophelia, is "frailty," not strength. And here, of course, the idealized father asserts *his* authority, since he has been betrayed by a woman. In planning "Gonzago," Hamlet penetrates to the depths of his creative being. But as Jacobi shows by "personalizing" the end of the "guilty creatures" soliloquy, that depth is erased by shallower levels of Hamlet's psyche, as material from the personal unconscious explodes and takes over consciousness.

"Gonzago" represents an act of projection for Hamlet. He is linked to his play as if it were his own dream, meaning, of course, that he can only become more rather than less involved in its unfolding scenario. His alter ego at the outset is the Player Queen, the boy actor who in the Olivier film looks so much like Ophelia (Jean Simmons). Here Hamlet, through the boy actor, is saying what should have been and what was, as he perceived it, *before* his father's death. "Gonzago" represents the rigidity and totality of Hamlet's concept of marriage ("O, but she'll keep *her* word": 3.2.231). But Baptista is also the betraying Gertrude, as the dumbshow has already mimied. The boy actor epitomizes androgyny, thus emblemizes what Carolyn Heilbrun calls the "problem of the reunification of the sexes."[36] But the boy actor speaks lines that Hamlet can only scorn as "wormwood" within the contaminated "reality" of his environment and psyche. We find a collision between conscious definition of what the play *might* do and the unconscious negatives that are flooding into Hamlet.

It is not so much that the deeper and positive unconscious energies of adrogyny, or the anima, are unavailable to Hamlet but that he denies them, as he does later, when he sneers at his premonitions about the coming "play" with Laertes: "'tis such a kind of gain-giving as would perhaps trouble a women" (5.2.215–16). Since he sneers at the woman in him, he can only condemn himself as the worst of the feminine stereotypes: "whore," "drab," and "scullion" (2.2.585–87). For the unintegrated male psyche, those are the only labels available. Hamlet is caught, as "Gonzago" shows, in the dichotomy of the split feminine, virgin and whore, as Othello will be. Christ, of course, healed the split via the two Marys (mother and Magdalene). In the deepest sense, then, it is Hamlet who betrays "the woman"—his androgynous selfhood. He projects this betrayal and the hatred it engenders onto Gertrude, Ophelia, *and* himself.

Hamlet's "it were better my mother had not borne me" (3.1.123) may reveal the deepest self-hatred of all. Hamlet was born a woman, as Shakespeare uncannily suggests, in describing the coding process whereby the female fetus is made male:

> And for a woman wert thou first created,
> Till Nature, as she wrought thee, feel a-doting,
> And by addition me of thee defeated,
> By adding one thing to my purpose nothing . . .
> She prick'd thee out for woman's pleasure . . .
>
> (Sonnet 20)

The "no-thing" word play continues in *Hamlet*, as Jacques Lacan notes,[37] but for Hamlet the feminine inheritance is only "frailty" in that he denies it as part of what "Nature wrought" in him, whether he likes it or not. The deepest Ur-Hamlet is inscribed as feminine. "Christ's solution" is available to Hamlet but it must crystallize within him before he can offer Claudius the energies of a drama that is masked so that it could *un*mask its auditor.

The Mousetrap confirms only repression in Hamlet, as the script suggests, and captures an incomplete and negative regression, as Jacobi shows. The failure of the grand plan is captured in

Hamlet's soliloquy as he prepares to confront Gertrude. He will "speak daggers to her, but use none" (3.2.396). Jacobi removes the theatrical dagger from the throat of Claudius's soul when Hamlet becomes a palpable threat and interferes with whatever Claudius's psychology of perception might have evoked from the King in response to "Gonzago." In a sense, the psychic sword that might have penetrated to "conscience" is already "up" as Hamlet contemplates the kneeling Claudius a few moments after the break up of "Gonzago." It will leap out again from Hamlet's repressed hand a few moments later to find only Polonius.

In the 1960 version of the play, produced for Austrian television, Hans Caninenberg's Claudius is provoked by Maximilian Schell's Hamlet, who is narrating from behind the King's throne, into ending the proceedings. The "official view"—that Hamlet has insulted both King and Queen—is also the production's view. In the 1970 production for Hallmark, with Richard Chamberlain as Hamlet, Richard Johnson's Claudius bashes his alter ego Player King from the stage. Claudius is enraged and drunk perhaps, but he tells everyone who is King around here. His fictional counterpart is subject to Claudius, as is the Crown Prince. The grotesque parody of play-within in the 1969 Tony Richardson film (with Nicol Williamson as Hamlet) finds "its strength and its truth in its duplicating in terms of visual style the insane discord in Hamlet's mind."[38] In the 1964 stage production in New York, directed by John Gielgud and starring Richard Burton, a startled Player King found himself onstage in the face of Claudius's anger. The Player King scuttled backstage like a found-out crab. Alfred Drake's Claudius departed from the splendid "musical comedy" subtext that Drake had employed and gave Hamlet a look of cold steel. Burton, like Jacobi, had failed in whatever he was trying to do. I cite these examples to suggest that "Gonzago" as Hamlet's *failure*, as opposed to the success most critics call it, is not unusual in performance. We may believe that Hamlet succeeds in the study, but performance has difficulty finding that success in the script.*

---

*Perhaps the alleged discrepancy between "study" and "stage" is best exemplified in the panic flight that the former attributes to Claudius as he responds to "Gonzago." "Claudius rises, crying for light and rushing out," says Alfred Harbage (*William Shakespeare: A Reader's Guide* [New York: The Noonday Press, 1963], 324), providing the academic "given" for this climactic moment. Those who deal with the scene *on stage*, however, refute the accepted version. "Claudius is upset not by the play but (reasonably enough) by the direct accusation which Hamlet blurts out, overcome with excitement at the progress of his plot. Rashly—and we cannot praise rashness for it—he has produced the right

Jacobi's Hamlet becomes the tragedy of the "detached" literary critic ambushed by his own psyche. It is appropriate that the psychic explosion shows Hamlet substituting the reportorial mode for representation. For us, the outer audience, that narration *becomes* representation as it depicts Hamlet's loss of control over what might have become more than just "theater." It does become more than that, of course, but only insofar as Hamlet falls into his own trap.

While I agree with Barber that "in his effort to find with Hamlet a nonaggressive way of being assertive, Shakespeare identifies with Hamlet's use of theatre to resolve his conflicts," I am not certain that Shakespeare "himself is making use of the play *Hamlet* to work out his own conflicts with authority."[39] Hamlet as character discovers the very medium in which Shakespeare has been working (regardless of his documented problems with "the authorities")—the assertive but nonaggressive genre of drama. I would suggest that Shakespeare moves toward us as audience even as he shows his character, Hamlet, plunging fatally into a mirror he has set up for someone else. Hamlet's action becomes a mirror for us at precisely the point at which he is no longer to be identified with his creator. Shakespeare knew, I believe, and demonstrates it through Hamlet, what the effect of drama can be:

> By projecting what is in the characters outward into externally visible events and actions, a play paves the way for the audience's own act of projection. We find in the external reality of a play what is hidden in ourselves. Drama shows virtue her own feature, scorn her own image, and the very age and body of the time his form and pressure. Watching a set of events in a play feels, for this reason, very different from reading them in a novel.[40]

"Gonzago" shows only Hamlet's conscious scorn and the turbulence of the unmediated depths of his psyche.

---

effect for the wrong reason: assured himself of Claudius's guilt only at the cost of making his own knowledge and consequent dangerousness quite explicit. . . . It is Hamlet, if anyone, who has been worked into a frenzy by this example of *mimesis*—and it is his own performance that brings the house down" (M. R. Woodhead, " 'The Murder of Gonzago,' " *Shakespeare Survey* 32 [1979]: 160–61). "Whichever way you play the scene, however, I am sure that it is wrong for Claudius to lose control at the climax. It is Hamlet, not he, who is excited. On the words 'you shall see anon how the murderer gets the love of Gonza[g]o's wife,' the second tooth is duly extracted; the King rises, pale and speechless; and then, with a brusque "Give me some lights—away" he strides—not rushes from the room" (Robert Speaight, "Shakespeare in Britain," *Shakespeare Quarterly* 21 [Autumn 1970]: 442).

In Hamlet the character, Shakespeare captures the central male psychic failure, one that makes *Hamlet* the play a tragedy:

> Material deriving from the collective unconscious is never "patholog-ical"; it can become pathological only if it comes from the personal unconscious, where it undergoes a specific transformation and colora-tion by being drawn into an area of individual conflict. . . . Only an interpretation on the symbolic level can strip the nucleus of the complex from its pathological covering and free it from the impedi-ment of its personalistic garb. . . . If a complex embedded in the material of the personal unconscious seems to stand in inexorable conflict with consciousness, its nucleus, once laid bare, may prove to be a content of the collective unconscious. For example, the individual is no longer confronted with his own mother, but with an archetype of the "maternal," no longer with the unique personal problem cre-ated by his own mother as a concrete reality, but with the universally human, impersonal problem of every man's dealings with the primor-dial maternal ground in himself . . . how much more bearable it is for a son to conceive the son-father problem no longer on the plane of individual guilt—in relation, for example, to his own desire for his father's death, his aggression and desire for revenge—but as a prob-lem of deliverance from the father, i.e. from a dominant principle of consciousness that is no longer adequate for the son: a problem that concerns all men, and has been disclosed in the myths and fairy tales as the slaying of the reigning old king and the son's accession to the throne. . . . Everything depends on whether the conscious mind is capable of understanding, assimilating, and integrating the complex, in order to ward off its harmful effects. If it does not succeed in this, the conscious mind falls victim to the complex, and is to a greater or lesser degree engulfed by it.[41]

Jacobi's donning of the skull-mask defines his role as the jester who serves as the king's unconscious, as "Gonzago" is meant to do. "Gonzago" has—or should have—"an archetypal meaning quite independent of any individual's conscious exploitation of it."[42] While "Gonzago" is not specifically "masked" drama, it shares what Harold Rosenberg calls "the Central Intuition of Greek Drama . . . there is one unique fact that each individual anxiously struggles to conceal from himself, and this is the very fact that is the root of his identity."[43] The play-within, however, becomes a projection of Hamlet's unconscious and forces him to reveal only negatively the fact of his feminine selfhood that he struggles so to conceal and thus reveals. As in the process of regression, Hamlet gets pulled in. He may come downstage with his plan ("I have heard that guilty creatures . . ."), but its execution yanks him upstage, away from the energy of the audience, both inner and outer, into his "dream of passion" (3.1.552), or symbolic representation, and thus blocks whatever response might have been activated in Claudius. The BBC production *represents* Hamlet's regression—a movement of libidinal energy that returns incomplete and empty-handed.

After the play breaks up, Jacobi's Hamlet turns to Horatio and gives a remorseful look, as if to say, I blew it, didn't I? It is to that assessment that this Horatio agrees.[44] This production does not show "Gonzago" as a "success." It becomes the locus of Hamlet's failure and thus the climax of the tragedy.

6

Edmund's Nature

Thou, nature, art my goddess; to thy law
My services are bound. Wherefore should I
Stand in the plague of custom, and permit
The curiosity of nations to deprive me,
For that I am some twelve or fourteen moonshines
Lag of a brother? Why bastard? Wherefore base?
When my dimensions are as well compact,
My mind as generous, and my shape as true,
As honest madam's issue? Why brand they us
With base? With baseness? Bastardy? Base, base?
Who, in the lusty stealth of nature, take
More composition and fierce quality
Than doth within a dull, stale, tired, bed
Go to th'creating a whole tribe of fops
Got 'tween asleep and wake? Well, then,
Legitimate Edgar, I must have your land.
Our father's love is to the bastard Edmund
As to th' legitimate. Fine word,"legitimate"!
Well, my legitimate, if this letter speed
And my invention thrive, Edmund the base
Shall top th' legitimate. I grow, I prosper.
Now, gods, stand up for bastards!

(1.2.1–22)

Edmund is hardly a revolutionary. He is biologically as good as honest madam's issue, even if a moonshine or two "lag" of legitimacy. But once he gets to be Earl of Gloucester—only the official investiture to be endured—he finds himself still on the wheel he set spinning. He can laugh at his father's version of determinism—a divine thrusting on—but he chains himself to another metaphor for the same conclusion. Malcolm Evans offers a challenge to the new-critical construct of what Evans calls "an idealized order in which the little world of the theatre stands in for a society which distills the virtues of national and cultural unity."[1] The paradigm here might be the model of late-sixteenth-century London over which the camera moves as it seeks the Globe in Olivier's 1944 *Henry V.* Evans commends "readings that take up committed positions contrary to that of the idealized universal reader of humanism."[2] That reader is an Eliot, a Leavis, a Tillyard, or even a Matthew Arnold, whose philosophy held no dreams of a death camp commandant winding down in the evening with Beethoven and a liter of good liebfraumilch. Committed readings, Evans argues, "compel the text to signify not 'in its own terms' but in the context of a discourse—feminist, Marxist, or anti-colonialist . . . which recognizes that any production of the text is for a particular interpretation of history, which is not simply a disinterested chronicle but a selective production of the past for the present with a stake in *making* or [in] prolonging the existing set of historical relations by transforming history into 'nature' " [his emphasis].[3]

Edmund would forge a metaphor between his own history and his version of nature, so that nature can be a goddess to be worshipped as the wild and unsanctified energy that Edmund claims to be as the quests for ironic legitimacy within the jungle Lear's "darker purpose" summons into being. And he laughs at maidenly stars when he wishes nature to be a male potency that will "stand up" for the "base" that Edmund reduces to nonsense by repetition. Any speech in which mere consciousness becomes absolute must refute itself.

While I would argue that a text *can* speak for itself, signifying the dialectic it creates between its voices (Chorus versus representation in *Henry V,* for example), the basic discourse that Shakespeare sets up for times subsequent to his own is that between his script and the theater in which the script is heard and seen.

Evans poses a basic question: "the concept of an absolute aesthetic value is itself subject to the quesiton, 'valuable for whom and for what?' "[4]

Lear had appropriated all value systems to himself. His shattering of his own totalizing mythology permits Edmund to seek value within the ruins. He will, of course, use the old values and will seek status within the system that no longer exists.

The isolation of a single speech and the focus on several versions permits us to interpret the speech as part of a *production,* as opposed to part of a *text,* where meanings may be manifold but must also be adulterated by their sheer multiplicity. The availability of different versions of the same speech permits us to "flip pages," as Berger says we cannot do with a production. But I submit that the process is potentially much richer when we look at several productions than it is when we read the same speech several times. We discover not what it "means," but *how* it means in dramatic context and how it means as framed by its medium. I select Edmund's speech partly because we do have a stage version—albeit televisied—available. The process of looking at a single speech in its various available manifestations can be amplified many-fold, as I have suggested. This is merely one example of the possibilities available to us as critics and, I might add, to our students.

Of the three television versions of *King Lear*—the Joseph Papp Central Park production of 1973 (PBS, February 1974), the BBC (1982), and the Olivier (Granada, 1983), only one can be said to have been motivated by the determinism of the mere box office. None of the Edmunds challenge the process of history. Like Claudius and Macbeth, who inhabit worlds different from that of the ambiguous sky over Britain in *Lear*, Edmund seeks a loophole whereby the shoulder that bears the zodiac can be made to pause for a brief inscription of the individual will. But each of these Edmunds bows to a different necessity. Each production depicts the "nature of history" and the "history of nature" in different ways. These Edmunds are worth considering because they show on a dull, sublunary level where feet plod on regardless of theory, that "the nature of television" does not necessarily dictate a diminished dispensation that captures only the glow of artificial sources of light. The medium proves itself worthy of exploration as it encounters the friction of the Shakespearean script.

The weakest Edmund is that of Robert Lindsay in the Granada production (1983). Lindsay is a good Lysander in the BBC-TV *Midsummer Night's Dream*, a fact that may say something about his Edmund. I believe, however, that he is a victim not of the politics of the script but of the politics of the production.

His father (Leo McKern) waves him away before Lear's entrance in 1.1. This is no place for you! Rouguish jokes and power politics alike made Edmund their victim here.

After Goneril and Regan have disagreed on the urgency of the father problem (1.1.282–308), the camera cuts abruptly to a man holding the bridles of two horses. Someone has gone somewhere far from the first scene. The camera pans across shadow and upright stones and finds a moon silvering a huge flat stone in the middle of all those phallic symbols. Edmund enters and casts a shadow over that center stone. Then he puts a foot on it. Ah ha!—it is his servant holding the horses while Edmund keeps a tryst with his white goddess. Edmund looks up at the moon over Stonehenge. But then we cannot tell what he is looking at, since the speech is shot almost exclusively in a radical close-up suggesting only that Edmund has a weak chin that he has tried to disguise with a whisper of beard. Lindsay *reads* the speech beautifully, but is given no *space* in which to read it, no room in which to feel the gathering fullness of his self-conception. Here, direction contradicts language.

Suddenly, Gloucester winds his way through the stones. What is *he* doing here? Why haven't we heard his horse approaching this remote ruin? Meanwhile, Edmund reads his letter by moonlight and buries it "by starlight." Surely Gloucester must be surprised to find him out here reading! Who is holding the horses—the Third Murderer?

This sequence is radically unconvincing. It is hard to believe that any director could turn so potent a moment into such a dull and confusing parenthesis. We ignore intention, however, at our peril. This production assembles what Peter Ustinov calls "the greatest cast ever." It is assembled to bow to Olivier, as it does from the beginning. Surely the original Edmund (Lowin?) mounted a challenge within the production to Burbage's Lear. Burbage grew and prospered, no doubt, by being challenged. No challenge is permitted here. Lindsay is victimized by the politics of production. He might not do well, but one is surprised to see Edmund done at all in a production that is primarily an homage to Olivier.

The most powerful of the three television Edmunds is Raul Julia's rendition in the 1973 Papp-Sherin production (shown on PBS in 1974). This, of course, is a televised version of a stage production. It uses the close-up for the better performers (Julia and James Earl Jones) and thus is often stronger than was the actual stage version.

Julia leads the way onstage with a torch, Kent and Gloucester following. As Lear enters, Gloucester merely turns to that urgent moment, leaving Edmund, we assume, to take a place downstage right.

Goneril and Regan exit to a nervous parody of "here comes the news" music. Edmund enters to a parody of Prokofiev's *Peter and the Wolf* theme—the wolf, of course. The audience out there has been established visually in 1.1. We hear them laugh at "fops" and at "top the legitimate." Julia's hooded brown eyes mock his own enjoyment of his verbal facility. This is no one to fool around with—he can command two levels of meaning simultaneously, while others in his world cannot even interpret the surface accurately. "I must have your lands" is delivered with the "sorry-about-that" cynicism typical of the mid-1970s. All of this is done in medium close-ups—so that some of the action with the letter is lost—but it is a more rewarding framing than the radical close-ups of the Granada version. Julia simply has a more interesting and expressive face than the blank Lindsay. Julia's Edmund is so strong that Paul Sorvino's Gloucester, still (it seems) struggling with his study of the lines, is instantly a victim. Gloucester, a great man of the former kingdom, should be permitted to have his tectonic plate brush briefly, at least, against Edmund's molten magnum.

Edmund's "Thou, nature . . ." is delivered with his right hand out, palm upward, swinging left to right across the audience, which must approve of the actor's imitation of an action, even if it may disapprove of the action. The audience is, after all, the god to which Prospero prays at the end of *The Tempest*. Julia's hair blows in the breeze of Central Park. The audience is "in nature" (as New York goes), and this Edmund, a Puerto Rican, represents the dangerous power of the mean streets beyond the zone of performance and, in a sense, the predatory dangers lurking in the pathways limned by the bright space of the Delacorte Theatre. Here is a creature of the jungle, svelt and beautiful, outlining his plan to his victims. This is a performance domesticated only by the script itself and overshadowed only by Jones's performance, which is superb until the very end, when he mutes the power toward which he has built so intelligently. Julia's performance is not undercut by the medium, which gives him the close-ups his stage performance has earned.

One critic comments of this production that "For reasons not entirely clear, but perhaps because it participates in the intimacy of theater, it enjoys greater success on the small TV screen than it might on the large screen of a movie house. Stage blocking and video frames equally call attention to the actors' movements. Only close-ups, medium shots, and camera angles separate the small screen from the live performance."[5] This production nicely correlates the space available for television production with that available for stage production—which is limited in each case, compared to film. It is not just that the inner space of performance is limited, but so is the size of the frame: the fifteenth row center of a theater, perhaps, gives us the same visual scale of nineteen diagonal inches of television "viewing space." Furthermore, stage performances can adapt effectively to the expectations of a television audience, given careful editing. The metadramatic element—we know this is a play and so do you—often translates better to television than does the "realistic" approach, as demonstrated by the Jane Howell First Henriad sequence for BBC, particularly *II Henry VI.*

The Papp-Sherin *Lear* is a stage production, pitched to some two thousand people, but it is not hyperbolic on the cool medium. Good acting seems to be good acting no matter what our aesthetic distance from it.

The Edmund best fitted to his medium is that of Michael Kitchen in the BBC version, directed by Jonathan Miller. Miller's sense of scale precisely matches that of television. He does not pretend that he is not pretending—he shows us actors on an obvious set, and a set that seems more like a stage set than a television studio. Edmund is domesticated, making much use of raised eyebrows and knowing nods. He is another—and elegant—courtier as Michael Hordern's tired CEO shambles in from downstage left. Edmund inclines his head. At the end of the scene, Goneril (Gillian Barge) and Regan (Penelope Wilton) discuss the issue of Lear's instability. Edmund wanders into the frame behind them, a rack-shot that creates one of the triangles that Miller employs so effectively in his "field-of-depth" approach to the script.[6] Edmund comes into focus as both Goneril (first) and Regan turn to notice him. He inclines his head. Goneril turns away with a smirk, slightly faster than does Regan. Regan's smile flashes past, saying, We'll see about that! The married women are getting just a bit restless. As they leave, the camera moves toward Edmund, who looks down at the map on the table, gazing, we assume, at Gloucestershire. This is not the huge cowhide rug that Olivier's minions had unrolled beneath his godlike survey. This map has been drawn on parchment by Hawkins or Raleigh and is the ancestor to the one we would discover at Citgo or Gulf.

Edmund delivers a thoughtful explanation of what he has already figured out. His discussion leads him to pause—as verbalizations often do—on the words he is using, words like "base" and "legitimate." This is a single shot, showing Edmund behind Lear's work table. The time is Rembrandtian. The production takes place within a highly established political dispensation where "upward mobility" has become a possibility. This is not a sinister or even threatening Edmund—the old men who inhabit this space should damned well give way to "younger strengths"!

The transition from Goneril and Regan to Edmund is brilliant here. These characters are part of the same play and will become the triangle that Miller's blocking predicts. Sheldon Zitner suggests that "Shakespeare's stage is a relational, not an essentializing or ideologizing, stage: not [a] stage pre-empted by convictions that must focus on one casual chain, psychological or sociological, but a stage closer to the tenor of encountered experience in which causes and motives of all sorts jostle."[7] Miller's technique captures this relational quality accurately and gives us a foretaste of the jostling of the motives of Goneril and Regan, even as Edmund's motives for looking at the map are complicated and augmented by his glimpse of these raven-lovely witches. Edmund may be a dark energy from outside the boundaries of social norms and from some blindspot in the zodiac, but so are this Goneril and this Regan. The effect is not of a sinister Edmund but of sinister forces gathering behind the complacency of the Dutch Masters and under the innocent map that seems to define limits.

Within the illuminated diagonal inches of that ideological medium known as television, Miller's Edmund is the most ideological. The demystification of evil and of the mythology that lies behind this conflated *Lear* script—the erasure that is Miller's goal—works to give us in Edmund the modern rationalist, indeed the modest, even clerkish mentality that Hannah Arendt assigns to Eichmann, and the wholly inoffensive nature of Auschwitz's Rudolph Höss and Treblinka's Franz Stangl.[8]

Like so many of the Nazis, Miller's Edmund is woven thread by thread into the web of institutionalized evil. When validated by power, it seems not to be evil at all—until Dachau's gates are swung open by the horrified outsiders (who are *inside* Shakespeare's script). "In prison," Höss says, 'several of the officials came at me and showed me their Auschwitz tattoo numbers. I could not understand them."[9] Kitchen's Edmund makes his character very believable within the space of a diminished medium which has become the only way of achieving and maintaining power. This Edmund knows what world he is in and knows that the only thing that counts is not getting caught.

At the end, Edmund would do "some good. . . . Despite of [his] own nature" (5.3.244–45). But the nature Edmund has embraced and would now contradict has merely been consciousness. She, the negative and stereotypic woman that man believes he possesses, must prove a fickle goddess, indeed must become, as Hamlet says, "a strumpet" (2.2.236).

7

Lear and Cordelia

Kathleen McLuskie observes that "Cordelia's saving love, so much admired by critics, works in the action less as a redemption for womankind than as an example of patriarchy restored."[1] "In the theatre," she suggests, "the tragic power of the play endorses its ideological position at every turn. . . . The figure of Cordelia is used as a channel for the response to her suffering father."[2] McLuskie is right, although any thesis—the redemption or the condemnation of women—tumbles into the abyss of "the promis'd end" or the theatrical "image of that horror." It has been argued, of course, that it is precisely Lear's reassertion of his wish to "set [his] rest on [Cordelia's] kind nursery" in 5.3 that dooms Cordelia.[3] A trick of the old rage takes command, even as Lear embraces the values that France recognized in Cordelia in 1.1: "She is herself a dowry." Having spent time in an "amorous sojourn" (1.1.47) of which we know nothing, France asserts his male prerogative within a "sub-auction" to which Cordelia, both before it has been established and once it is finished, is allowed no response. France, however, rejects Lear's sense of "price" (1.1.97). But it is not Cordelia of whom Lear is thinking as he commands, "No, no, no, no! Come, let's away to prison" (5.3.8). It is himself, and he reasserts the old authority. Given McLuskie's thesis, it is surprising that she does not deal with 5.3.

It may be worthwhile, then, to look at the Lear-Cordelia story, as depicted in the reconciliation scene (4.7.) and in 5.3 and as represented in five different productions. The interpretations vary widely among the films by Kozintsev (1970) and Brook (1971), the tape of the live Papp-Sherin production (1973; PBS, 1974), and the two television productions, BBC (1982) and Granada (1983). Of these, only the Papp-Sherin production is currently unavailable commercially, but perhaps it can be encouraged out of the vault, since it is a worthwhile addition to the experience of *King Lear* as production, indeed the only televised production of a stage version of *Lear* on tape.

My own descriptions of these productions are inevitably selective and subjective. I offer them merely as a starting point for discussion. As productions are themselves interpretations of a script, responses to productions involve a further reification in which the experience and the psyche of the critic are necessarily, but often unconsciously, involved.

I shall begin slightly out of chronological order with the Brook version, itself a product of Brook's experience with *Lear* on television (1953) and on stage (1962), his film being a radical version of what was in the early 1960s a radical staging of the play. The Brook film, however, helps frame the discussion by unframing it. The film challenges conceptions of the script to which the Granada version (with Olivier) returned as if Brook's challenge to received opinion had never been mounted.

The film emerges not just from the obvious Brechtian-Kottian premises of "alienation" but also from Brook's outrage with the war in Vietnam. A product of *zeitgeist,* it remains powerful today. It may be that the production makes one "feel dead while you watch," as Pauline Kael complains,[4] but it may also be, as William Chaplin suggests, that the Brook version isolates "those who might secretly prefer Tate's fairy tale happy ending."[5]

I find the film even more "political" than its bleak vision would make it—its deletion of Cordelia's asides in 1.1, of France's sudden insights, of the humanity of Cornwall's servants after Gloucester's blinding, and on and on. The conflict is between an older aristocracy that can dump its "darker purpose" on its supposed beneficiaries and a new bourgeoisie with no need to "reason the need." In this world of easy assumption, the enunciation of ethical norms and personal moral codes would be as laughable as they are today. "Love" must "be silent" in such an environment, and Brook silences it. If uttered—as in the sections of 1.1 that Brook cuts—it can only be hypocrisy. The film shows outcasts and carcasses pelted by wind-driven rain. The analogy is to modern societies that "deinstitutionalize" the mad and the helpless while the yuppies warm by the fireside. Brook's world reflects the one in which we live. It is a world without mercy. (I am not speaking of the smugness of the "born again," with their appropriation of virtue and automatic embrace of petty-bourgeois patterns.)

As the script tends to rebuff confident assumptions about "justice," Brook's film defeats our expectations for film. The camera incorporates irrelevance, as in an off-center shot of Lear in 1.1, with nothing significant on the left side of the frame. "Nothing" becomes significant here, becomes "all," as the film ends with a blank pitiless sky, Lear's head having finally dropped from the frame. It is as if an amateur stands behind the camera—or a sadist. A sadist, if anything, seems to be behind the "cosmic plan." Gloucester's complaint about "flies," "the gods," and "wanton boys" becomes normative here. Kael objects to Brook's technique: "the cutting has become jaggedly mannered, with sudden shifts from one angle to another and from long shots to closeups, often when someone is speaking. [It] seems designed as an alienation device, but who wants to be alienated from Shakespeare?"[6] Kael objects to Brook's intention while appealing implicitly to "Shakespeare's intention," as other critics do explicitly in attacking the film.[7]

Given what Jack Jorgens describes as "a bleak, existential tale of meaningless violence in a cold, empty universe,"[8] Brook inherits the problem of Cordelia. She is, Normand Berlin claims, "a spring shower in a world of storms . . . the child who redeems nature."[9] But, Berlin continues, "Brook *wants* Cordelia to be sullen or arrogant (I'm not sure which); he *wants* her to be as cold as her sisters; he seems to want to give Lear a cause for banishing her—all, I submit, clashing with the spirit of the text".[10] Brook's opening scene can also be read as showing Cordelia totally isolated and able only to refuse to step into the trap Lear has set for her. While that may play against a script that must be heavily excised for filmic purposes, I am not convinced that the concept conflicts with "the spirit of the text."

Brook's reconciliation permits Lear and Cordelia to share the frame only after Lear's "my child, Cordelia" and until her "No cause, no cause." Lear comes back into the frame for a moment to touch his forehead to hers. The earlier part of the scene shows Lear in close-up, lying back, objecting, with Scofield's almost offhanded understatement at being a victim of graverobbers. We perceive Cordelia via close-up, but Lear seems not to wake up until he wonders about where he "did lodge last night." Brook emphasizes not reconciliation and forgiveness but the terror of awakening into a zone between absolute nightmare and incomplete consciousness. That phenomenology captured, Brook's Cordelia (Anne-lise Gabold) is content to recognize that Lear has fully awakened. She has done her duty.

While the scene "seems perfunctory," as Berlin notes,[11] it avoids the sentiment that can easily overload into sentimentality. Brook refuses to provide the music the script calls for. The scene blends with his bleak vision. It does, as Berlin complains, "minimalize . . . Shakespeare's rich dialectic and inclusiveness [down to] a single-minded conception."[12] But that is partly the effect of a black-and-white film. We get no transition from grim Kansas to the technicolor Land of Oz. I think, for example, of George Stevens's powerful 1951 film *A Place in the Sun*, in which a fleeting glimpse of possibility—motor boats and vacation lakes—becomes a newspaper photograph that promotes George Eastman's (Clyde Griffith's) inevitable movement down the corridor that terminates at the door to Sing Sing's death house. The camera is the remorseless chronicler, knowing the ending and not trying to delude us into hope, even if the characters we watch are enticed into pleasant delusions. The scene is, as McLuskie says, "an emblem of possible harmony, briefly glimpsed before the tragic debacle."[13] Brook's camera already has the debacle in view as it records the scenes that lead to it.

As Lear and Cordelia emerge from a hut (5.3), Edmund meets them. Burning ships crackle in the background and the foreground shrouds in smoke. Cordelia asks Edmund, "Shall we not see these daughters and these sisters?" (5.3.7). He is not sure what to do. He has not been near royalty. Cordelia accedes to Lear's demand that they go off to prison. She seems willing to humor him, even if she would select another direction. As Lear says "great ones" (5.3.18), he turns his back on Edmund. Cordelia would confront him, but Lear is above dealing with such "half-blooded fellows" (5.3.80). Lear's attitude is that of Suffolk in *II Henry VI* (4.1). Lear conveys the arrogance of the older aristocracy—hubris—even within a speech that delineates a new set of nonmaterialistic values. While Edmund has the note for the Captain already written, it is a contingency that Cordelia and Lear, each in different ways, motivate into transmission. It does not matter, then, which decision they make. They are going only one way.

This production shows what the script shows—that Cordelia is as much a victim of Lear in 5.3. as she was in 1.1. But here it is the "old Lear"—still a vigorous man as Scofield plays him—who reasserts himself, not a "new Lear," elevating himself on the steps of a new set of principles to the status of one of "God's spies" (5.3.17). The moment is hubristic, however interpreted. Lear does "reappropriate" Cordelia here. But the emphasis is on his return to inner attitudes for which his words are rationalizations. Lear's reassumption of attitudes he had encouraged and of a position he had rendered obsolete dooms both him and Cordelia. While I disagree strongly with Brook's interpretation of the text, it is right for this film. If the cosmos is bleak, Lear remains blind. This environment permits only "nothing" to be learned. Barbara Hodgdon accurately defines Brook's technique as one that "frustrates our ability to see and to know."[14] The characters we see are similarly frustrated. Thus, as Lillian Wilds argues, the film is "coherent" and achieves a "terrifying unity."[15]

The Kozintsev version reveals huddled masses of poor people picking across the fields and hillsides outside the great, protected fortress, as opposed to the static and unhappy faces over which Brook's camera pans at his opening. Kozintsev's ragged proletariat soon absorbs Edgar, Lear, and Gloucester, the aristocrats.

The reconciliation and capture scenes are part of the sweep of this production. The scenes convey both the huge sway of battle and the nuance of individual motivations, showing both victory in defeat and defeat in victory.

Cordelia breaks away from her marching army to attend to Lear. As commander, she has little, if anything, to do with the conduct of the battle. She walks beside Lear's litter, past fire and a twisting bole of river, through the counterpush of the conflict. Lear is transferred to a cart. The Fool provides music with his mournful recorder. Lear and Cordelia kneel to each other. Lear tastes one of Cordelia's tears, learning, as Kozintsev says, "the value of salt."[16] An alarum forces them to vacate the moment of their reunion.

"In Shakespeare's poetry," Kozintsev says, "love is a martial concept, a challenge addressed to the ideas of the iron age."[17] The landscape for 5.3 resembles that depicted by Nazi cameras in the early 1940s. Flames flicker. People die at the edges of the frame and the camera does not pause to consider them. Cordelia and Lear are trapped within the panic press of a retreat. The scene resembles the retreat from Caporetto depicted in Hemingway's *A Farewell to Arms*, where battle police sort out the officers for summary execution. A guard pauses as he stops Lear. The guard turns to Edmund. Cordelia kisses Lear's hand. "Take them away!" Edmund commands—they are saying dangerous things. They move off, robes flowing, a frail old man (Yuri Jarvet) and his daughter (Valentina Shandrikova) surrounded by a phalanx of beefy soldiers in armor and helmets, holding studded spikes. But Lear and Cordelia assert a joyous power over their environment. Kozintsev shows that "these vulnerable two are the victors."[18] Edmund observes their faces—don't they realize that they have *lost?* Disturbed, he gives his "men are as the time are" speech from a cart (perhaps a brief, ironic allusion to Olivier's "band of brothers" speech in his filmic *Henry V*).[19] The soldiers chant "Edmund! Edmund!" He whispers to the Captain. But he moves into his combat still musing about what he had seen in the faces of Lear and Cordelia—something that puzzled him. Like a heavy-weight preoccupied with something else when the bell rings, Edmund is knocked out.

Kozintsev's emphasis is on the joyous reunion of daughter and father. "Their love is more than the passion of lovers, or the affection between father and daughter; it is an illustration of wisdom."[20] Edmund cannot fathom that wisdom, though he can order it executed. In an ironic way, however, that wisdom also kills him. While Lear and Cordelia are trapped in a pattern of fatality, they transcend it. Their transcendence dooms Edmund, indeed denies him the very physical power that is his premise. He has seen something that denies his premise, and it puzzles him, fatally.

While some still prefer the Kozintsev version, with its emphasis on the "positive text," to the Brook, I am not making that judg-ment. Each is a different film, and each is powerful in different ways.

Kozintsev's final scene is worth a brief comment. As Albany's command (5.3.234) and the original stage direction dictate, the bodies of Goneril and Regan are produced. The effect of this family reunion in death—clearly "Shakespeare's intention"—is powerful. Brook's Lear falls gradually out of the frame, leaving us only a blank and pitiless sky to observe. In Kozintsev's coda, the Fool, a Treblinka survivor, plays his recorder but is roughly pushed aside by a soldier. The peasants flow back through the smoke and pick through the smolder. A little girl finds a doll, smudged and grimy, beneath a flame-wrinkled bedboard. She hugs it to her unformed bosom. The story of Lear and Cordelia is absorbed into an ongoing drama of survival. The returning peas-ants do not know the story. They do not even ask why what little they had has been consumed in battle. The question is thus projected at us. It is not those within the mimetic frame who must understand, but as Kozintsev says, "The spectator is to believe that he grasps everything."[21]

The Joseph Papp production of 1973 suffers, as reviewers note, from uneven acting.[22] While the television version was taped during a live performance in Central Park, it helps the weaker actors by focusing on James Earl Jones (Lear) and Raul Julia (Edmund). They are privileged with close-ups they have earned. At moments, as in the opening scene, the outer audience is incorporated as part of the fabric of the production. At other times, as in the reconciliation scene, they are an intrusion.

Lee Chamberlin (Cordelia) is tall and dominant, certainly not a stereotypical Cordelia, but one Kozintsev might have admired: "The figure of Cordelia lacks susceptible softness or incorporeal dreaminess. . . . Her poetry is close to folk balladry in its tension; the rhythm is severe, the colors subdued, the images often cruel."[23] Such a Cordelia could only be defeated in battle by an even more powerful Edmund, which Julia provides.

The music accompanying Lear's awakening is tom-tom and pipe, somehow appropriate to a production that blends ethnicity as brilliantly as this production does. This Cordelia tries to insist that Lear *"know"* who she is. She turns to the Doctor in frustration on "Still, still, far wide!" She pleads with Lear on "*No* cause, *no* cause!" She is putting pressure on Lear—don't you understand? She offers an arm to him, but Lear has to put an arm around her as he exits. This is not a signal of appropriation. It is a sign of physical weakness.

As prisoner, Lear is dragged in on the end of a rope, victim of "a murderous slave master," as Jack Jorgens notes.[24] The image is of a Joe Louis being led to the ring where his destructive power would be released to make a fortune for his white managers. The image emerges from Cleaver's *Soul on Ice,* which, of course, emerges from the black man's experience of being "sold to slavery." Cordelia, member of a younger and more militant black generation, says, "Shall we not *see* these daughters and these sisters?" She swings her head around the stage at Lear's "No, no, no, no!" suggesting that he is making the wrong political decision in surrendering to Edmund. She does not accord with docility. The conflict reminded me of Bettelheim's indictment of Jewish passivity in the face of Nazi genocide.[25] This Cordelia is not ignoring "the lesson of Anne Frank." But Lear shakes the rope like a giant rein, as if urging his captors forward. Julia's Edmund has his letter for the Captain ready, and holds it as he had held the forgery he had foisted on Gloucester earlier.

While Jones is often a powerful and effective Lear, he plays submissiveness against Cordelia's strength. He thus denies the identity she is trying to assert. She, too, is Lear's daughter, but one who has integrated his strength into her own system of intentions. She neither understands nor shares Lear's "discovery" of the irrelevancy of "great ones." She is a young queen with her future ahead of her. While such an interpretation may contradict the Cordelia who has rejected Lear's opening auction sale, it suggests that the Queen of France has grown in her way, even as Lear has come to accept the meaninglessness of the competitive premises he had enunciated earlier. Lear seems to regress in 5.3, however. His daughter, meanwhile, has marched at Selma.

Uneven as this production may be, and difficult as it is to convey nuance and detail in a main-stage, outdoor performance, the Lear-Cordelia story refutes more conventional approaches. The racial subtext, which reviewers tended to ignore, lends a poignancy to the Lear-Cordelia conflict that goes well beyond mere topicality. They cannot communicate at the outset. They cannot communicate in 5.3. Lear's latter scenario ignores a Cordelia who has changed since act 1. Cordelia is dragged back into a past to which Lear submits, a past in which uppity blacks were lynched. This production suggests that that past is still with us.

Miller's production for BBC is another of his efforts to "de-mythologize" the text. He gives us, in Michael Hordern, a shambling old CEO turning the family business he has built over to "younger strengths" (1.1.40). The youngsters, though, have been enjoying their status, as opposed to having worked for the corporation, as Kent and Gloucester have been doing.

The ensemble acting was condemned by Steven Urkowitz as resembling a football huddle.[26] But this anachronistic script can absorb many styles and many different placements in time. It does demand the scaling down that the medium also demands. One result of Miller's decision to set the play in relatively modern times is to reduce the element of patriarchy and to concentrate instead upon a single parent—and an old man—who is trying to deal with his family as best he can. He does not do well, obviously, but Miller's many-peopled frames capture his sense of family, that staple out of which so much television emerges.

The camera moves almost imperceptibly during Lear's awakening and incorporates Kent and the Doctor, as well as Lear and Cordelia. Hordern looks at Brenda Blethyn when she asks, "Sir, do you know me?" He isn't sure, and refuses to jump to the conclusions of his senses. Her "*look* upon me!" means Recognize me, please! She weeps as he cannot remember where he lodged last night, so that his "Do not laugh at me" is bitingly ironic. He is still a crusty old man. His "Am I in France?" is a sudden question, accompanied by a jerk of the head, the question one asks when awakening on a sick bed. All of the others help Lear up. Cordelia and the Doctor help him to walk, leaving Kent with the French Gentleman, in another of the splendid transitions that this production's "field-of-depth" technique permits.[27]

In 5.3, Edmund plays the busy officer catching up on paperwork. Cordelia's "We are not the first / Who, with best meaning, have incurr'd the worst" is directed at Edmund, as if to remind him of his own former condition. But Edmund is concentrating on his future. Lear's "No" surprises Cordelia, but she is pleased at his recovery. He wipes her eyes. She holds her chin up. She will be brave. Edmund gives the Captain a letter already sealed and orders the Captain to "Follow them to prison."

This production dismisses whatever cosmic issues there may be in *Lear* and closes in on the family. In 5.3 Lear reasserts his role as father, recognizing his earlier failure. It does not matter that Cordelia is married and a queen. Failed fathers ignore the present and try to compensate for what they should have done long before. It is too late for that, of course, but this Cordelia is happy to have found her father at last and to play the role of daughter that, we assume, the opening of the play has interrupted. We observe here the flowing of positive energies that should have come together years before and *then* been permitted to diverge, even as the generations separate naturally from each other. The positive evolution, however, would have required the eradication of Lear's patriarchal and egotistical attitudes, an erasure that could not have occurred while he was king. This production shows us that positive personal insights must coincide with the time when they can emerge positively into the familial context. Here, the interchange occurs within an environment that denies it. It is like falling in love at Dachau.

This production shows that the small scale of television can work when the focus is on the personal issues inherent in this script.

The effort to "scale up" via Stonehenge and despotism can meet ironic diminution on the small screen. The Olivier production, with its absolute monarch demanding debasement from his subjects and its huge rug of a map (of some zone other than Britain) over which Lear presides like God above Eden, emphasizes patriarchal values to the extreme and a king who enjoys his role as puppeteer.

The reconciliation scene is backed by a mixed consort—recorder, harp, and viola da gamba (possibly a cello)—that vamps till ready. Anna Calder-Marshall kisses Lear's hand, then his cheek. Lear finds it wrong to "wake" him out of the grave. He knows how old he is—"not a *hour* more nor less" (although Olivier says "day"). He sits up on "mightily abus'd," as if abuse could be countered by his frailty—who could abuse such vulnerability? He has barely been able to raise his great sword against Kent in 1.1. After putting his hands to Cordelia's damp face, Lear kisses her cheek on "Be your tears wet?" Cordelia's "No *cause, no cause,*" seemed to come from the edge of exasperation. The vaguely liturgical music plays on as Lear and Cordelia embrace. Elliot's montage cuts to the next scene.

I find the music obtrusive here, though the script calls for it— "louder." Here it is a Hollywood cuing of a lovers' meeting after all that misunderstanding.

In 5.3, Edmund takes his helmet off amid a circle of swords. Calder-Marshall's "Shall we not see these daughters and these sisters?" is an appeal to Edmund. "Take them away!" he responds. Olivier puts his manacled arms over Cordelia's shoulders on "Upon such sacrifices" and removes them on "Wipe thine eyes." He is angry that she should be seen weeping, even as he fights back his own tears on "starv'd first."

The Captain looks up after reading Edmund's letter—not considering moral scruple but figuring out how to follow his orders. Edmund holds his helmet in his hands, like a skull.

Cordelia seems as much Lear's prisoner here as Edmund's. But Elliott's compulsive use of close-ups often seems like a nervous tic rather than camera work motivated by the script, and it makes no sense of relationships. Perhaps we are meant to observe all of this from Lear's point of view, as he foolishly gives away what was his at the outset and blindly reappropriates what he thinks to be his at the end. But the script offers vantage points other than Lear's, including that which we infer from Cordelia at the beginning. Here she is captured in 5.3 by a Lear who was little changed from 1.1—except that he has grown physically weaker.

At the end, amid the lugubrious strokes of that viola da gamba, the camera circles Lear and Cordelia with the old Hollywood cliché for lovers. The script may suggest that Lear harbors an incestuous desire foir Cordelia, disguised in his wish to set his "rest in her kind nursery." The opening scene shows, then, a Cordelia who refuses the almost literal prostitution Lear would force upon her. This production brings the sexual agenda to the surface and in my opinion destroys the unexamined resonance that may exist in any father-daughter relationship. At the very least, this Lear is a sexist who can evoke little pity—in spite of Olivier's virtuoso performance. We pity his victim, Cordelia.[28]

By ignoring the feminist thesis that McLuskie sets forth, this production tends to prove it.

The two films, given the amplitude of the medium and granted Brook's minimalist approach, give us more to observe, therefore more to describe and evaluate. The television versions are, necessarily, far less "visual," and, given the smaller size of the screen and the heritage of radio, incorporate more of the language of this conflated script. Because the translation from script to film is so radical, however, the films force us to consider the script more than do the television productions. What language is omitted for the sake of the imagery? How adequate is the visualization of language that the film demands? Brook fills in the language as his written scenario dictated.[29] Kozintsev sees "half of the text of any play . . . as a diffused remark that the author wrote in order to acquaint actors as thoroughly as possible with the heart of the action to be played."[30] For a film, "The flow of the verse must become a swarm of images of the same poetic quality."[31] Perhaps ironically, the radical translation from script to film captures, in Brook and Kozintsev, a larger fragment of whatever the Shakespearean vision may have been than does the more literal medium of television. Brook and Kozintsev themselves have different visions, but they bring them to truth on their screens. Television, a more pedestrian medium, because of what it is and because of what we have made it, lacks the scope for genius— whether it be Shakespeare's or that of his interpreters—to recreate and to be creative. As Kozintsev says, "It is quite possible to speak all the words and to say little."[32] For all of the good things in the productions of *Lear* on television, Kozintsev delivers their epitaph.[33]

8

Shakespeare and History

I

Malcolm Evans advocates "readings that take up committed positions contrary to that of the idealized universal reader of humanism. These compel the text to signify not 'in its own terms' but in the context of a discourse—feminist, Marxist, or anti-colonialist, for example—which recognizes that any production of the text is *for* a particular interpretation of history, which is not simply a disinterested chronicle but a selective production of the past for the present with a stake in *making* history or, in the case of the discourse under attack, prolonging the existing set of historical relations by transforming history into 'nature' " [his emphasis].[1]

As I have suggested already, production per se creates its own dialectic. It certainly eliminates "the idealized universal reader of humanism" by making the reader witness an interpretation that, in turn, should excite her or his own subjectivity into action. But as I have also suggested, the spectator may arrive at the theater with televisual expectations and find those expectations met by cretin-directors; or the reader may be that universal reader that Levin's consensus posits. If so, a good production will quickly erase "universal expectations" with the specificity of its interpretation.

One reason why production is not often employed as a mode of interpretation is that productions are usually nonretrievable. Another reason is that production *is* interpretation and has therefore already robbed the theorist of his or her chance to examine the text. But the text in this case is a script, and production is a representation of that script.

A basic question to be asked of any production is Does it enhance one's sense of the vitality of the inherited script? Or, Is one's sense of the script diminished? "One," of course, is a subjective entity carrying all the biases and unexamined assumptions

140

that that construct entails. I would share, however, the distinction that Graham Holderness makes between the BBC-TV versions of Second and First Henriads: "[The *Henry VI–Richard III*] plays . . . are not a dramatisation of the Elizabethan World Picture but a sustained interrogation of residual and emergent ideologies in a changing society."[2]

I was fortunate to see two history-making productions, perhaps the most famous productions of the 1970s—the John Barton *Richard II* and the Terry Hands *Henry V*. Each created its own dialectic. One was overlaid with gimmicks that coerced momentary attention—even shock. Direction masked the profound issues the script explores and the absolute transition that it depicts. That was Barton's frivolous *Richard II*. The other emerged from a depth of consideration, as if a palimpsest under whose clear surface resided many complimentary inscriptions. That was Hand's *Henry V*.

I will deal briefly with these productions because one of the potential ironies in cultural materialism, useful as the approach is in exploring the premises of production, is that its practitioners might well have preferred the Barton over the Hands. The former did, indeed, trivialize both medieval and modern political process. The latter took its modern politics very seriously but perhaps reinforced our sense of the manifest ideology of King and Chorus.

Although John Barton clothed his *Richard II* in conventional costumes, the production represented a series of impositions upon the inherited text. Since that production has been treated at length by Stanley Wells,[3] my objections can be brief. To have Bolingbroke and Mowbray mince about inside toy horses, making each protagonist look as if he had been amputated from a merry-go-round, was to invalidate the seriousness of the medieval trial-by-combat convention and to erase the symbolic import of Richard's interruption of it. We may laugh today at a trial-by-combat as a means of arriving at justice when we know that justice is a purchased commodity. We may learn that both Bolingbroke and Mowbray know that no intrinsic justice can emerge from a ceremony that Richard's complicity undercuts. Mowbray and Bolingbroke must, however, believe that they are about to fight to the death. Here, even that expectation was erased. To give Northumberland the outfit of an Hitchcockian bird and to allow him to grow into a giant upstage crow as the production continued was to make some point about Northumberland as his own "ladder" at the expense of our believing in the literal facts the play presents.

A willing suspension of disbelief was further violated when a snowman, complete with top hat and carrot nose, melted away behind York's sorrowful speech about the different entrances and exits of Bolingbroke and Richard. That "bright idea" forced a collision between language and stage image—Richard's "mockery king of snow" is *not* York's metaphor—and simply obliterated York's fine speech. (What is that *snowman* doing there? Did it miss its cue earlier?) To have Richard smash the mirror over his own head and wear it as a silly necklace of thorns was to rob the play of the superb moment when Richard dashes the mirror down at the feet of "silent king" Bolingbroke. To make Bolingbroke the Groom who visits Richard at Pomfret was to make some premature point about Bolingbroke's conscience perhaps, but was to eradicate the several different points the scene itself makes. To import Henry IV's "uneasy head" speech all the way from act 3 of *II Henry IV* and place it in *Richard II* was to miss many points, not the least of which is that the speech captures the frustrations of the career of Henry IV after the full ramifications of regicide have echoed through England and returned to Bolingbroke in a series of potent rebellions. Exton has not yet entered with the corpse of Richard, so we had to accept Bolingbroke's speech as the product of an insomniac who had read other works of Shakespeare.[4] *Richard II* has world enough and language to explore intelligently. The play becomes unintelligible if forced into the facile atmosphere of a series of incoherent *tour de forces*. As Joseph Price says of this production, "The stage devices that were used to blur the personalities of Richard [and Bolingbroke] into one personality ran counter to the psychological foils these characters are to each other."[5] Indeed, the production represented a blurring of emphasis, of conflict, and of characterization and became for me a prime example of the evils attendant upon the "director's theater," where fallacy can obscure even what *is* demonstrable in the text.

While a director must make choices, he cannot be self-indulgent. The script itself limits the range of choices available. One of the assumptions implicit in my response to Barton's *Richard II* is that of a "good audience," a group alert and alive, interacting emotionally as well as intellectually as performance develops through the evening. The positive energy transmitted by the audience is basic to good production, but that force can only emerge if the production permits it. When a director insists on telling us only what *he* sees in the play, he behaves like Hamlet, limiting the meaning of the play and denying the uniqueness of an imagination other than his own. Modern directors too often embrace the very pretentiousness, arrogance, even hubris that the plays themselves expose.

If Barton made mostly wrong decisions in his *Richard II*, Hands made mostly right decisions in his *Henry V.* The latter production fulfilled the absolute criterion of allowing individual performance to emerge—superbly, in the case of Alan Howard. His Henry was a master of rhetoric, and Henry knew it. He smiled at himself after his seemingly angry reaction to the Dauphin's tennis balls. Hey—not bad! he seemed to say, allowing the spectator to observe a personality the King cannot show those on stage. Henry V displayed the fine formal education he had received so informally with Falstaff yet allowed us to remember that this Henry *had* been Prince Hal. We knew that no one had much to dread later at Harfleur, when Henry vented his blank verse before the gates. Although he could not know the time or the place, Henry was getting his troops ready for Agincourt, building a reality out of rhetoric, like Tamburlaine or like Cassius Clay before his first fight with Liston. Howard's self-aware, even self-amused conception gave the role an "interiority" the text does not always suggest. The script has awaited an Alan Howard to release its potentiality. Henry's humble admission to Mountjoy that the English do not seek battle at Agincourt, his sad survey of the slaughter behind his own lines, and the amusement he shared with Katherine in the wooing scene were all anticipated in a play that became the unfolding of a complex and believable character—to be sure, a collusionist with the Church, a promoter of the very war that kills defenseless boys and disarmed prisoners, and a consummate rhetorician, but also a man aware of the humanity the King must keep to himself.

Hand's production was more than merely a "starring vehicle." Howard's Henry was the energetic builder of a community rising anew over the wreckage of the sacramental, medieval kingship Richard had conspired with Bolingbroke to destroy. The "band of brothers" speech in this production was not an oratorical set piece delivered from a cart à la Olivier but the impromptu inspiration of the commander moving among his troops, uniting them into more than just another army. This sense of community and common purpose had to have an impact on a modern British audience experiencing the erosion of that rapport which England has always seemed to hold within its sceptered isle.

But lest Hands be accused of modernization—and he has been, in that his production began randomly, as a rehearsal—recall that the brief moment of Henry V, taking a united England off into dubious battle in France, followed the uneasy reign of his father, hammered by the civil wars attendant upon deposition and regicide, and preceded the reign of his son and the internecine collision of the roses. The moment of Henry V represented an instant of commonality, a parenthesis of national coherence within the civil butchery that killed off most of the fifteenth century. This production might also have appealed to the Englishman of 1599. The reference to Essex in the Chorus to act 5 is perhaps Shakespeare's most specific allusion to his own times. The end of the sixteenth century was also uneasy. Doubts about what would happen when the age of Elizabeth ended were rife in the London that first heard Henry V, the London that soon enough would see a nonvictorious and rebellious Earl of Essex beheaded at the Tower. It may also be, as James Shapiro has suggested, that England in 1599 was facing renewed threats from Spain.[6] This production may have been topical in one way, but it was historical in the deepest sense.

If we explore further, we discover that the concept for this Henry V emerged from the problems of that microcosm of Great Britain, the Royal Shakespeare Company. The play, says director Hands, "is about improvisation, interdependence, and unity . . . essential qualities if the company was to surmount its present difficulties."[7] Did Shakespeare face threats to his theater in 1599—rampant plague on one side and rising Puritanism on the other? He could not know then that he and his company would become the original Royal Shakespeare Company, to be known after May 1603 as the King's Men.

Olivier cut the scene with the traitors from his filmscript, apparently because treason was not to be bruited with Lord Haw-Haw beaming his subversion into England.[8] In Hand's production, King Henry greeted his friend, Scroop, his fellow aristocrat, Cambridge, and groped for the name Grey. Coming up with it, he held Grey by the hand and indulged in chit-chat while poor Grey glanced helplessly at his as yet unindicted co-conspirators. The soldier Henry had just freed became the officer who took Scroop into custody. The soldier was loyal, "excess of wine" having worn off and left him in his better senses. The explicitly sober Scroop was a traitor. The question of loyalty and treason was raised again when Williams and Bates were portrayed by the actors who had played Scroop and Grey, a piece of doubling Shakespeare himself might have employed. The doubling raised a subtle question. The goal of the Cambridge conspiracy, after all, was to replace Henry V with Mortimer, the heir Richard II had named long before. The Cambridge group expresses loyalty to a de jure precedent they believe violated by a merely *de facto* king. So consummate is Henry V's stage management of the Southampton sequence that the real issue—Henry's right to his own throne—scarcely surfaces (cf. Cambridge: 2.2.155–57). But this production raised the question delicately, simply by using valid theatrical technique. And this production did not presume to give an answer.

The soldiers by the campfire do not engage legalisms like *de jure* and *de facto* within the format of their fundamentalism. One wonders, however, how they might have responded later to Henry VI. The former king asks his keepers, "have you not broke your oaths?" "No," replies the First Keeper, "For we were subjects but while you were king." (*III Henry VI*: 3.1.79–80). The doubling in this *Henry V*, the later scene echoing the former, evoked a sense of historical process and reminded us that the Cambridge or Yorkist branch would have its revenge in the next generation against the Lancastrian son of Henry V, a sequence Shakespeare has already dramatized. Once basic loyalties have been sundered—loyalties to principle, not just person—superb individual leadership must substitute for sacramental kingship. That leadership can incorporate the subject's continuing belief in the anachronistic "ceremony" the King perceives as "farcical." But the skill Henry V has labored to acquire and that he deploys so brilliantly is not transferable. It dies with him, and "hung be the heavens with black."

Such considerations of the ultimate reaches of Shakespeare's history plays—indeed of history itself—do emerge from productions as carefully conceived as this *Henry V*. To say that one critic will see a rabbit and another a duck, as Norman Rabkin suggests, is accurate, in that this text, like *Hamlet*, is a kind of dramatic Rorschach test.[9] But Hands did not force the text into a rigid "pro or con" configuration. His production explored its issues, leaving us to construe that exploration as we would. "The inscrutability of *Henry V*," Rabkin says, "is the inscrutability of history. And for a unique moment in Shakespeare's work ambiguity is the heart of the matter, the single most important fact we must confront in plucking out the mystery of the world we live in."[10] While one might quarrel with the unique ambiguity of *Henry V*—the play from which Rabkin wisely steals a line, *Hamlet*, would seem to have a claim—Hands's *Henry V*, a product of countless decisions, most of them deeply valid, opened out to confront us with mysteries that required no explicit modernization to be recognized as ours. By avoiding the fallacy of overt directorial imposition, Hands bestowed upon us the responsibility Shakespeare gave his audience—we must ponder these things in our own way. Our response is our own, however gropingly articulated and however much consensus might wish to produce our words for us.

Hands's production tended to reflect a paradox to its audience. Robin Wells articulates the paradox in describing Robert Parsons, who "dismantles with ruthless logic the 'absurd paradoxes' of the establishment doctrine of absolute obedience, [but] at the same time . . . acknowledges that 'of all other governments the monarchy is the best and least subject to the inconveniences that other governments have.' "[11]

One poblem with ideological approaches is that they tend to ignore dynamics *within* the plays. The script may not be able to speak for itself, but these critics (like most) tend to speak for it. Tensions do exist within the scripts, after all, that are exclusive of Marxist critiques of society and of documents contemporary to Shakespeare's time. John of Gaunt's idealized and sacramental England—as he describes it at length to York in *Richard II* (2.1)—no doubt was an ancien régime full of rationalized brutalities like crusades and "chivalric" combats. That world, however, is juxtaposed in the script against the equivocal "modern world" that Richard and Bolingbroke, each against his will, usher in. No doubt exists about the ruthlessness of Richard and Bolingbroke, but emphasis on the flaws of hierarchal and monarchical models blurs the action of the play. It depicts a paradigm shift. A different England comes in with Gloucester's murder and Richard's leasing out of royal lands—each an anti-sacramental action. We move from Gaunt's memory of an "other Eden" to Carlisle's prediction of "another Golgotha." The script does speak for itself, often in what Harry Berger calls "the retrospective mode of structural irony."[12] We must make something of that speaking, I think, before we impose ideological positions upon the dramatic materials before us. The cultural materialist who watched Barton's *Richard II* might have found his own predilections confirmed and thus might have favored that production over the profound exploration of the script that Hands' *Henry V* represented. Hands did not challenge the script with *his* meanings. He challenged it for *its* meanings and captured at least a glimpse of "the Shakespearean moment."

II

At the beginning of Leni Reifenstahl's 1934 film *The Triumph of the Will*, Hitler's plane flies over Nuremberg—although we do not yet know whose plane it is. Its shadow rides down a thronged thoroughfare, the crowd receiving the benediction of a moving swastika. The two-engined Junkers is buoyed by a soaring Wagnerian theme. A god is coming to earth. He rides an open Mercedes through an ocean of cheers. Thousands of right arms disable themselves as they vector their power towards the stern and brown-shirted messiah. The Night of the Long Knives has just passed. Hitler's murky metaphors will allude to it, and the sweaty new head of the emasculated SA will give a speech pledging absolute loyalty to Hitler—the same speech that Rohm might have given in the spring of that year.

At the beginning of Olivier's 1944 film *Henry V*, a camera in the sky roves over a model of London. The mighty heart is lying still, the unchartered Thames flows gently, a placid ribbon. This is, one assumes, a model to England's inward greatness. A glimpse of the Tower on its hill across the river is—as we will learn—the only allusion to treason the film will provide. The camera is seeking something, makes a wrong guess as it dips toward the Swan, then corrects itself to capture the flag rising above the Globe. The camera is not bringing a god to the groundlings. It is making a discovery.

The sense of community created by the two films is obviously very different. "The Will" enunciates order, and "Ordnung ist nie falsch," as Erwin Rommell once said. The masses stand as if in cast iron. Actual statues stare out from their squares. Only Hitler moves. In London, the crowd jostles within the wooden O; wenches hawk oranges; noblemen take their places. The actors rush about backstage adjusting costumes and forgetting props. But the stage pulls the audience into a single focus as the Chorus (Leslie Banks) pleads for a flaming muse. A few moments later, however, the Archbishop (Felix Aylmer) must rebuke an audience suddenly demanding their Falstaff. The film, of course, is dedicated to "The Commandos and Airbourne Troops of Great Britain." But the film shows that those highly disciplined branches were defending not outstretched obedience but a culture and its rich diversity.

The play moves toward France, of course, as does the film toward its rendezvous with a fully representational Agincourt. At Harfleur, Henry delivers his speech from astride a restless charger. The camera moves back to include the hundreds of men surrounding the king and even the crosslike mast of a ship. Henry is at the center and, as the camera shows us, the creator of the mimesis—"the action of the tiger"—that this ragtag and not uniformly valorous group must achieve. The waves of the Channel punctuate Henry's words. The only direction is "into the breach." It is D-Day, and the enemy is really Germany, as the film's "sliding symbolism" would have it.[13] Later, of course, the camera rises above Henry until he is a tiny figure with a huge voice creating victory in advance for the troops surrounding him. God has not come to earth. Rather, He is looking down upon this great king, endowing him with the strength to lead his beggars to victory at dawn.

In 1944, German troops were refusing to watch the films of the strangulation by piano wire of the generals implicated in the Stauffenberg Plot.

Reifenstahl's "documentary" and Olivier's filmic recreation of Shakespeare's play within the context of another invasion of France are superb films. They are propaganda, of course, but perhaps any depiction of history is propaganda.

Critics complain of the BBC's treatment of the *Richard II–Henry V* sequence. It "reinforces the political status quo by presenting an image of a world without change and thereby helping to prevent change."[14] BBC was motivated "by a desire to improve the company image."[15] "Exxon, envying the Mobil Oil Corporation's sponsorship of *Masterpiece Theatre,*" was similarly motivated.[16] It follows, then, that Hal-Henry V will have "an unthreatening mien [that] suits the BBC's intentions perfectly. This Henry is a peach. Telling us he will dump his companions when the time comes, Gwillim makes it seem not like a calculated step but like a cute idea that's just occurring to him."[17] This Henry becomes the CEO of a multinational enterprise, "sent by his father about some merchandise." That metaphor may be appropriate enough, but in the BBC *Henry V* it is not seen as metaphor. The production permits no ironic vision, no subversion of the overt text. While television is hardly a vehicle for irony, it fails when it tells us that Henry V is "but a man." He is "but a man as *I* am," but that means not "as *we* are," but as *he* can employ "we," and "us" (and *us*) in his royal manipulations.

Gwillim may, however, be a victim of a vision of the medium. Jonathan Miller argues that "the television medium is incurably naturalistic and TV Shakespeare productions should eschew any mixing of conventions, any techniques of alienation, any devices of self-reflection: the audience should be unaware that it is in the presence of an art form."[18] Miller is seconded by David Giles, director of the BBC's *Richard II–Henry V* cycle: "I do not think [that the television audience is] ready to use [its] imagination because

[it] is never asked to. . . . You can't do [1.3 of *Richard II*] realistically in a television studio and yet we didn't want it to get too stylized: that's why we used real horses. If we had gone too stylized with the list scene we would have had to stylize the play all the way through, and stylization on television is very difficult."[19] And Giles, of course, was just following the rules, as laid down by Cedric Messina: "We've not done anything too sensational in the shooting of it—there's no arty-crafty shooting at all. All of them are, for want of a better word, straightforward productions."[20] One irony of Giles's approach to 1.3 is that real horses in a studio are as ludicrous as Barton's toy horses on the stage. The toy-horse technique works a little better in Jane Howell's *I Henry VI*, where, silly as it is, it does trivialize Winchester. Unfortunately, it also makes Gloucester look equally foolish. The "style" erases the contrast between the characters, a problem that Howell gradually works out, as Barton consistently did not.

Of the BBC style for the *Richard II–Henry V* plays, Graham Holderness says, "where this policy is carried out, the viewer is given no space to reflect critically on the nature of what is being offered, or to become aware of Shakespearean drama's capacity for disclosing contradiction."[21] While that is true, we must also consider television's capacity for erasing contradiction—unless unintentionally, as when Nixon chose to have a bust of Lincoln at his shoulder during one of his final Watergate chats. Holderness is right, however—the BBC Second Henriad did not undercut the postures and pretensions of its politicians. An American audience, at least, might have been more ready to deploy its imagination than Giles suggests. When I asked Ian Richardson in 1972 how he explained the responses of an American audience to the *Richard II* in which he was co-starring with Richard Pasco, Richardson said, "It's Watergate!" I have a feeling that only this contemporary American parallel to a long-ago British monarch's effort to adjudicate his own crime saved that production from the tongues of many serpents. A coincidental and borrowed history saved a bad production from the hissing that should have driven it from the stage.

Mark Crispin Miller suggests how the BBC Second Henriad rebuffs any opportunity for the kind of alienation for which Holderness calls, indeed keeps us from any sense that we are in the presence of an art form: "Struggling to create the proper aura, the BBC has blown a wad on late medieval bric-a-brac: hogsheads, cross-bows, goblets, scrolls. . . . These irrelevant items clutter irrelevant sets, all those dungeons and taverns and banquet halls which Shakespeare mentions, but which the BBC has meticulously reconstituted."[22] We were, these critics argue, thrust into the worst of normative television, where as much is sold—attitudes, things, "life-style," the perception of a status quo within which we alone have mobility—*between* commercials as within them. " 'The Shakespeare Plays,' Miller says, "reflects the corporate approach, hiring lots of 'experts,' spending too much money and making something deadly out of something good. Each play is just another useless product meant for quick consumption."[23] It follows that these productions tend not to deliver "the struggle between true and false discourses,"[24] except insofar as the scripts do—accidentally. Television becomes, then, what Norman Rabkin calls "the special pleader for a particular ideology."[25] The ideology is consumption—within the product and of the product itself. Erased is what Rabkin calls "the dramatic structure [that] sets up the opposed elements as equally valid, equally desirable, and equally impossible."[26] As depicted in the BBC Second Henriad, then, the issues have been domesticated, as if BBC had followed Levin's advice on consensus. The consent of the viewers is so effectively numbed that, as Stuart Hall suggests, "oppositional ideologies cannot be theorized from this position."[27] Any "sense of position" has been absorbed into the "non-style" that has become at once a denial and an enforcer of ideology. Must we wander through a museum, guided by a camera as we listen to vaguely familiar words? Let us instead move in silence through the Cloisters, for example, and ponder the magnificence produced in the name of faith. The velvet showcase, as enhanced by indirect lighting, knows better.

While I tend to agree with the critics of BBC's Second Henriad— and shall extend my agreement in the next section of this chapter—I do find the *Richard II* a splendid production. Derek Jacobi takes on the remarkably difficult role of Richard and is the best Richard I have ever seen. He takes a simple declarative line and turns it into a dramatic question. Salisbury kneels with his bad news about the dispersal of his "twelve thousand fighting men." Jacobi responds to Aumerle's appeal for "Comfort" by saying, "But now the blood of twenty thousand men / Did triumph in my face." He pauses and looks down at Salisbury, as if not believing the news Salisbury has just delivered. "And they are *fled?*" Salisbury can but nod.

The production emerges from the BBC "received standard" mode and thus has that "reinforcing" quality to which Holderness rightly objects. But the production does have much to say about

Shakespeare's contact with television, as that medium is approached by its practitioners *and* by Shakespearean actors like Jacobi. The conservative production values of the BBC *Richard II* and the success it achieves within its limiting premises help us appreciate Jane Howell's radical approach to history, which I will consider at the end of this section.

Henry Fenwick and Jacobi discuss the problems an actor encounters when working on television: " 'Down, down I come'— the speech at Flint Castle—was begun on one set, interrupted, then finished on another set. 'The freedom that you get on stage [says Jacobi] when the juices are really flowing, you don't get on television. There are too many technical things to worry about— the sound, the camera.' "[28] Moreover, the sequence for shooting scenes imposes strains: "In the theatre," says Jacobi, "Shakespeare gave you time off, little breaks before your crescendos. Here we were doing the big scenes one after another. The orchestration of an actor's tempo is thrown out of gear—but it always is by television."[29] Indeed, Shakespeare usually gives his leading actor a breathing space during act 4, just before the often energetic final scenes. My own surmise is that Richard Burbage said to Shakespeare just after the opening of *Richard III*, "Will, you have got to give me time to catch my breath." What seems a structural principle reflects dramatic necessity.

But, Fenwick continues, television offers advantages: "Television makes it possible to take a scene in a much lower key than is possible in an auditorium: the camera will catch it. And a performance can be improved by the director in editing."[30] As McLuhan says of the television actor, "He must be alert to improvise and to embellish every phrase and verbal resonance with details of gesture and posture, sustaining that intimacy with the viewer which is not possible on the massive movie screen or on the stage."[31]

In the BBC-TV version of *Richard II*, the scene between Northumberland, Ross, and Willoughby (2.1), which creates a seemingly impossible time sequence wherein John of Gaunt's death and Bolingbroke's return to claim his inheritance seem to occur simultaneously, occurs at Gaunt's funeral. The scene's improbabilities are not noticed within the undifferentiated space of Shakespeare's stage, but they might prove disturbing within the mechanical zone of the television screen. Director Giles allows "time to pass" and cuts to Northumberland's fishing line, "Well, lords, the Duke of Lancaster is dead." Shakespeare renders the timing and the reason for Bolingbroke's return ambiguous in this ambiguity of a play—so full of what students used to call "hidden meanings." While stage and television may both be "cool" media, insisting on our participation to complete the experience, television is *not* a medium for ambiguity. As we once objected to the "snow" that often reached blizzard proportions on early television, we will not now accept any obscurity behind or beyond the image. Television is a medium of clarity. It can leave no loose ends. It is designed to send us to bed sleepy, not abuzz with stinging questions.

The BBC-TV *Richard II* deals effectively with Richard's self-deceiving and inconclusive soliloquy at Pomfret (5.5). Director David Giles breaks it up into a series of dissolves, allowing Jacobi to deliver sections of it from various places in Richard's cell, and, as shadows tell us, at different times of day. Such a sequence could not be worked out on stage without calling attention to the gimmickry necessary to suggest the passage of time. On television the effect is exactly right. The speech represents an aimless brooding over the course of a long dull period that proves to Richard that "time doth waste" him. Except for the almost willful paradox Richard creates out of the New Testament—the solution to which an attentive auditor perceives—the speech, like Richard, goes nowhere. Here the medium allows for an interpretation not possible on the stage for which Richard's soliloquy was written. Television provides the best context for the speech that I have ever experienced.

Peter Saccio comments on the difference between "historical" time, as depicted on a stage which allows us to suspend our disbelief and "psychological" time, which in its shallow way television tends to imitate: "Richard's prison soliloquy . . . is interrupted by five ostentatious camera dissolves. . . . Shakespeare's single written scene compresses historical time. The BBC's decompression allows more history—at least the fact and the sense of passing time—to peep through the interstices. . . . A modern audience expects a slower process: our models for character change derive from the theories of Freud or Piaget or Erikson about childhood and maturation. For us those things just don't happen that fast. Richard [is] therefore given days (according to the conventions of the camera) . . . of psychological time that we would consider necessary for self-examination, for the shifts in mood, for the changes and advances of thought that the words reveal. The assumption of a modern notion about psychic change has made the material *seem* more historical."[32]

Jack Jorgens offers a further telling commentary on why the *Richard II* succeeds and other BBC-TV productions do not:

In the earlier efforts, one feels the pressures of time and money as directors rush past "small" scenes in order to spend more effort on the big ones. But some of Shakespeare's best work is in those "small" scenes, and it is in their quality that this production really shines. To take but one example, in the scene where Bolingbroke sentences Bushy and Green to death, we get all three perspectives: (1) Bolingbroke's righteous indignation at being stripped on his lands and title, his straight-faced lies, and his casual indifference to the beheadings; (2) York's silent protests as Bolingbroke accuses the prisoners of causing not only the rift between Richard and the Queen but that between Richard and Bolingbroke, and his shock at the sound of the beheadings off-frame as Bolingbroke calmly instructs him to send "fair entreaties" and "kind commends"; and (3) Bushy and Green's vulnerability, their shirts and bare chests contrasting with their armor of their captors, and their Richard-like impotence as they insult Bolingbroke before being taken away. The confident use of the camera, which includes and excludes characters with precision and moves when Bolingbroke motivates it to move, provides a striking contrast with the randomness of earlier productions.[33]

And a final instance: as the camera dollies back to follow Northumberland's arrest of Carlisle, it catches York looking at Carlisle in stupefied admiration for the Bishop's round denunciation of Bolingbroke's usurpation. "That's what *I* should have said!" York's expression says. Two characters not brought together by the text are united in a telling frame by Giles's vivid sense of what the script suggests. That York and Carlisle represent a "conservative" point of view does not make them wrong or despicable. They are not, say, a Bush and Dukakis avoiding the issue of the CIA during the 1988 presidential campaign lest they be assassinated by the very government for which they offer themselves as leaders. Bush, of course, as former head of the CIA, favors the principle, except as it might apply to him.

For all of the virtues of the BBC *Richard II*, however, the Jane Howell First Henriad is a revelation. It reverses the pattern that Jerry Mander describes, a description true of too many of the stultifying BBC productions:

Programs concerned with the arts . . . are . . . distorted by television's inability to convey their several aspects. . . . Some people argue that television delivers a new world of art to people in, say, Omaha, who might otherwise never see the Stuttgart Ballet or the New York Philharmonic. They say this stimulates interest in the arts. I find this very unlikely. . . . On television the depths are flattened, the spaces edited, the movements distorted and fuzzed-up, the music thinned and the scale reduced. . . . Seeing the Stuttgart Ballet performing on television leaves one with such a reduced notion of ballet as to reduce the appeal of Ballet itself. The result is likely to be boredom and switched channels. To say that such a program stimulates new interest in the arts is to believe, as Howard Gossage put it, "That it's possible to convince an eight-year-old that making love is more fun than ice cream cones."[34]

Howell's *Henry VI, Part 1* so lampoons politics that serious issues are left unarticulated. That approach, however, is consistent with Howell's notion that the plays get increasingly serious as they go along. Part 2, at any rate, is superb. It is a great play, with its intricate patternings of deceptions, discoveries, and punishments, working out on all levels of the social and cosmic structure and in its "mirroring" of stand-ins—Suffolk for Henry early, Cade for York late, pretenders who impose their own temporary reality upon the equivocal politics of England. Howell integrates this superbly interrelated script via a playground set—ramps, ladders, and platforms. As she says, "Some sets you find in your head, some sets are in books. I knew this one was in the street. I did not know what it was. Then one day, I was out in a car, and suddenly I saw the top of an adventure playground which had been crudely painted in medieval colours by the kids. It was lovely. I was in such a hurry I couldn't stop, but I knew I had solved it. It was some strange area in which you could play, in which you could pretend, which is an equivalent of Shakespeare's theatre."[35]

Howell also worked with the same talented company throughout the production of the tetralogy, so that doubling becomes an effective device within the plays—David Burke as Gloucester and Dick the Butcher, Antony Brown as Whitmore and Iden, for example. As in Terry Hands's *Henry V*, the doubling creates the texture and irony that one may inevitably attribute to Shakespeare's dramaturgy.

The acting is superb and depends on the ensemble technique that makes sense of what Sheldon Zitner calls Shakespeare's "relational" stage.[36] The vacuum of power that Peter Benson's Henry VI creates is the opposite of the circles of strength that Olivier's Henry V throws out to incorporate his army. At one point, Benson shambles in and turns in surprise as a trumpet heralds his entrance—it is a moment both metadramatic and "in character." Julia Foster is drawn into Henry VI's vacuum—the play is centripetal, a variety of characters imploding against the empty center. But Foster is also pulled into the zone of affection that

Suffolk's embassy has cleared. She conveys both motives superbly, but she needs Benson's soft-spoken piety against which to play her lust for power and her lust per se. But as Foster plays the latter, it is "first love."

Howell charges her set with a visual excitement that television seldom provides. For the opening procession and Margaret's arrival, the balconies are hung with pennants and banners that conceal the rough boards of the set. Margaret is showered by pink roses (an ironic mutation of white and red). The petals fall from her as she recognizes that her synechdoche (Suffolk) had not stood for England. At times the richness of the costumes creates opulent irony amid the unpainted planks and two-by-fours. That "modern statement" is one that the script also supports. The unadorned set reflects Eleanor's ramshackle wishes. The Petitioners sneak through a board in a fence—like kids stealing into a ball game in 1911. A net on the set's outer circumference becomes ribbed cloud formations drifting across a sunset in a patterning never to be repeated and, later, the outlines of modern buildings in city darkness, as if history is peering down on all of this even as we in the television audience are looking in. It is also, quite simply, a net within which ambitions are played out against surrounding mortality. At times the colors of the playground— purple, pink, blue, rose, and mustard—coordinate with the richer textures of the costumes and the dull sheen of chains and crowns. The variations in lighting are splendidly cued to what Howell's spaces depict at any given moment.

The set embraces Thump's victory over Horner, Cade's rebellion (with a madly-laughing Cade superimposed over the burning books and framed between the kissing heads of Say and Cromer), and a wonderfully hokey sorcery scene in which Margery Jourdain is born into the future amid a ring of fire, fire that will come nearer to her at Smithfield.

Howell, then, evokes the sense of relationships in the script— between persons and between scenes—without denying the production the elements that are subordinated, as Zitner sees it, in Shakespeare's scripts:

> Shakespeare's plays were written for Shakespeare's theatre. And what his theatre provided most often was humanity seen not in the all-defining close-up of psychology or at the far and narrowed distance of sociology or through the historical retrospect of montage but in the open middle distance of social relation. Shakespeare's is a relational not an essentializing or ideologizing stage: not [a] stage pre-empted

by convictions that must focus on one causal chain, psychological or
sociological, but a stage closer to the tenor of encountered experience
in which causes and motives of all sorts jostle. It offers whole human
figures disposed in patterns that exhibit what is primarily a social
(often familial) meaning. . . . What the camera can instantly suggest—enclosing sociology with a long shot, defining private states
with a close-up—Shakespeare must do by other, more elaborate,
means, and usually does not do at all. In sum, the simplicity and
flexibility of the Elizabethan stage do not provide encompassing environments. But film and more emphatically, television . . . give a
priority to time, place, and objects, and so create environments in
which human actors are expressions of a context rather than its
creators. To re-define the locus of dramatic action, its characters, its
size, its depth, the angle from which it is viewed, is thus to tamper
with the conceptual foundations of the Elizabethan text. It is also to
create a new medium. . . . But if one wants to preserve the old words,
one has to discover in the new medium some equivalents of the old.
This, rather than the conventional problems of interpretation, is the
challenge of televising Shakespeare's plays.[37]

The television director does indeed inherit the issues of the plays
in very specific ways. Television itself creates a set of problems
that, we can safely assume, had already been worked out within
the dimensions and conventions of the Shakespearean stage—a
space "in which you could pretend." Shakespeare, of course, was
exploring the nature of his stage even as he wrote for it. Howell is
doing much the same thing as she explores her set with the
scripts.

What we experience here is relationship. Bernard Hill's York is
upset by "The Duke yet lives that Henry shall depose" (*II Henry
VI*: 1.4.59) and hands the scroll to Buckingham to complete, as
York ponders an ominous ambiguity that might pertain to him.
The link between York's first soliloquy and Hume's—each dealing
with overthrow—is neatly established by giving each character
the close-up ability to speak directly to us. Henry's piety at the
"miracle" of Simpcox's sudden sight plays against the Cardinal's
cynical amusement. Frank Middlemass's Cardinal seems to say
Oh, God! to himself as Henry takes the miracle at face value.
Middlemass struggles to keep a straight face. Foster's Margaret,
having transcended her own impecunity, is delighted at the exposure of Simpcox and his wife. Margaret does not notice that *they*
have come in under a shower of rose petals or that Simpcox's wife
looks enough like Margaret to link the latter to the former's plea of
"pure need." Foster is superb in her open-mouthed public dis-

belief at what she already knows (or suspects) and in her extended torture of a despondent and slumped King (3.2.142–71), in which she creates a self-pitying martyrdom for herself. Gloucester's one-by-one condemnation of Henry's entire court is superbly conducted by David Burke. Middlemass's Winchester begins to break down at the side of Gloucester's deathbed, as Warwick delivers a detailed postmortem. That scene is echoed—as in the script—at Winchester's death. An ironic crucifix stands in the background and monks sing irrelevant hymns just outside the chamber. Winchester hallucinates atop a handworked silken pillow, damp with the sweat of fear. Benson's King prays fervently, while Mark Wing-Davey's Warwick staves off helpless hilarity. He has never seen or heard anything like *this* before!

Here is a series of productions that eschews "realism," "naturalism," and "literalism." The set's versatility serves for indoor/outdoor, nighttime/daytime sequences and instantly undercuts—just by its being there—the posturing of the politicians, particularly York and Cade. It also shows that Henry does not know what world he is in. His childlike nature should be at home here, but he is bedeviled by his childish subjects. The set renders ludicrous the efforts of a man at once shrewd and good: Gloucester. He is caught in a children's scenario worthy of that evil empire known as the CIA.

Howell says that she "never know[s] what naturalism means. I did attempt to obey the ground rules by which the plays were written. They were written for a known space, for a known company."[38] Gary Waller's suggestions about television would seem to define precisely what Howell does with her Henriad:

Inherent in television are features that do, in fact, challenge the dominance of bourgeois realism and embody . . . forms of experience that break with those approved by the dominant socio-economic forces of corporate capitalist society. Ironically it is in commercials, in live sports television, and in some "fringe" programming where the most sophisticated, disruptive and dislocative techniques . . . can be found: discontinuity, irrealism, dislocating effects of sound, colour, perceptive changes, split-screens, slow-motion and instant replays from a variety of angles—all ways of exposing the ideological repression of bourgeois realism. . . . What the bulk of television does is to limit the responses of its audience to the known, the approved, to the consensus outlook of the dominant classes of society. But just as a text ravels itself together at one end while always unravelling at the other, so television, in spite of itself, contains the seeds of transformation, the possibility of opening its audience to experiences and forms that go beyond its declared or desired intentions.[39]

Howell's First Henriad provides many of the "dislocating effects" for which Waller calls, stopping short of "instant replay," although that might have worked well during some of her fight scenes. If "alienation devices" call attention to *our* relationship to the script—a summoning that television normally wishes to avoid— Howell's techniques work well. That the scripts themselves are among the most unfamiliar in the canon (with the exception of *Richard III*, of course) is also a factor in Howell's success—though they could have been deadened by another director under all that bric-a-brac that Miller mentions. Graham Holderness credits Howell, rightly, with an "awareness of the multiplicity of potential meanings in the play[s]," a view that "required a decisive and scrupulous avoidance of television or theatrical naturalism." Holderness asserts that "methods of production should operate to open the plays out, rather than close them into the immediately recognisable familiarity of Shakespearean production." Holderness maintains that this approach frees the actor, "who is no longer imprisoned within the naturalist concept of a coherent psychological identity, but [is] able to play out those psychological incoherences which can disclose sociological truths."[40]

My own feeling is that we do not want to trap our actors into some expectation of "sociological truths." Such "truths" become another version of "imposed vision." But Holderness is right. Psychological consistency is not attainable—though its attainment is one of the controlling myths of Western Civilization. Howell's production emerges from *the language of the script* and the script provides the psychology of the sociology of these plays. The friction of word and action against her splintery boards—the superb articulation and movement of her company—are subversive in the best way. They open up new possibilities for Shakespeare on television. As Howell says, "The Shakespearean space is where they say it is." For the time being, at least, the *Henry VI* plays are where she says they are. These productions combat the fallacy of the "text." They produce the "truth" of the script (though that truth is subject to a variety of interpretations). As David Burke (Howell's Gloucester and Dick the Butcher) says, "These plays were never meant to be just read. Though most scholars would say they're not first-class Shakespeare, that's because they are *reading* them. . . . In performance some magical element is added to these plays."[41] Performance is, of course, the alchemy whereby text changes to script and becomes our experience.

III

The Second Part of Henry IV is rarely produced. One would have loved to see what Jane Howell, her company and format, would have done with the play. We do, however, have three versions of Falstaff's rejection available. The depictions of this great scene are radically different, inevitably, and the differences are partly due to the medium in which each appears—a film into which the scene is interpolated (Olivier's *Henry V*), a film in which the scene is the climax of years of history (Welles's *Chimes at Midnight*), and the BBC-TV version of the play.

Olivier's camera moves upwards toward a lighted window and discovers the Hostess sitting beside Falstaff's bed. She leaves. He awakes and says, "God save thy grace, King Hal! My royal Hal! God save thee, my sweet boy! My king! My Jove! I speak to thee my heart!" Olivier's voice—obviously in the mode of public pronouncement—cuts across Falstaff's face:

> I know thee not, old man. Fall to thy prayers.
> How ill white hairs become a fool and jester!
> I have long dream'd of such a kind of man,
> So surfeit-swell'd, so old, and so profane;
> But, being awaked, I do despise my dream.
> Reply not to me with a fool-born jest:
> Presume not that I am the thing I was;
> For God doth know, so shall the world perceive,
> That I have turned away my former self
> So [shall] I those that kept me company.

While Olivier's editing cuts the cruel reference to the grave that gapes so wide for Falstaff, George Robey's face registers the absolute rejection that the lines emphasize.

This inset does bring us Falstaff dying "of a sweat," not in France, but above a mean street in London. The scene fulfills the Archbishop's inclusion of lines cobbled from the end of *II Henry IV* and placed in this film in 1.1. ("Sir John Falstaff, and all his company / Along with him, he banish'd under pain of death / Not to come near his person by ten mile."). The lines, of course, draw anger from Olivier's Globe audience, who have come back to see Falstaff. That audience and the Globe frame are gone by the time we, now the audience of a film, see Falstaff dying. As in other things, the film provides what the script and even a staged version of *this* script cannot.

Leni Reifenstahl does not give us a vignette of Hitler's old supporter Rohm demanding to see the Führer before Rohm is executed. Why does Olivier make Falstaff himself central to the scenes that report his sickness and death, scenes that sandwich Henry's entrapment and execution of some of his supporters (though Olivier excises the scene with the traitors)? Part of the reason, of course, is that representation in film is preferable to presentation. Part of the reason is to provide a part of the story not available to those who do not know *II Henry IV*.

But Olivier includes other material that might not make it into a straight propaganda film. Williams's speech, "But if his cause be not good . . ." (4.1.139 ff.) is delivered almost intact, although transferred to a very young Court. (He says "afraid" and not "afeard," and does not say "who to disobey were against all proportion of subjection."). The speech is given a single medium close-up and is followed by a pause, punctuated by a pondering "Ay," then an assenting "Ay!" from Williams.

One must admire Olivier's daring in putting these pacific sentiments so prominently in his film. Propaganda must seem plausible. Many soldiers have had time on the eve of battle to think about dying the next day and of whether their own lives are worth spending for whatever cause it may be. Certainly the commandos and airborne troops to whom the film was dedicated would have had such thoughts. Their chances of getting killed were the greater for their being volunteers. The speech says what many soldiers think and thus includes them and their personal doubts within the film's message. If England was being democratized in the subways under the nineteen hundred and forty nails being driven down upon London, the film continues that emphasis. And the film moves on. The victory the next day shows night thoughts for what they are.

And, of course, soldiers sitting around before battle is a cliché from *The Red Badge of Courage* and a stock film situation that Shakespeare anticipated. Olivier capitalizes on one of the best written examples of the genre. The pacifist *All Quiet on the Western Front* (1930) is the archetypal war film and introduces almost all of the motifs that subsequent films focusing on the individual infantryman would incorporate. (The film, however, apparently convinced only Lew Ayers, its star, who became a conscientious objector in World War II). By 1944, many American movies had rendered the night before battle, almost invariably peopling the foxhole with a kid from Brooklyn and a blonde young giant known as "Nebraska." Olivier provides what was, for the time, an almost obligatory scene. And by tolerating personal doubts, the film's political message becomes more potent. It reflects "the dominant ideology," but one that was combating another version of domination—that of Nazi Germany.

The Falstaff material also reinforces the "truth" of the film. We assume from the early sequences that Olivier's Globe audience has heard the rejection scene and has responded to it. Yet as he who was Hal, Burbage-Henry V, enters the Globe stage he is greeted with enthusiastic applause. Falstaff's death and the broken record of his shattered memory become a parenthesis of personality within the declarative sentence of Henry's career. In war, no time exists to "jest and dally." Personal idiosyncracies and indulgences must give way to the imitation of the tiger's action. All must surrender to the "blood, sweat [of struggle, not sack-induced fever], toil, and tears" of the total effort. All people and all traits within people must move in one direction or be discarded. Olivier finds his example in his "source" and exploits it brilliantly. As Henry Geduld says:

> Olivier's addition of the death scene [is] an unequivocal reminder that Henry has renounced his former waywardness, and secondly . . . an indication that corruption in the attractive guise of frivolous responsibility has been exorcised from the kingdom. . . . Falstaff's rascality is a distraction that must be removed before the campaign begins.[42]

The scene may reflect what Jack Jorgens calls "the *cost* of kingship," (his emphasis)[43] but it also shows a jester in a world that cannot afford irony. Such a world creates its own ironies, of course, but cannot tolerate what Jorgens calls "Falstaff's way of smelling out the lies hiding behind official abstractions [and] of riddling sophistries with holes."[44] That subversion continues in the script, however, and Jorgens includes Court's speech as evidence that Henry must "face things he would rather not face."[45] One would have had to have been alive and conscious during World War II to remember how absolute the effort was against the archetypal evil of Hitler and "the Japs," how close the issue came to an opposite conclusion many times, and how much was repressed about our own conduct of the war.

Olivier's film remains great because, beyond propaganda, it reminds us what war is. A script already full of ambushes for its manifest content is permitted, as Jorgens says, to include "a reminder of the darker side of Henry's character."[46] He cannot try his battle with unspotted soldiers, of course, but there is a human cost behind every "political necessity." The old man in the bed is doomed to hear the killing words over and over again until they kill his heart for good.

The bells celebrating Henry V's coronation have already begun to widen across Gloucestershire as Welles's Falstaff capers through a snowy landscape and cries that the laws of England are at his commandment. The King rides toward his coronation, distanced from us by ranks of soldiers, staffs, and flags. As elsewhere in the film, the effects are borrowed from Eisenstein, particularly from *Alexander Nevsky*, it seems. The King, now dismounted, strides to liturgical music as an acolyte swings a censer of incense. The King enters the cathedral.

The camera tracks Falstaff moving eagerly behind masses of troops. The effect is of the tremendous power that attends kingship and of the insignificance of personality. Falstaff breaks through and shouts, creating an obscene disturbance. The bishops attending Henry are shocked. Falstaff kneels, even crawls a step or two toward Henry. The King keeps his back to Falstaff on "I know thee not, old man. Fall to thy prayers." The line is intensely ironic, since Falstaff is kneeling inside a cathedral, but not to pray. Falstaff seems puzzled at first. He laughs and rises at the King's joke about the grave, but kneels again, a subject now, on Henry's "I banish thee." He hears out the speech, even seems to smile grimly at the King, as if to say, So that's how it is, is it? This evader of so many traps appreciates the absolute springing shut of the trap he himself had helped to build.[47]

Welles's camera cuts from speech to reaction, looking up at the King, who is crowned and wears a cross and shares the frame with heraldic banners to his left. The camera angles slightly down at Falstaff, behind whom range the massed shields of Henry's myriad knights. The Lord Chief Justice appears in the frame at Falstaff's back as Henry's speech ends. Jorgens, who sees the scene much as I do, gives this impression of its ending:

Shifting from the high-angled shots of bewildered, hurt Falstaff to a low angle which restores him to his kingly stature, we see the jester smile for the last time—in recognition of the grim humor that this is the way it must be, that Hal must play the comedy in earnest, betray both Falstaff and himself in order to follow his father's path. Henry studies the understanding smile and, unable to bear it, turns to go off into legendary history.[48]

My own sense of Keith Baxter's reaction to Welles's reaction is that Henry V can bear Falstaff's glint of understanding quite well. The King has turned this frightful moment into the high point of his long, ceremonial day. He spins away and moves down a long line of noblemen into the world he has been choosing all along. The film's landscape—the bleak midwinter in which words make vapor even indoors—comments upon what Henry has chosen. Falstaff's huge piano case of a coffin shows what Henry has not chosen. The film's irony is that Falstaff offers Hal/Henry only a variation of a world onto which snow falls and night falls, fast oh fast until it becomes a whiteness with no expression, nothing to express.

Of the rejection scene in the BBC version, Peter Saccio offers this comment: "The historical fact of [Henry V's] soupbowl haircut has been used trenchantly. With the locks of supposedly madcap youth shorn away, and with his plain openthroated jerkin replaced by a full ermine collar, his face appears as an unfamiliar mask through which emerges the obligatory words. The screen image of the newly crowned Henry V resembles the late portraits of Elizabeth I, where the face is but a stylized oval surrounded by emblems of monarchy. The king is an icon, and sweaty, quirky, living bystanders are given their orders and left to cope as best they may."[49]

M. C. Miller, however, sees the scene as depicting something opposite to what Saccio describes. Miller has Gwillim rejecting Falstaff "weepily, with Henry doing what he must despite his breaking heart."[50] Miller overstates the case here. He is correct to say that Gwillim indicts Cambridge, Scroop, and Grey while "choking back the tears and sinking to a bitter whisper."[51] The Henry V of the rejection scene, however, is the zombie that Saccio says he is. But Miller is also right—this Henry is much too personal. The wild bells spilling in the background proclaim a public event. Gwillim reads the speech as if it were being thought up on the spot (as he reads his soliloquy at the end of 1.2). Most lines in Shakespeare should have a feel of spontaneity about them, but some are calculated and, like a politician's speeches, "un-natural"—like those of Claudius and Lear as they bang their agendas down on their helpless courts. The same can be said of Henry V's speech to Falstaff. He cannot know that Falstaff will interrupt the coronation procession (or recession, as the script suggests it is), but he knows what he will say if that moment should occur. The

Prince has learned how to destroy Falstaff *from* Falstaff, once "Hal" becomes the "fiction" he has been all along as he plans to become the illusory "reality" known as King. The intimacy of the scene in BBC's version is scaled perhaps to the perceived necessities of television, but the diminution thus engendered wipes out the moment's sense of political necessity. It is as if this waxen figure were saying, I told you never to call me here! We get a dehumanized being delivering a personal message. It is like hearing a replay of one's words falteringly spoken into one of those maddening answering machines from which no response can come. The script shows a public pronouncement—body politic all the way. What we get is only a sad young man sorry that he is king. That is Bolingbroke, perhaps, and for a moment it may be Henry V, pondering kingship as dawn cracks open the field of Agincourt. But it is not Henry V as he assumes the kingship for which Falstaff has trained him.

Henry V has the transitional scene with the Chief Justice, in which the King listens to the arguments he has elicited and then agrees with them. We are prepared for this "voice of history" to speak to Falstaff, should the latter show up. Instead we get the *face* of history speaking but "as a man." The conflict between the iconographic and the personal defeats our effort to respond to the scene. The "king's two bodies" are confused here, incoherently conflated.

I agree with Jonathan Dollimore and Alan Sinfield when they say that "Henry engrosses in himself the ideological coherence of the state and then, asked to take responsibility for the likely defeat of Agincourt, claims to be an effect of the structure which he seemed to guarantee."[52] While Henry does just happen to win the battle, the play does "reveal not only the strategies of power but the anxieties informing both them and their ideological representation."[53]

Both Welles and Olivier, in very different ways and for somewhat different purposes, capture the ways, subtle and unsubtle, in which the brutality of power hides its motives and silences its critics. Henry V does not neglect to tell Falstaff that he—the King—is doing all of this for Falstaff's own good.

IV

Two of Shakespeare's most minor characters suffer executions. Each makes a decision—one to suppress what he knows to be the truth, the other to express what he knows to be the truth. And each dies because of the decision he makes.

Vernon departs upon three words delivered by King Henry IV: "Bear Worcester to the death, *and Vernon too*" (5.5.14). Colevile of the Dale exits upon Prince John's command: "Send Colevile with his confederates / To York, to present execution" (4.3.73–74).

Vernon deserves beheading, as King Henry sees things. Vernon, after all, was one of the emissaries who turned the King's "terms of love" to the "contrary" (5.5.3–4). In the BBC production, directed by David Giles, both Worcester and Vernon are brought before Henry for judgment. Vernon stands perhaps a half pace behind Worcester's left shoulder. Jon Finch's pause after "death" is intended to balance Vernon's complicity and guilt with Worcester's. The alacrity with which the soldiers push Worcester and Vernon off to the block shows that the order for both executions has been expected.

The comma in F1 represents a fairly heavy form of punctuation for Elizabethan texts, and certainly indicates a pause. It could be that Henry makes his mind up as he looks at Vernon. Certainly Henry emphasizes, with Holinshed, that Worcester was "the procurer and setter forth of all this mischief." Although Vernon is listed as a member of the rebel army by Holinshed "with divers other stout and right valiant captains," so is Douglas. The King says, "Other offenders we will pause upon" (5.5.15), but that pause comes after the pause between the order for Worcester's execution and Vernon's. As they go off to the block, Hal reveals that Douglas is at Prince Hal's tent. Hal requests that John "deliver [Douglas] / Up to his pleasure, ransomless and free" (5.5.28). Douglas is pardoned for his "valour" and "high deeds" (5.5.30–31), but he fled from Hal at a crucial moment in the battle and his injuries are the result of his "falling from a hill" (5.5.21) during the panic flight of the Percy forces. In *A Farewell to Arms*, a full colonel of the line becomes separated from his command and asks the battle police, "Have you ever been in a retreat?" While he isn't asking for a medal, he suggests that summary execution is not appropriate during a debacle like the retreat from Caporetto. He is shot anyway. Douglas, for all his exploits against psuedo-kings early in the battle, hardly seems a candidate for honors. But Shrewsbury has more than its share of misprisions. Douglas is a Scot—a "giddy neighbor"—and Scots are apparently not responsible for their actions. Douglas gets the pardon that Worcester predicted would have been Hotspur's had the King's offer been reported aright.

It may be that Henry's pause before condemning Vernon means merely that Henry is toying with Vernon. He is not above acting like Richard and making people wait upon his word. Such is the breath of kings. Henry plays with Carlisle at the end of *Richard II* ("Carlisle, this is your doom"). He goes on to pardon Carlisle because of his "High sparks of honor" (5.4.24–29). But the word "doom" had begun to differentiate from its inclusive Anglo Saxon meaning because of its competition with the French word "judgment," toward negative judgment, or "sentence." As Carlisle hears Bolingbroke's pardon, the former says (to himself), Oh, he meant "doom" in the old fashioned sense of the word.

Vernon would have Hotspur know of what Worcester calls "The liberal and kind offer of the king." "'Twere best he did," says Vernon. Worcester argues against disclosure because Hotspur "hath the excuse of youth," as Worcester, Northumberland, and, presumably, Vernon do not (5.2.2ff.). BBC cuts most of Worcester's rationale (from "Suspicion all our lives" to "shall pay for all"), perhaps because Vernon (Terence Wilton) is easily as young as Tim Piggot-Smith's Hotspur. Vernon's "Deliver what you will, I'll say 'tis so" (5.2.26) is inaudible in the BBC production, one way of suggesting grudging assent, but not the best way. Even the mumble, however, means that Vernon must share the consequences of Worcester's self-serving deception, once deceit leads to defeat.

We notice, however, that Vernon does not support, verbally at least, Worcester's depiction of the parley. Vernon doesn't have to, of course, since Hotspur has worked himself up to a defiant mood, contrary to his pacific response to Sir Walter Blunt's previous embassy. Vernon, however, has glimpsed Prince Hal's intention—to "imitate the sun, / Who doth permit the base contagious clouds / To smother up his beauty from the world" (2.2.197–99). After permitting Worcester to spew his falsehoods, Vernon says of Hal, "If he outlive the envy of this day, / England did never owe so sweet a hope, / So much misconstrued in his wantonness" (5.2.66–68). Indeed, Vernon's description of Hal predicts that of Canterbury, after Hal has become King Henry V:

> [He] chid his truant youth with such a grace,
> As if mast'red there a double spirit
> Of teaching and of learning instantly.
>
> (5.2.62–64)

Vernon's praise can be seen as compensation for his surrender to the Worcester agenda. Vernon becomes, then, one of the many choric voices of the history plays. But as actor in history, rather than commentator upon it, his voice is quickly stilled.

Before the battle, when questioned by Hotspur about "The nimble-footed madcap Prince of Wales" (4.1.95), Vernon describes the soldiers of the King as "gorgeous as the sun at mid-summer," and "young Harry," mounting his horse, as "an angel dropped down from the clouds." The English, "glittering in golden coats like images" (4.1.97–110), manifest Hal's previous metaphor about himself: "like bright metal on a sullen ground / My reformation glitt'ring o'er my fault" (1.2.212–13). Vernon has somehow gotten close enough to the King's forces to observe this reformation, the first character in the play to do so.

Hal has made a premature but necessary emergence from the clouds. Vernon recognizes it, and expresses it with Hal's imagery. Vernon seems to believe in the imagery, as Hal wants his ultimate audience to do, once he is King. Hal's mimesis is designed to summon such belief. But in subscribing to the Worcester thesis, Vernon yields himself to Henry IV's decision and denies himself the possibilities of his own perceptions. Vernon will not be among the "band of brothers" at Agincourt.

Vernon is a virtually unnoticed actor in the "closure" of *I Henry IV*. Worcester, Henry's enemy, is defeated and executed. Hotspur—the energy Hal must confront and dispatch—is dead, as Falstaff—the energy Hal must confront and destroy in the sequel—will be, soon after Hal becomes a Henry himself. Having seen the possibilities in future history (if Hal outlive "the envy of this day"), Vernon surrenders to Worcester's "ill-spirited" counsel. He yields in spite of his own perceptions and their attendant insights and, in doing so, condemns himself.

In his way, Vernon predicts the English victory at Agincourt. He contains a strain of the heartwood that even Richard II could not deracinate. But Vernon is an existential man in a world that has lost its contact with essence—except as a Henry V can imitate it and encourage it into a semblance of being. Vernon ends up on the wrong side and proves unwilling to defect from it, in spite of what he has glimpsed in Hal. What he has seen is not just the afternoon of Shrewsbury, but the morning of Agincourt as well.

That Vernon's positive sense of what Hal represents for England could be canceled with a shoulder shrug in the face of duplicity, indeed in the face of deceiving one's leader, makes Vernon more than just a member of a losing faction. He shows—as does so much in *Richard II*—why Hal's "reformation" can only be existential, that is, can live only as long as Henry V is there to manage it. The opportunism that Bolingbroke has ushered in confronts him from the very faction that helped him—for its own advantage—to the throne. Bolingbroke—and Richard—deny Henry V any opportunity to return to "essentialism," as Hal knows and as Vernon shows. Douglas may represent an energy that Hal hopes to nurture under his politics. Vernon, too, could have been an ally but denies himself the chance.

The way in which this dimension of a minor character can be developed on stage is suggested by Arthur Colby Sprague:

> Peace is beginning to seem possible, after all, when Worcester acts to prevent it. Their offence, he explains to Vernon, is not of a sort to be forgiven. . . . Vernon does not oppose him when he concludes . . . that the King's offer must be suppressed. . . . When, however, he must listen to Worcester's careful misrepresentation of what was said at the parley, it will be for the actor to bring out his sense of humiliation and disgust. Then comes the mention of how Harry Monmouth had challenged Hotspur to single combat, and Vernon is happy in the chance to speak out at last. . . . In the theatre, all this can become transparently clear. It is not always so, in the study.[54]

Giles misses an opportunity to demonstrate the buildup of anger by excluding Vernon from the frame in which Worcester (Clive Swift) misrepresents the parley. But Vernon *is* angry as he helps Worcester tighten the straps of his cuirass. Vernon's "of teaching and of learning instantly" is a rebuke that Worcester registers with a warning roll of the eyes. This interpretation makes the omission of Worcester's immediately prior "we did train him [Hotspur] on" curious, since Vernon's emphasis points at the bad education Worcester and Northumberland have given Hotspur ("Well, I am schooled"), in contrast to Hal's having "mast'red there a double spirit." Vernon's is a "double spirit" that recognizes Hal's emergence but accepts Worcester's duplicity. The duality working within Vernon needs a fuller chance to express itself in the BBC production. He does, however, pick up his sword reluctantly as he enters the battle that will send him to the block.

Giles handles the Colevile episode with some effect and some defect. It is unfortunate that Falstaff (Anthony Quayle) and the Boy (John Fowler) rig a rope by which to trip Colevile (Salvin Stewart). This privileges Falstaff, but by this time in the series we are as tired of Quayle as Shakespeare apparently was of Falstaff. Colevile surrenders while lying on his back in his armor. He had seemed to be making a cautious retreat through Gaultree but suddenly is as helpless as a turtle on its back. Thus his effort to identify Falstaff and his statement "I think you are Sir John Falstaff, and in that thought yield me" (4.3.16–17) makes no sense at all. His yielding would have been more a matter of "thought" had his own sword point been at Falstaff's throat. Whether Falstaff's Shrewsbury reputation causes Colevile to yield or, as I believe, Colevile has been seeking an enemy captain to whom to surrender ("his courtesy," as Prince John asserts: 4.3.43), the rope trick is one of those extratextual directorial additions that defeat whatever the script may be trying to say.

Falstaff is allowed to steal the scene once Prince John arrives. Colevile should have been given a close-up free of Quayle's florid wheezing on:

> I am, my lord, but as my betters are
> That led me hither. Had they been rul'd by me,
> You should have won them dearer than you have.
>   (4.3.65–67)

Giles does cut to John (Rob Edwards) and Westmorland (David Buck). The latter has already found Colevile's name on a list of prominent rebels. The scroll sets up John's flat statement, "A famous rebel art thou, Colevile" (4.3.63). Some actors read the line as a question that pursues an interrogation ("Is thy name Colevile?": 4.3.61) and that elicits Colevile's response. At "You should have won them dearer," John and Westmorland exchange a glance. While John is the chief perpetrator of Gaultree (Holinshed gives Westmorland credit), this is a "joint command . . . the theoretical aspects [of which Shakespeare] commented vigorously upon . . . both by dramatic situation and by dialogue."[55] The wordless exchange between co-commanders says, *We* will show you who your betters are! John's sentence emerges from a little boy's impulse suddenly empowered.

John pauses before he says "to present execution," as the F1 comma suggests he should. Colevile is surprised—he, after all, is an underling, well below the august level of those John has already dispatched—though Colevile is mentioned by Holinshed among those Henry IV executed at Durham. Falstaff's reaction is remorseful, almost as if he is sorry he made the capture in the first place. In the 1982 RSC production, "When Prince John smirkingly sentenced Colevile to death, Falstaff registered horror."[56] While Falstaff responds similarly in BBC, Edwards sends Colevile off with a sneer and not a smirk. Edwards only smiles much later, as he jokes about the good intentions his brother has toward those he has banished.

C. G. Thayer says that Colevile's "execution is both gratuitous (why kill so grotesquely harmless an enemy?) and a parody of justice (even if Colevile is only a parody of a prisoner of war)."[57] Both in the script and in the BBC production, Colevile's continued defiance insults Prince John. That defiance can be incited by Falstaff's effort to mythologize his triumph, although I did not see that happening in the BBC production. What Colevile should do, of course, is to kneel, acknowledge power, and beg forgiveness. But he does not and dies for precisely the qualities of courage and honesty that John's "victory" at Gaultree has denied. The execution of Colevile, although he invites it, is merely a final reflex of John's "policy."

Few characters have any control over their destinies in the Second Henriad. They are trapped in the history that others put into motion, as the releasers of history find themselves trapped as well. The lesser figures, even including Falstaff, are contained by the dominant ideology. But Vernon and Colevile do have choices. Vernon's compliance and Colevile's defiance make each a victim of the realpolitik that rules Lancastrian England. Vernon betrays himself and his vision of "so sweet a hope" as Hal. At the point that Bolingbroke attempts to introduce an ethic other than just the mean strain of extemporaneous and pragmatic politics, that strain emerges from nasty Worcester, and Vernon says, "I'll say 'tis so." Colevile, betrayed by the fatuity of his leaders, remains true to himself. Both go to the block.

BBC captures only a portion of the possibilities inherent in these minor characters. Small adjustments—the inclusion of Vernon's reaction as Worcester misconstrues Henry IV's generosity and a close-up of Colevile as he reminds John of the battle that John has greasily avoided—would have added vividly to the few moments during which these characters live. Performance is made up of such tiny but vital increments.

V

In the late 1960s I watched a powerful documentary called *The Anderson Platoon*. It was neither pro- nor antiwar, though in its grim detail it tended as it had to toward the latter stance. In fact, when I asked a question of Captain Anderson, the platoon leader who was there at the showing, it turned out that one of the men we had seen carried off in a bodybag had been mistakenly killed by his own men, although that fact had not emerged in the film. The film conveyed a strong sense of male bonding. One would have liked to be with these men, regardless of death and the deprivations of the jungle. The film had an understated but therefore very persuasive appeal as a means of recruitment. It was, of course, an appeal to a very specialized and superficial facet of masculinity, but it came through to me in spite of my having served in a combat billet (in a branch other than the infantry) and in spite of my rage at the Vietnam War. The film made me weep for the victims of a politics-gone-mad and admire their dogged willingness to fight and die for nothing and absolutely in vain. But it also triggered memories of the feeling I and my friends and as we walked from movie theaters in, say, 1943.

I am describing ambivalence, of course, and am also describing my response to the Branagh *Henry V*. While our perception of the film is probably conditioned by Vietnam, Panama, Nicaragua, the Falklands, and other recent events, I don't believe with Richard Corliss that Branagh's is an "anti-war war movie."[58] I agree, rather, with Amy E. Schwartz, who says that the film "reflects the complex intertwined pro- and anti-war themes" of the script.[59] Schwartz attributes the balance to Branagh's age: "he fits the generation that came along just when unthinking patriotism and unthinking protest had fought each other to a standstill."[60] The Vietnam analogy, for me, is that of the platoon and its leader. War is a brutal business. It ennobles no one. But neither does it necessarily brutalize its participants. Henry V is not a hero in the way that Hal was at Shrewsbury or in the way that Olivier was as he squared off against the Constable. Branagh's Henry may be a "hero," as Stuart Klawans says, "because he knows the cost of victory."[61] I would suggest, however, that the cost seems not to inhibit the process of war, even if Branagh, like Shakespeare's Henry, prohibits the celebration after the victory. Instead, to the sound of a growing chorus of "Te Deum," Branagh carries the Boy, "his last link to the past,"[62] as Klawans says, for four minutes through the mess and mourning of the battlefield.

Even the battle itself provides no sense of victory. Henry's speech is erased by the gasp of fear from the English line as it takes in the magnitude of the French charge. The battle is a muddy mess. The English archers seem to shoot their volleys indiscriminately into the combatants. That so few Englishmen die—Branagh leaves the list in his script—seems incomprehensible. Whether the script explains Henry's victory or not, Jonathan Yardley is correct to complain about Branagh's "inability to show why the British triumphed at Agincourt."[63] I do not believe that we are left to infer that the reasons are the same as for the victory of the Vietcong and North Vietnamese against the powerful armor and air forces of the United States.

Suffice it that, as Branagh says of the inevitable comparisons with Olivier, "our acting styles . . . belong to different worlds."[64] So do the two films. Olivier was responding not just to World War II but to Edward VI's destruction of the British monarchical system. He reminded England that it was a monarchy, even if Churchill was its primary figure. While Branagh interviewed Prince Charles as background for his film—and not Margaret Thatcher—his production had to pick up the colorations of recent international criminality, whether it did so consciously or not.

Also belonging to two different worlds but closer in time to each other are Branagh's film and the BBC-TV version of *Henry V* (1980), starring David Gwillim.

It is a commonplace that art resists the dominant ideology, though in most cases it is a tolerated dissent that proves how "liberal" the power structure is and that thus reinforces power. Certainly most "Hollywood" films present a unified and comforting point of view similar to that of landscape painting, with a relaxed shepherd in the corner of the canvas, half asleep in the browse of the sun. Escapist films of the 1930s, in which Fred and Ginger danced in ritzy nightclubs, allowed people to forget what rampant capitalism was doing to them even as it made them modest consumers of an escape from "depression." Television is seldom if ever subversive. It is meant to sell something. Thus Miller complains of David Grillim's Henry V: "This Henry is a peach. . . . It is doubtful . . . that a group of corporations can produce a work criticial of, even objective about, the mighty. Moreover, the profit-making habit is hard to break: Exxon would surely prefer a hero with broad and immediate appeal. BBC has therefore bowdlerized this difficult character, turning 'the warlike Harry' into a really nice person."[65]

Miller suggests that Gwillim's indictment of Cambridge, Scroop, and Grey is "mawkish." Gwillim "chokes . . . back the tears and sinks . . . to a bitter whisper."[66] That is a fairly accurate description, particularly when contrasted with the rage with which Branagh pounces on Scroop, pinioning him and shouting from within an inch or two of Scroop's head. Branagh's scene seethes with gut-wrenching violence, the traitors, for example, going for their swords when they realise they have been descried. Gwillim's three traitors kneel for their praise of Henry and his triumph over treason in a single frame, the camera at their level, Scroop, Cambridge, and Grey angled toward us in the order of their final words. It is all rather passive, all rehearsed. But if Branagh gets at the latent danger expressed by Bedford in the scene's opening line, Gwillim gets at the King's management of the traitors. One of the scene's points is not the danger they represent but the protection of God who "so graciously hath brought to light / This dangerous treason, lurking in our way" (2.2.185–86). One of the scene's points is Henry's superb management—via written indictments—of a conspiracy aimed at replacing a *de facto* king with one whose claim may be *de jure*. Henry further uses the threat to his own throne as a happy augury in his quest for another throne he dubiously claims. While Gwillim's Henry does kneel beside Scroop and deliver a seemingly rehearsed "Why, thus didst thou" sequence, that is a moment of calculated personality within a scene in which the traitors go along with Henry's scenario as if their own lines have been memorized in advance rather than dictated by Henry. Much as I admire the power of Branagh's version of the scene, the blandness of the BBC version may make its *political* point more effectively. It permits us to remember that "Official discourse on treason always invests heavily in improbable providential explanations."[67] It also permits us to recall that "Official conspiratorial narrative was always questionable precisely because it arose as a site of contestation attempting to mask itself as an elucidation of the truth."[68] Gwillim shows us how superbly Henry controls the mechanisms of "truth" in the traitors' scene. The scene's straightforward conflict and limited number of characters means that it is nicely calibrated to television's scale and three-camera format.

Branagh's "Crispin's Day" speech is framed with a few soldiers in view—including Nym, Pistol, and the Boy. Here is a leader on the same plane as his men. The camera makes the point that Zdenek Stribrny makes: "Shakespeare lays special stress on the fact that the French lords at Agincourt refuse to lean upon their own people and rely solely on their own chivalric bravery. Whereas in the English host gentlemen fight side by side with their yeomen as one compact national army."[69] Olivier makes the same point, but his camera suggests a leadership in which we no longer believe today and a rhetoric perhaps more likely to raise laughter than a cheer. A tracking shot has shown Henry gathering troops behind him as he walks, and the camera has boomed out from the cart in which Henry orates to include his army and the embrace of an approving God.

The script can support at least two very different styles of leadership, and seemingly contains a manifest content and its subversion—though a debate would ensue as soon as surface meaning and refutation were defined. The play, obviously, means differently according to *zeitgeist* and *weltanschauung*, partaking of the qualities that Ann Thompson attributes to *King Lear:* "In some sense all future readings could be said to be already 'there' in the text, but we have to wait for the historical circumstances which will make them visible."[70]

The same can be said of most of the plays I have discussed in this book. That they keep getting rediscovered suggests why so many productions of some of the scripts are available. But we need more. Branagh's Henry shows us Olivier's and the place of Olivier's Henry in history. We need another *Measure for Measure* and a director who can show us how *Twelfth Night* can work on film or television. We need a history comprehensive enough to incorporate Shakespeare into its modernity. And even if World War II permits us to understand *King Lear* at last, and if no subsequent history will permit the ending to be reinscribed with the optimism of the heroic couplet, the play shifts along its plates and the molten lava itself rides underneath waiting to break through and scald the script in ways we cannot anticipate.

Much has been made and will be made about Branagh's flashback technique. As Bardolph sits pathetically in a cart, his already executed nose trickling blood, Branagh recalls the scene in which Bardolph had asked about the hanging of thieves. Falstaff's question has been shifted to Bardolph and Hal's answer, "No, thou shalt" is directed at Bardolph. The flashbacks, says Stuart Klawans, "endow . . . Henry with a whole range of emotions without his having to speak a word."[71] Branagh nods, Bardolph swings aloft, clutching at his neck, and gives a final spasm, and Henry forces his speech about "lenity and cruelty" past his personal response to the sign of an old crony hanged from a tree in France.

Gwillim, in the BBC production, pauses while cleaning his boots as Fluellen describes Bardolph (3.6.107–112), letting the wash of memory play behind his face. Gwillim's Henry is silent for almost four seconds after Fluellen has finished and then says, "We would have all such offenders so cut off." The effect—typical of Gwillim's performance—is of extemporaneous politics emerging from the premises of a practicality that absorbs personality. Gwillim's approach seems consistently mild compared to Branagh's, but the former's style and attitude are often effective on television. We are forced to fill in what personal details may color the cold politics of Gwillim's Henry. The advantages provided by the neglected BBC version of *Henry V* are that we have remarkable contrasts between the cool and introverted Henry of Gwillim and the passionate, extroverted Henry of Branagh, and a contrast between the media that each interpretation of the character is designed to serve.

Probably the most interesting flashback in the Branagh film occurs within Henry's psyche as Burgundy discourses on peace. Olivier provides trite visual equivalents for Burgundy's words. Branagh's Henry, forced to listen to a politician extolling pie à la mother, recalls all that has gotten him to this moment—York's death at Agincourt, the discovered treason of Scroop, the bleary light of the tavern, friends and former friends, almost all dead now. While the sequence is consistent chronologically and thematically, it shows Henry "spacing out" (as one of my students said). We experience something like the hallucination that sleeplessness can induce, a sudden and unwilled moment in which the psyche intercepts one of the first and only moments for which Henry's control of the moment is not demanded.

The final Chorus tells us powerfully that Henry could control neither time nor history. The door swings shut on a narrative that occurred long ago, during a time shrouded in Medieval darkness, filled with the butchery of hand-to-hand combat, lightened perhaps by a romantic interlude whose result has been dictated in advance, and suffused with a yearning for peace. The ending erases any sense of comic ending. "Yet," says Branagh, "it was all for nothing, as the Chorus tells us right at the end."[72]

VI

We cannot reconstruct any sense of an audience's response in, say, 1601 to the boy actor playing a woman's role. My own belief is that the boy actor de-eroticized the female character, permitting a spectator of *any* sexual orientation to contemplate the character's words and actions with some detachment. The boy actor, then, served as an "alienation device," creating a zone for a spectator's recognition of, perhaps even analysis of, his or her response. Here I agree with Catherine Belsey's suggestion that the boy actor creates a "third entity," neither male nor female, and certainly not hemaphroditic, but asexual or transsexual, "where the notion of identity itself is disrupted to display a difference within subjectivity."[73] Theater is an illusion that tricks our imagination out of the hiding demanded by the numbness of consensus. The actor, boy or otherwise, is the puppet who lifts its skirt in *Bartholomew Fair* for Busy (5.5.132). The boy actor becomes, to paraphrase Barthes, a site being traversed and speaking words. The decision for gender resides in our response.

Here I find myself in disagreement with what I take to be Madelon Sprengnether's point that "The tragedies, on the whole, enact the hero's resistance to femininity, as manifest in his responses to women whom he regards as powerful. His story tends to climax in his acknowledgement of the femininity within, though such an awareness takes an enormous toll, destroying himself along with the female 'other.' Thus while the tragedies on the whole support the values associated with femininity, the apparent price of the hero's appropriation of femininity is death."[74] If the critic emerges from stereotypical definitions of femininity based upon physical premises of "frailty," then this very shallow conception of what Sprengnether calls "the feminine (or androgynous man)"[75] is inevitable. But it is precisely the tragic hero's inability (as characterized) to communicate with the transpersonal energy within his psyche that forces Hamlet to "fall a cursing" like the worst of stereotypical women. Macbeth represents a corollary. He abandons a nature "full of the milk of human kindness" for a "mind . . . full of scorpions." It is no doubt true, as Jean Howard suggests, that "while dressed as a man, Rosalind impersonates a woman, and that woman is herself or, rather, a self that is the logical conclusion of Orlando's romantic, Petrarchan construction of her. Saucy, imperious, and fickle by turns, Rosalind plays out masculine constructions of femininity, in the process showing Orlando their limitations."[76]

Indeed, Orlando does get below the artificial constructs that have dictated and refuted his love, making it into an affectation that can only be parodied by pressing it to bawdiness (as Touchstone shows). When Orlando says that he "can live no longer by thinking" (5.2.55), he is saying that he cannot cloy his need for Rosalind by bare imagination of her *and* that artificial, mindforged conceits no longer serve his turn. He is saying that Rosalind-as-Ganymede-as Rosalind has forced him to scour down to his own androgyny, to that feminine quality that is deeper than, prior to, and inexpressible in male ballads made to a mistress's eyebrow. It is precisely Rosalind's neutrality as specific sexual object that has created the "alienation" that has permitted Orlando his insights. As we experience Rosalind "teaching her future mate how to get beyond certain ideologies of gender to more enabling ones," as Howard says,[77] we spectators experience the process through and *because* of the boy actor.

We cannot, unfortunately, test the thesis.* Not only have our own theatrical conventions changed with the Restoration but the link between the de-eroticized boy actor and the neoplatonic conception of love that goes back to *The Symposium* has been lost. But I do wish to cite two instances of male actors playing a woman.

In the powerful 1989 RSC *Dr. Faustus* at Stratford, Helen was played by Vincent Regan. Regan's cold and detached attitude suggested the chilly bargain Faustus had made and the unnaturalness of Faustus's love-without-sacrament, which becomes merely lust and the damnable nature of demonolatry, an argument made long ago by W. W. Greg. The convention created a zone for analysis rather than mere response to Regan's physical presence.

In the 1980 BBC *Hamlet* we get probably the fullest version of "Gonzago" we are likely to experience and thus the most complete opportunity to respond to a boy actor playing a woman (Jason Kemp as Baptista). Admittedly, "Gonzago" is a stylized melodrama, trapped in sententious couples and "distanced" from the more "naturalistic" play surrounding it. That granted however, the boy actor becomes a metaphor, an implied comparison between his characterization and women, as the anonymous author of "Gonzago," Gonzago himself, and Hamlet see women. We may accept the connection with Gertrude ("Oh, but she'll keep *her* word," as Jacobi emphasized it), but that is Hamlet's metaphor, based on stereotype and probably generically a function of the

---

*Although it will never be proved, I believe that A. M. Nagler is correct to suggest that "if the young player stylized Lady Macbeth, the adult Burbage must also have stylized. An inconsistency of technique is inconceivable." The actors shared "a common denominator—style. Such stylization did not exclude an emotional reaction on the part of the audience" (*Shakespeare's Stage* [New Haven: Yale University Press, 1958], 81). Indeed, we can think of Ferdinand's reaction to the highly stylized Masque in *The Tempest*, where the almost exclusively feminine cast would have been made up of boy actors, regardless of the practice of masque productions at aristocratic entertainments. "Gonzago," of course, draws plenty of emotional response, but its principal spectators are too "under-distanced" to suggest that they could do otherwise than to react emotionally, and the range of possible reactions is large. Perhaps the best example in Shakespeare is Sly's "emotional reponse" to his boy-actor "wife." There, indeed, we do perceive "an inconsistency of technique." That inconsistency results from Sly's being "taken in" by the illusion of the boy actor, as I believe Shakespeare's audience was not, here, or in the inner "history" by Kate or Bianca.

melodrama dictated by the oedipal unconscious that blocks the male from the energy of his own androgyny. Suffice it that the boy actor forces us to make a metaphor between the obvious fiction of the stage and our own flesh-and-blood reality, and to find on our side of the equation the truth of the imitation, the ways in which our own stereotypical visions block our enablement as human beings. Disbelief is the zone across which the arc of imagination leaps. The return vector brings insight. The modern camera, if informed merely by the "male gaze," confirms stereotype. Shakespeare's practice challenges stereotype. One of our challenges, as modern practitioners of Shakespeare, is to allow our own media to continue to challenge stereotypes as the scripts do. This challenge is particularly difficult given the tendency of television toward farce ("situation comedy") and melodrama, which, like most mystery stories, are most disappointing in their closures, since their technique and the reason for our interest has been misdirection. In a sense, Rosalind's Epilogue continues the discourse, demanding a dialogic response even after her/his final curtsey/bow. What may have happened in 1601 is irrelevant, except as a play has survived to be translated into an interrogation of today's spectator.*

---

*One effort to suggest androgyny occurs at the end of Czinner's 1936 *As You Like It*, in which Rosalind's Epilogue is presented in a series of dissolves between Rosalind (Elizabeth Bergner) in her wedding dress and Rosalind in doublet and hose. This filmic technique could not be done on stage and would not work on television, but it suggests Czinner's understanding of a central aspect of the inherited script and his willingness to address it.

9

A Space for Shakespeare

I

Television's evolution from radio combines with its small screen to make it as much a verbal as a visual medium, as its appropriation by politicians suggests. One of the first things the anti-Marcos faction in the Philippines did was to pull the plug on Marcos's television station. The television image augments the words, and the words seem often to demand the augmentation of canned laughter, a holdover from the live studio broadcasts of Jack Benny, Fred Allen, Abbott and Costello, and others. Even film, with its evolution from the silent screen and its emphasis on the image, can use words effectively, as in Fitzgerald's prose voiced over the opulent images of the film *The Great Gatsby.* One of the flaws of the film *Deliverance* is that it erases the lyricism of Dickey's descriptions of the river, which is splendid without reminding anyone of Twain or T. S. Eliot. On-location camera work does not capture the resonance of Dickey's prose.

If television is a limited but "perfected" medium that can recreate literary texts like *Pride and Prejudice, Our Mutual Friend,* and *The Golden Bowl* in an elegant version of "Classic Comics," then Shakespeare and his ready-made script should be easily adaptable to it. Not so. A script "in being," particularly of a famous play, represents a rigidity, a centuries-old codification that one tampers with at one's peril. The fact of a script "in being" demands an adjustment to the dialogue. The director cannot say, Rewrite this scene. Furthermore, television tends to create a space for the language, while Shakespeare's language creates the space within which the action occurs. As Sheldon Zitner says, television gives "a priority to time, place, and objects, and so create[s] environments in which human actors are expressions of a context rather than its creators. To re-define the locus of dramatic action, its characters,

179

its size, its depth, the angle from which it is viewed, is thus to tamper with the conceptual foundations of the Elizabethan text."[1]

Shakespeare's plays were produced out of doors, with the possible exception of "command performances" that some scholars posit for *A Midsummer Night's Dream* and *Macbeth*, and before Shakespeare moved to the indoor Blackfriars Theatre late in his career. Shakespeare's stage was unencumbered by sets, depended upon available lighting, and was subject to sudden squalls, as depicted in Olivier's *Henry V* (the storm a synecdoche for World War II). The language augments our willing suspension of disbelief and helps us compensate for what the stage cannot represent—Verona's dawns; Scotland's murky darkness; Egypt's heat; the sunless dawn at Bosworth Field ("Not shine today!" Richard complains, searching for his lucky talisman, the shadow of the hump on his back); the bloody sun that illuminates the showdown at Shrewsbury; the storms that sink Turks, counterpoint the madness of an ex-monarch, predict the fall of princes and kings, and evaporate at the wave of a magician's wand.

Stephen Hearst points at the problems of the spoken word on television. His observations apply particularly to that troublesome entity of a script "in being":

> A written text on the right-hand side of any script page which makes complete sense in itself is a bad text. What are the pictures there for? . . . The words, except in exceptional circumstances, need to follow the pictures. . . . Pictures have their own grammar, their own logic . . . and cannot easily be kept waiting. . . . To such a picture you could speak no more than about 25 words . . . language seems to play a secondary role in television.[2]

Hearst, of course, is speaking of the problem of language in production, not of the *effect* of language and image upon the viewer. In that regard, I believe that Adrian Mitchell is more accurate to say that "most television depends on the choice of sentences and silences as much as the selection of pictures. This is often acknowledged by script editors of individual plays, more rarely by the producers of drama series."[3] But Hearst is correct to say, as Zitner does, that "Television is a medium whose form dominates its content."[4] This domination increases as television moves further away from its strictly audio origins and becomes more and more a filmic medium.

"Words," say Joseph Papp and Elizabeth Kirkland, "are the core of what Shakespeare and his theater are all about."[5] Arthur

Holmberg disagrees: "The core of Shakespeare's art is his ability to generate theatrical metaphors by mobilizing all the resources of the stage—visual and verbal."[6] But the visualization and the cues for action are *in* the words that are, of course, also metaphors. "The deep of night is crept upon our talk" was a line heard by an audience in a theater open to a summer afternoon's sky. As Lois Potter says, "darkness was metaphorical at the Globe. . . . The characters might be in physical darkness. . . . The peculiar horror of Othello . . . is that we are forced to watch in helpless clarity as the hero walks blindly, in his private darkness, over a precipice."[7] Holmberg is correct to suggest that Shakespeare's scripts explored his stage and found meanings in it, or, perhaps, an exposure of the vanity of human wishes: "look you, this brave o'erhanging firmament, this majestical roof fretted with golden fire. . . ."

We follow Hamlet's arm as he points up at the actual roof of the Globe. In television, the camera moves for us. The camera does not require a line like "Look where it comes again!" Indeed, entrance lines can usually be cut on television. "Here comes your cousin," is cut, for example, in the BBC *I Henry IV*. The camera easily shows that Hotspur is there. Since space is not a dimension that television is framed to explore, the television director must create a space for the language, as Jane Howell did so brilliantly in her First Henriad sequence. In most cases a relatively bare set—resembling a stage set—is the best staging area for the words. As Rodney Bennett, director of the BBC *Hamlet* says, "Just before I began working on [*Hamlet*] I went to see *The Merchant of Venice* at the Warehouse, and that was a very useful experience. . . . there was Shakespeare being done with the absolute minimum of furniture: no settings at all, and yet it was absolutely satisfactory. One didn't want any more than that. It was a very timely reminder, really, that the way to do it is to start with nothing and gradually feed in only what's actually required."[8]

But exceptions do exist. The production of *Merchant* to which Bennett refers, which I saw at The Other Place in Stratford in 1978, was done "in the round" (or square) and would have translated well to television, as did the similarly mounted *Macbeth* of the same era, which I saw at the Warehouse (in 1977) and which became a Thames television production (with Judi Dench and Ian McKellen: 1979). The opulent Victorian settings for the Miller *Merchant* (with Olivier: BBC, 1973; ABC, 1974)—an elaborate lazy susan for the caskets, for example—creates a world of "thingness" that is definitely riding the humankind of this version. Regardless of the problems that anachronism can produce, the background is

remarkably consistent with the mercenary and materialistic premises to be found in the script. References to "argosies" and "Ja-
sons" seems odd, of course, and it is off-putting to find Belmont
right around the corner from Bond Street. Belmont may have
overlooked Regent's Park, but one does not have to cross even the
Thames to get there.

I cite Miller's production simply to suggest that no absolute
ground rules apply to televised Shakespeare. It is a matter of what
works for this script. The contrast between the elegant courtiers of
the BBC *Merchant* (1980) and the actually gabardined Shylock
(Warren Mitchell) is much more sharply drawn than in the Miller
version. But Miller is getting at the anti-Semitism still virulent in
modern society, beneath its trappings of "civilization." The BBC
production makes another equally valid point by depicting
Shylock as an obvious alien, a visible candidate for scapegoating.
Olivier's effort to simulate in Shylock upper-class mannerisms
and speech patterns "disdains the easy process of making Shylock
'sympathetic'; instead it shows the kind of monster into which
Christian societies transform their shame."[9] It is a powerful and
valid interpretation, perhaps one that only Olivier could have
brought off. Mitchell is powerful as well, but for reasons having to
do with a different interpretation.

The issue is—how is Shakespeare accommodated to the limited
dimensions of television so that the inherited script still works for
an audience not familiar with stage productions and conditioned
to the inevitably diminished expectations of television, the result
of its bondage to the vice president's interpretation of "what the
people want." Shakespeare had remarkable respect for his audience; indeed, he educated them over the course of his career to
an unparalleled level of expectation.

To explore the issue, I shall look at the Papp-Antoon *Much Ado
About Nothing* (1973), two versions of *Julius Caesar* (Monmouth,
1975; RSC, 1987), two versions of *Antony and Cleopatra* (the Nunn-
Schoffield, shown on ABC in January 1975, and the Miller BBC
version, 1981), the Desmond Davis *Measure for Measure* (BBC,
1979), the stage used as television studio, and the Trevor Nunn
Othello (1989). I shall also discuss filmic and televisual treatments
of Hamlet's "now might I do't" soliloquy and will explore the
question of television and special effects.

Response to television is immediate and a result of *zeitgeist*. I
have seen each of the television productions again recently and
find that my original reactions have not altered significantly. One
problem, of course, is that my attack upon Papp's anachronistic

approach to *Much Ado* is itself anachronistic, but that is a function of the "disposable" quality of television. The Papp-Antoon production was highly praised and, like the superb Nunn-Schoffield *Antony and Cleopatra*, deserves to be made commercially available. The two BBC productions are, of course, on the market.

II Papp's *Much Ado:* The Perils of Anachronism

Perhaps the production I have most disliked during the past two decades was the celebrated Papp-Antoon *Much Ado About Nothing*.

It is not anachronism to which I object. My response emerges from the script's subjugation to the metaphor of 1910 America. The setting *exposes* bad acting, rather than permitting it to get absorbed into all that detail. Superb acting, like that delivered by Olivier, Plowright, and Carteret in Miller's *Merchant*, might have transcended the clutter. As it is, the setting must be treated as the focal point of the production rather than as an adjunct to the script, as was Miller's Victorian conception of *Merchant*.

Peter Brook told Roger Manvell of how Brook took *King Lear* apart, even asked Ted Hughes to render a modern version, and finally became convinced of the power and validity of the Shakespearean treatment.[10] The process worked. For all of its flaws and for all of the adverse critical reaction it has received, Brook's *Lear* is a moving reintegration of the inherited text. The Papp-Antoon *Much Ado About Nothing*, aired on CBS, effectively demolishes Shakespeare's play but leaves in its place a cultural disaster.

For some incomprehensible reason, this *Much Ado* is set in 1910 America. The production is defeated at the outset by its conception. Aristocratic love and Italianate intrigue collide in midair with small-town America, bands, balloons, and Blue Ribbon Beer. Language, "by my troth," clashes with spats and gramophones, turkey trots, and Keystone Kops. The cops might almost be forgiven were they capable of some of the superb visual jokes that Mack Sennett achieved, but these police are embarrassing parodies of a silent screen whose conventions director Antoon has not studied. A trombone and banjo accompaniment of "Hey, nonny nonny" competes for first place as the production's worst moment against a host of strong contenders. The others would demand a tedious listing, but surely Beatrice's vibrant soliloquy ("What fire is in mine ears?") becomes a trifle dampened when delivered into the splatter and spray of a Victorian sprinkler system. Such gimmicks quench what fire is in the play. The Elizabethan cuckold's horns simply don't suit a set for *Ah, Wilderness!*—and vice versa.

Conceptual problems are augmented by Antoon's inability to pursue the play's dramatic curve. *Much Ado* is intricately but carefully crafted, creating its structure primarily by contrast, insight against obliviousness, one character against another, these lovers against those, this scene against the one before and the one after. As in so many of Shakespeare's plays, genre plays against genre, the melodrama of Claudio-Hero, the valid comedy of Beatrice-Benedick, the farce of Dogberry-Verges. Antoon delivers what Sedulus in *The New Republic* accurately calls "a big, loud, indiscriminate bundle of farce, tragedy, melodrama, and fairy tale."[11] With equal accuracy, Day Thorpe of the *Washington Evening Star* asserts that "Papp's travesty of Shakespeare has no wit, no pace, no point."[12] Antoon so overpowers the inherited text with his 1910 clutter that, while the production may work for someone not acquainted with the text, it must baffle someone who is. Here, even a little knowledge is a dangerous thing. For example, Dogberry tends not merely to confuse words but to reverse meanings ("benefactor" for "malefactor"). While he *might* say "monocles" for "manacles," as Antoon has him say, the confusion is hardly Dogberry's linguistic best. Knowledge of optics would suggest that "monocle" cannot be within the Shakespearean canon: The first entry of the word in the *Oxford English Dictionary* is dated 1858.

The question of "monocle" might seem a quibble, but it raises the question implicit in Papp's production, that of anachronism. Brook sets his *Lear* in some prehistoric era shortly after the invention of the wheel, thus surrendering the opportunity to project the play's Renaissance opulence. But *Lear* does seem to emerge from some dim folkloric landscape, when Stonehenge stood unscarred on Salisbury Plain. Brook makes a choice, giving something up and, one hopes, gaining something else. One may criticize that choice but must recognize it as a valid option. *Much Ado About Nothing* does not offer 1910 America as option, any more than *Troilus and Cressida* offers Civil War America or *Julius Caesar* the Italy of Mussolini. Yet the problem with Welles's fascist *Caesar* was not merely its displacement in time, but rather that the displacement defined the very complications which Shakespeare leaves unresolved in his play. Brutus may be a kind of Woodrow Wilson, but Shakespeare's Julius Caesar is hardly a Mussolini. When the director, even someone as brilliant as Welles, replaces the Shakespearean imagination with his own, rather than attempting to recapture some of its dimensions, as Brook does in his *Lear*, the result is almost always disappointing. Occasionally, sheer visual brilliance can atone for obtuse editing and amateur acting, as in Zeffirelli's *Romeo and Juliet*. While Zeffirelli allows Rembrandt and Vermeer to vie with Raphael and Botticelli, his Verona is realized in a way that magnificently complements his admittedly controversial conception of the play.

Yet, one may ask, how can Antoon be indicted for cultural miscegenation or anachronism? Is not Dogberry as out of place in Sicily as Elizabethan spirits in Athens or striking clocks in preimperial Rome? Or *Much Ado* in 1910? Shakespeare's anachronisms have with the passing of time blended into the fabrics of his plays. It is the province of scholars to tell us that striking clocks were a medieval invention and that Elizabethan fairies were survivals of pagan gods treated very differently by historical Athenians like Aeschylus and Sophocles. And the question of Shakespeare's anachronisms misses a vital point. As Anthony Burgess says in his tongue-in-cheek book on Shakespeare, "Our heads swim at the ease with which the Elizabethans fuse, or confuse, disparate times and cultures."[13] There, Burgess is being serious. Historical accuracy was hardly Shakespeare's concern. He went behind and beyond history, ignoring chronology and cultural distinctions when he could make a better play, when he could penetrate more deeply into the motives of his characters, as in his making contemporaries of Prince Hal and Hotspur. If true of Shakespeare, however, why can it not be true of Antoon?

Shakespeare's scripts have an uncanny ability to capture *zeitgeist*, even when performed in Elizabethan costumes. They can lose that quality, however, if framed too specifically. Then the work of imagination is done for us. We are robbed of our response as we absorb 1910 America or Raj India, as in the RSC *Much Ado* of the late 1970s with Donald Sinden as a superannuated Benedict or Kahn's 1989 *Twelfth Night*, with Kelly McGillis as Viola. Setting and conception must illuminate the script, not erase it. The balance between conception and script can be delicate, and obviously, different persons with different criteria will disagree with each other. The goal of the Papp-Antoon production is historical accuracy. This fidelity to detail is not suggestive but oppressive. What we see is "the message." The cluttered space permits us to hear very little. That problem is partly a result of the acting, of course.

When we claim we suddenly "understand Shakespeare" because some director, disciple of Jan Kott or not, has delivered an updating to us, we are kidding ourselves. At best we understand something about our posthuman era that Shakespeare also perceived. We may understand in new ways the Oedipus, Orestes, Electra, or Antigone myths when they are recreated by a Cocteau, Sartre, Giraudoux, or Anouilh, but we do not thereby understand the Greek plays on *their* terms. We may glimpse the myth of ambition more completely when we see Kurosawa's superb *Throne of Blood*, but the film is a complement to *Macbeth*, not a substitute for it. A "modern" Shakespeare will move us closer to the mystery of *the* Shakespeare primarily by chasing us back to the script to rediscover the complexity and suggestiveness that modernizing tends to insult and flatten. Antoon's *Much Ado* reproduces with incredible fidelity the form and pressure of 1910 America but, in doing so, it obliterates whatever Shakespeare may still be saying to us with *his* play.

Sedulus suggests that Antoon produces a schizophrenic combination "with the Shakespearean play rendered hysterical by its competitor [the play about 1910 America]."[14] Certainly this is one impression the production produces. My own non-psychoanalytic theory is that someone said something like, Nothing can come of *Much Ado About Nothing*—so let's ignore it as much as possible, and do *our* play. This, too, is an impression the production produces.

Acting, along with conception and direction, would normally be a vital component of almost any review of a Shakespearean production. Here, it is a virtually irrelevant consideration. Day Thorpe says that "to say it is amateurish is to insult many nonprofessionals."[15] I am kinder (in the Elizabethan sense of the word) and suggest the acting at times reaches the level of daytime serials. Claudio is hardly an admirable character, but the actor playing the role should not make us cringe every time he clears his voice to speak. April Shawhan's Hero is lost somewhere between her natural inflection and the schooled voice she has yet to master. Sam Waterston gives us a Benedick from Brooklyn, when the late Dodgers were the Superbas, and at one point is upstaged by the nineteenth-century print behind him. Some of Kate Widdoes's bad scenes as Beatrice can probably be attributed to bad direction and to the impossible format that, to her credit, seems to bewilder her.

A reviewer of a television production must account for the medium into which the play is projected. Conceivably, this *Much Ado* might have been less disturbing on a full screen, which could have accommodated the amount of junk that crowded the foreground, background, and middle distance. True, the bust of Shakespeare on Don Pedro's mantlepiece is wryly amusing, but the introduction of a plastic bard is finally an archetype for this production. Sedulus tells us that he saw the production on a movie screen at the Folger Library. It was too much for him, and when it was crammed into my area of some 350 square inches it was much too much for me. Watching a television production on a large screen usually creates palpable distortion—close-ups are too large, and suggestive background cries for explicit detail. Still, the size of the larger image might have helped this production accommodate its "grandmother's attic." A larger picture, however, would probably have made the acting even more painful than it was. Antoon and Papp have much to learn from Howard Zieff, director of Alka Seltzer television ads, in which background is suggestive but authentic, not overly specific, not dominant. Not only do Papp and Antoon not know their play, they do not know their medium. The medium is not totally the message, but its dimensions dictate an intelligent response, which, in this case, we have not got.

Conception, direction, acting and voice, accommodation to the medium—these are criteria a reviewer must consider. Papp and Antoon fail vividly in each area. They neatly destroy the Shakespearean play, but they do not put it together again.

Nevertheless, this production was praised. Here, for example, is part of Gerald Clarke's 1973 *Time* review of Papp's *Much Ado*: "Papp scored a clear triumph. . . . this brilliant TV version [was] a dazzling reward for actor . . . and audience alike. Set with happy incongruity in Teddy Roosevelt's America [William Howard Taft's?], this *Much Ado* was all gingerbread and gingham. . . . As presented by Director A. J. Antoon, the play proved ideal for the small screen. Indeed the incessant closeups made for intimate scenes of discovered emotion while the plotting was as easy to follow as *Mission: Impossible*. With telling closeups, like Fabergé-crafted Easter eggs, Antoon created an almost three-dimensional illusion of depth. Like the Fabergé egg itself, this *Much Ado* was a jewel."[16] Perhaps this is the only time that Shakespeare's play has been compared with "Mission: Impossible," a television show that at least understood the clichés it manipulated (suppose what's-his-name had chosen *not* to accept his mission?). I believe that Papp's production lays an egg worthy of neither a bunny nor a czarina. *Time*, one must recognize, is engaged in promoting what it purports to be critiquing. *TV Guide* is even more obviously in shill-biz and reported (next to an ad for Midol) that Papp's *Much*

Ado was "a triumph." The *Guide* quoted critics who called the production " 'splendid' and 'stunning' and 'superb' and 'joyful' and 'dazzling' and 'glorious.' "

The *Shakespeare on Film Newsletter* is not similarly obligated, however. Here are excerpts from Edward T. Jones's 1978 review of Papp's *Much Ado:*

> the brash ardor and winsome intelligibility of the . . . determinedly American *Much Ado* . . . preserved the timeless world of the text. . . . Indeed, few productions of Shakespearean comedy so admirably relate jest to earnestness as this version does. . . . Antoon's 1910 setting permits a recognition of ordinary behavior beneath the theatricality and acting that forever rise to the surface in the play. The world of carousels, bandstands, Victorian Gothic houses and gazebos, rustic bridges and player pianos, barber shops and village squares, has at once nostalgic distance and familiarity. This ambience further offers the necessary nooks, crannies, and conservatories where characters may be concealed in order to overhear—perhaps the principal action of *Much Ado.* . . . What emerges is a romantic *Much Ado*, impressive for its eros of wit, good nature, and richness of texture.[17]

But a player piano plinking away, even if programmed by a virtuoso and performing with a great orchestra (as player pianos once did) still represents a mechanical reproduction, even of a work of genius. The Papp-Antoon *Much Ado* was not even faithful to the mechanics of the cliché-machine known as "the tube."[18]

III   *Julius Caesar:* Live and Otherwise

The Theater at Monmouth was in the 1970s the equal of any theater in the world. Others more expert than I share what would otherwise be branded provincial hubris. The structure itself was partly responsible for what happened within it. A small auditorium, oblong rather than long, so that most seats were close to the rake stage thrusting from under the ornate proscenium, and a huge decorative center piece on the ceiling, around which floated busty Victorian deities—this space did not seem ideal for the sheeted posturings of *Julius Caesar* in 1975. But Monmouth's production remains the best I have ever seen.

The play seems to belong to the genre of the History, which concentrates not on a single overpowering figure, but on a sequence of events that deal with the disposition of political power. The point was made superbly by Monmouth's Director, Earl Mc-

Carroll, after Octavius's final speech, when Antony and Octavius went up a set of steps side by side, turned, stared at each other, then exited in opposite directions. We scented Actium in the winds.

The play's power emerged from its staging and from William Wight's potent Antony. Mr. McCarroll placed the citizens gathered for the orations first in the balcony that extends over part of the auditorium, then in the back of the auditorium, then in front of the stage to view Caesar's body, then on stage to move off to their rampage. Thus McCarroll reframed the proscenium for us, having permitted the play for the moment to overflow its fictive boundaries and to invade *our* space. Brutus and Antony delivered their orations directly to the audience. Responses came from behind and within the audience. The effect was, as it was meant to be—profoundly disturbing. No huddled group of Romans in togas stood on stage absorbing rhetoric while we looked on. The dangers of such "under-distancing" were neatly absorbed by having the mob exit off stage, rather than back through the audience, and by the eerie scene following the orations and preceding the interval—the murder of Cinna. Audience emotion was drawn into the questions closing in on Cinna and back under the dramatic frame. Thus we did not rush out under Antony's spell to rip down the refreshment stand or put the ticket booth to the torch. One of McCarroll's neat touches was to have Brutus listen to the first and seemingly unironic lines of Antony's speech. Certain that all was under control, Brutus left Antony alone with captive and captivated crowd-becoming-mob.

My sense of the quality of the Monmouth production was enhanced by my experience of Terry Hands's *Julius Caesar* for RSC in 1987. The production virtually self-destructed during the orations. Hands chose to convey the response of the crowd via loudspeakers, an effort, one assumed, to simulate the manipulations of modern politicians. Both Brutus and Antony delivered their orations center-stage, front. The curious result of the use of loudspeakers was that Brutus's speech, obviously rhetorical and mechanical, was enhanced by artificial noise. He needed no "None, Brutus, none!" though I, gnawed by a sense of the script, almost provided it from the second row. But Antony asks for and *needs* human response. He releases emotions—for political purposes, of course—not just a sound-track. In the National Theatre production of 1977, featuring Ronald Pickup's splendid Cassius and Gielgud's superb hook-nosed fellow, the citizens were grouped downstage right so that they could respond on cue to "straight-on" orations. In the Hands's production, without the response of flesh-and-blood to Antony's strategically contrived and tactically dictated speech, this sequence fell flat. Brutus came off the winner. Antony's translation of crowd to mob fell back into the script.

The difference between Monmouth and RSC productions was, of course, a function of the difference between a small and potentially intimate auditorium and the huge and often alienating expanse of the Stratford main stage. The Hands's production did not attempt to expand into the dimensions of its space. At the very moment it might have done so its failure became most vivid. McCarroll opened into his space and violated our sense of disbelief. He pulled us back into fictive premises, but with our hearts still pounding from our experience as mob.

IV   The RSC, Nunn-Schoffield *Antony and Cleopatra:* Freeing the Script

The Nunn-Schoffield *Antony and Cleopatra,* presented on American commercial TV (ABC, 1975) had the advantage of a stage history behind it, as did the Thames *Macbeth* and Jacobi as Hamlet. Robert Speaight called the 1972 stage production "the best production of the play I have ever seen." Speaight praised Janet Suzman: "[she] has the breadth which the part demands. She enchants the eye and ear, and satisfies the mind." Speaight found that Richard Johnson's Antony "had a careless grandeur and irresistible largesse."[19]

The translation to television incorporates all of the things that television can do well. The "varying shores of the world" are not reached for here, but they are not missed, so luminous are the individual performances.

A sense of place is achieved by both camera and sound. Philo's opening "Nay!" is delivered to black and white, helmeted and sober centurions, and cuts to the in-color caperings of Antony chasing Cleopatra, while she wears his Roman helmet. While the production never reverts to documentary black and white, it shows Caesar in Rome, striding under an overhead camera, in and out of shadows, pulling his subordinates with him. In Egypt, Cleopatra pulls Antony toward her. The faces around Caesar are of unsmiling marble. Those around Cleopatra are of women, mostly seen in profile, and of poulter-breasted and round-faced eunuchs, whom she insults with her remark about Octavia's round-faced foolishness. Her world is of silken tents, pink and restless, and of a molten desert brushed by the feathers of slow fans, plinking strings, and effeminate singing. Few stand in that world—they lounge on rich rugs and pillows as Antony and Enobarbus do, sniggering at Fulvia's death and draining their goblets. Messages, entrances, and departures are rendered through the diaphanous, decidedly feminine film of curtains. The early frames in Egypt are blurred at the edges, as if seen through an alcoholic haze or the shimmer of heat from sand. The concept is that, for Rome, this is a world that exists in the imagination, in a story being told—as it is to the Romans by Enobarbus. When Caesar and Antony confront each other in 2.2, the latter has five supporters with him. Caesar has ten, including a back line of five in Falangist blue. They create an ominous sense of power and context. As John J. O'Connor says, "The visual structure, relying more on suggestion than literal definition, provides an unusually effective vehicle for the [many] brief scenes flowing between Egypt and Rome."[20]

Sound is not used as "sound effect" but as a kind of cueing. We hear the lapping of Mediterranean waves outside Cleopatra's Alexandrian tent. We hear female laughter behind Antony's hearing of Caesar's first messenger, then waves again: Caesar's rhythm. Dogs bark behind Enobarbus's description, an ironic counterpointing, as is Agrippa's deadpan encouragement of Enobarbus's enchantment with his own articulation of the events on Cydnus. The neighs of horses make their prediction as Caesar and Octavia part. A trace of thunder rumbles under Octavia's prophetic speech about "Wars betwixt you twain." The winds grow high and the parting comes finally in a sandstorm that is repeated on the second day of battle. Flies buzz in the tent where Antony responds incredulously to Caesar's celerity. The winds blow darkness across Cleopatra's monument as, shot by shot, she looks out as the dying Antony is borne to her until finally they inhabit the same frame.

The design of this production turns television into a suggestive medium and demonstrates how the vivid contrasts of this huge script can be fitted to the small screen. The design does not try for "mythology," but it captures those who inhabit the "irreconcilable" zones of Rome and Egypt. The settings, augmented by background sounds, are effectively allegorical, seldom explicit.

The production benefits from that fitting of word to action, action to word that must occur at every instant of a Shakespeare production. Antony's "now" is a demand for immediate sexual gratification. Rebuffed, he pauses to ask, "What sport tonight?" But wandering through the streets had been what Cleopatra had "desire[d] *last* night." She is forever a hop ahead of Antony. He stuffs a fig into the mouth of Caesar's first messenger, who spits it out and deplores another member of the empire who has "gone native."[21] Cleopatra's "wrinkled deep in time" is spoken into a wrinkled mirror of bronze foil. She "already looks back on those salad days with Caesar and an earlier, simpler relationship with Antony with a touching wistfulness, as at a youth that can't be regained. Possibly she does not love the 'old ruffian' as she did."[22] Agrippa's speech in 2.2 is obviously rehearsed—"not a present thought." Antony hears him out reluctantly, knowing he can claim nothing for his relationship with Cleopatra in *this* company. Lepidus's effort to place his hands on top of those of Caesar and Antony as they conclude their agreement is interrupted by applause in which he belatedly joins. Enobarbus's speech about Cleopatra is amused, even cynical, but certain about Cleopatra's indefinable power, so unlike the reality of sword and phalanx. Agrippa eggs him on as if reading from a prepared papyrus. But Enobarbus suddenly realizes that these officers—the ones who had been standing behind the great men a moment before for the official photograph—really believe that Antony must leave Cleopatra "utterly." Enobarbus's "Never! He will *not!*" sends a nervous stir through the Romans. Maybe this "accord" doesn't mean peace after all! Antony finishes Caesar's cup for him at the party, which is not on Pompey's galley but is a bachelor party *after* the wedding, a placement in time that does not suggest Antony's eagerness to be with his new wife. The parting of Caesar and Octavia is nicely framed by Enobarbus and Agrippa trading cynical comments about their leaders. Octavia's coy and cuddly efforts at affection obviously make Antony wish to shrug her off and contrast with the sensuously confident slide of Cleopatra's arms over Antony's shoulders. Cleopatra appears with her entourage out of sheer fire and air to greet Antony coming from the world's great snare, uncaught after his land victory. She materializes after the third day's disaster on Antony's cry of "Eros!" as if sent by a mocking god of love. Enobarbus says, " 'Tis better playing with a lion's whelp / Than with an old one dying," directly to a Thidias, who is being led off to be whipped. This is an effective translation of an aside into the dramatic context, though Enobarbus is allowed most of his choric asides in close-up, looking directly at the camera. Caesar's stark Rome cuts back and forth from his complaint to hazy close-ups of Cleopatra, Antony, and

Cesarion, all in cloth-of-gold Eastern habiliments. This sequence reminds us of Philo's opening commentary, but it raises the odds in that it is spoken by Caesar and shows Antony and Cleopatra clothed as divinities. The sea battles are observed and reported, with oars, waves, and seabirds suggesting what is happening off-camera. The land battle is fought in a televisually convenient sand storm, full of violent thrust and counterthrust (as in Welles's Shrewsbury) and allowing only an occasional quick identification of a specific figure. The battle is impersonal, not heroic, and thereafter whatever is said about it or claimed for it is either ironic or merely tactical. After the last battle, Antony walks unsteadily downhill, away from his promontory. After his confrontation and reconciliation with Cleopatra, wine spills on his beard. The camera cuts to Caesar taking a quick sip of some milder potation and preparing to meet with Antony's Schoolmaster. Cleopatra is momentarily furious with Antony for dying on her. Cleopatra is robed for her exit via a close-up in which we see only her golden crown and headdress put on. The camera moves back to reveal a mosaic of queenliness—"the fury and mire of human veins" now ready for a trip back through time to Cydnus, to begin the story again without Octavius in it.

Caesar kneels in front of Cleopatra, who is close to the camera in her best attires, like a goddess newly painted atop a sarcophagus. He does not ask how she had died but goes right into "She looks like sleep." He raises his voice just enough to give order for the double funeral, then realizes he must make a political statement and launches into "high events." The Romans, some of whom had not seen Cleopatra, take a last, surreptitious look at her, spellbinding even in death, magnificent in profile as she had been moments before as she stood in the robes of her voyage into immortality. "I call it death-in-life and life-in-death."

The editing is relatively unobtrusive, although one notices the cut in the middle of Octavius's "greeting" of Octavia's market-maid return to the camera's panning across the faces of the threadbare kinglings Antony has gathered around him. The former scene is already powerful and should be allowed to develop the perhaps too-late modulation of Caesar's cruelty toward this adoring sister. Cuts like this one reveal Shakespeare's intention more than can a hundred critics. Antony does not get the fine speech about "black vesper's pageants," perhaps because he was back among the pillows that Cleopatra had abandoned for her monument. Octavius is not permitted to express how patient he has been with Antony, after Octavius hears of his partner's death.

Pompey is gone, as is Seleucus, but the scene in which Hercules deserts Antony is retained with eerie effect. Antony, dying, looks at Cleopatra on "noblest"—she had had a noble or two in her time—and receives an assenting nod. He has passed the test, and thus Cleopatra does not get jealous as Iris topples. The lines beginning "If first she meet the curled Antony" are cut. Cleopatra's belief in his love—and hers for him—has grown absolute.

The ending is edited, as the play is, toward Cleopatra. As Charles Shattuck says of Suzman's version, "Such were her personal beauty, her breadth of style, her vocal range, and her realization of the total Cleopatra from heroism to depravity, as such too were the equally right responses of Richard Johnson, that 'politics' seemed only secondary to the humanity of the protagonists."[23] This relegating of "politics" is particularly vivid on television, where intimacy could overweigh the talking head of Caesar. Suzman's domination of the ending is so hypnotic that this ending—Caesar kneeling and uttering an unrehearsed pagan prayer that arrives on his tongue unbidden and against his will, and the others, including detached Agrippa, staring down in wonder—is utterly convincing. There was a great spirit gone. Having seen Colin Blakely and Anthony Hopkins struggle with the part—and Robert Ryan obliterate it—I recognize how good Johnson is, and how much his role depends upon response to Cleopatra. This production built out from that central insight.

The rest of the cast is uniformly excellent. Raymond Westwell is a weak Ledipus, although he really does wish to be a peacemaker. But he is a Henry VI or a Neville Chamberlain in a world of wolves. Corin Redgrave's Octavius plays his "Ledipus had grown too cruel" as a joke that evokes derisive Roman laughter in a world where to do good is only dangerous folly. Redgrave's icy-blue Octavius has defined the role for our time, although Tim Piggot-Smith tried to redefine it in London in 1987.[24] Redgrave does permit his Caesar to release a little carefully dictated emotion when Caesar can afford so to do. As his rivals kill themselves, he befriends them, even admires Cleopatra's decision for death. Mary Rutherford's Octavia is fine as the woman her brother can't have, and doesn't want—his passion is politics—and as the wife that Antony doesn't want either. Patrick Stewart's amused and amusing Scottish Enobarbus is won over by a "Roman thought" at precisely the point where his cynicism might have discovered his idealism or at least have scoured down to the necessary existential identity before he allows it to attack and kill him. Pigott-Smith plays Proculeius here as a passive mirror of Caesar, as if that were the way to get ahead. Ben Kingsley's splendid Thidias has other ideas. He would woo the Egyptian queen. But he and Cleopatra turn as he bends over the inside of her arm. There stands Antony. Thidias is vividly thrashed. Martin Millman's Dollabella does not tumble into Cleopatra's web but is troubled by her plight and resents Caesar's game with her. He is a Roman, but a "kind" one in the old-fashioned sense of the word. These three minor roles are beautifully played and precisely contrasted with each other.

This was probably the finest Shakespearean production on television up to 1975. It has been rivaled since by only two or three BBC productions and possibly by the Thames *Macbeth*. On American television, however, it was destroyed by commercials, which consumed only 10 percent of the three hours, although it seemed like much more. John J. O'Connor, television critic of the *New York Times* gave a rave review—"marvelously imaginative interpretation, beautifully performed."[25] But O'Connor had seen the production sans commercials. One viewer wrote in to complain:

> At the end of the play, the split-second cut from the dead Queen of Egypt to a middle-aged man in pyjamas announcing "That's my last cough" would have been incredible, except by then, after three hours of similarly ludicrous hi-jinks, not even a plug for an asp-antidote would have been surprising.[26]

I too objected to the commercials when I first reviewed the production years ago: "The worst of daytime television [seemed to be] emerging from one of Shakespeare's three or four most brilliant scripts. . . . This production deserves a mounting free of the seductions of Lysol, Noxema, Prell, Wizard, Cascade, Geritol, and Grecian Formula."[27]

It deserves to be made available in the United States in cassette format. Nunn and Schoffield, Suzman and Johnson permit us to recreate this superb play within the matrix of our own imaginations. As Leonard Buckley said, "television lifted the production off the stage and into its own ethereal element."[28] At rare moments, hyperbole is the truth.[29]

V   The BBC-TV *Antony and Cleopatra:* Plastering the Script

In addressing a disaster as unmitigated and as monumental as Miller's *Antony and Cleopatra*, one is at a loss as to where to begin. This production is bound to contaminate the attitudes of thousands of students toward this magnificent script. I hope that it is only thousands—it may be millions who will reject Shakespeare on the basis of their dismal experience of one of his masterworks. Faced with this production, we teachers can only claim, Believe it or not, this *is* a great play! Students, however, tend to believe what they see on television more than what they hear from teachers.

Miller insists on coming out in advance of his productions to chat with the audience. The chatter is arrogant, patronizing, and reductive. Viewers learn that *Shrew* will be hollowed out to conform with Miller's conceptions of late sixteenth-century male-female norms. Thus is Sarah Badel robbed of her role at the outset by directorial fiat. They learn that *Merchant* should not even be produced, since it is anti-Semitic. We are told that Cleopatra is a "treacherous slut," even as the actress playing the part asserts that Cleopatra is "fun to be with."

Miller's approach is all wrong from the outset. Instead of giving viewers an imaginative entrance to the production, he subjects them to opinion, a quasi-ideational format delivered, literally, off-the-cuff, a revelation of directorial intention that defeats whatever dramatic intentions the production might reveal. Framing is vital, as Shakespeare shows so often via choruses, misdirected challenges, Weird Sisters, and apparent shipwrecks and as Olivier demonstrates in that superb approach to the Globe Theater at the beginning of his *Henry V* and in his return to it at the end. Miller might have employed an old map of the world—Italy's boot separated from tropic Alexandria by "mare nostrum." The world is the issue, and divisions within it the drama. The map might absorb color, and the camera might zoom in toward Egypt, where, perhaps unexpectedly, Philo's Roman thought might strike us. The framing I suggest might have prepared us for Miller's awkward and confusing treatment of Actium. Ah, but I am designing an alternative production, as I did with increasing impatience throughout Miller's version.

By imposing the old masters—Paolo Veronese (of the Venetian school), in this case—upon his production, Miller erases the distinction the play makes between Rome and Egypt. Thus Miller also erases the conflict suffered by the play's hero, Marc Antony. Cleopatra and her court-with the exception of dusky Iris—could have been in Rome. Octavia could have been Cleopatra. Rome is of swords and columns; of the eagle; of consciousness, sobriety, and control; of precise measurement and efficient logistics; of military intelligence; and of power in this world. Its complete figure is cool Octavius. Rome is yang. Egypt is of recumbent pleasure, fertility, excess, of Keats's grape bursting against the palate; it is the zone of the serpent. It is warm and sensuous, a place where men lose their swords and soldiership, where Roman phallicism yields to liquidity, to ooze and slime. Egypt is yin: Cleopatra. Torn between these extremes is Antony, who would remain a triumvir, who would retain Cleopatra. He can find no mid-way between these extremes.

Miller shows us none of this. In his effort to escape the Holly-wood, Elizabeth Taylor vision of Egypt, Miller forgets that Cleopatra's production on the River Cydnus—if Enobarbus be accurate—outworks even the fancies of C. B. DeMille. Miller, it would seem, is simply not up to an imaginative recreation of a central contrast that defines the central conflict.

In his effort to create the patina of an old master, Miller forgets that he is working with drama. Not painting. It is as if he took his scene designer and lighting director to the National Gallery, pointed at a canvas, and said, There! That's what I want. Such an approach *can* work in some of the static set-piece scenes of *Merchant*, a play that offers, after all, a High Renaissance setting and style. But the approach fails in this *Antony and Cleopatra*. Drama is stifled beneath canvas. The confrontation between Caesar and Antony (2.2), for example, *is* pictorially beautiful, ornate goblets and bowls of fruit glinting and glowing in the foreground. But what happens in the scene? One could argue that Caesar manipulates Antony adroitly into condemning Egypt's "poisoned hours," then, via Agrippa, springs the trap of marriage to Octavia. Caesar draws his great competitor into the "double bind" that typifies poor Antony's conflict.

This reading is certainly not the only one the scene will bear, but any sense of anything dramatic happening was trapped behind the beautiful picture. We are given a tour through a museum, not a play, and certainly not *this* play.

While good acting could not have struggled free from ancient oil, the casting for this production is egregious: a short, pathetic Antony, who, never having been on the hill, could not be over it and a sexless Cleopatra. Whatever the field of her infinite variety, a depth of female sensuality lies close to the heart of her mystery. Whatever ironies abound within and around each character, they must convince us that one is a "Herculean Roman," the other suited to "the habiliments of the goddess Isis." Since neither tries to touch mythology, we cannot believe that such diminished beings are capable of the grand passion the play explores. At their best they are, as Jack Kroll suggested, "like Wilbur Mills and

Fanne Fox."[30] At their worst, they bicker petulantly, this treacherous slut and this sad old man. It is Edward Albee, not William Shakespeare. We are subjected again, as in *Shrew,* to the "bright idea" that glows dimly from directorial ego and that casts Shakespeare into the outer darkness.

If we cannot believe that something other than game-playing and manipulation lies below the surface, if we cannot believe in the love, or passion at least, of these two great figures—however destructive and self-destructive—we cannot believe the play itself. Cleopatra's arias to and about Antony in act 5 become, then, efforts to create what was never there in the first place—self-refuting rationalizations. She becomes as pathetic in her hyperbole as was the silly, self-deluded drunk she claims to have loved. The "god, Hercules" never leaves Antony in this production—that wonderful scene (4.3) is cut. Wisely is it cut, for Hercules had never visited this Antony, except perhaps in his fantasies.

Beautiful pictures cannot compensate for bad casting, obvious underrehearsal, or the director's unwillingness to seek the tensions and conflicts of the play and its every scene. As Kroll says, "Miller, like many modern skeptics, is suspicious of the very idea of greatness and passion." Well, so am I, existentially. But our own narrowness meets its compensatory energy in a great and passionate play like *Antony and Cleopatra.* Miller's defense against what Shakespeare understood is to filter the play to us via Veronese, thereby rendering the play static, passionless, undramatic, and frozen in a time that Shakespeare should be allowed to transcend.

In a review of BBC-TV's excellent *Richard II,* I expressed this hope:

> If the tube has become "America's unconscious," replacing individual dreams and fantasies, then perhaps Shakespeare can deepen our expectations for a medium that usually transmits only vapidity and puerility to its public. Perhaps Shakespeare can challenge successfully the very norms of the medium on which he appears.[31]

That hope grows ever more forlorn, assuming it were ever possible. The best that I can do now, as a teacher of Shakespeare, is to attempt to mitigate the damage done by a production as misguided as Miller's *Antony and Cleopatra.* One way to do that is to insist that its "great competitor," the Nunn-Schoffield version, be made available.[32]

VI *Measure for Measure:* **Balancing the Scale**

It remains a puzzle for some viewers that BBC-TV's *Measure for Measure,* one of the first productions in the Shakespeare Series, remains one of the best. I would suggest that it is not merely because subsequent productions, including Miller's *Taming of the Shrew* and *Antony and Cleopatra,* have been, to put it gracefully, less than satisfactory. Assuming good casting and intelligent direction—warranted assumptions in the case of Desmond Davis's BBC-TV production—the script per se proves excellent for television. Before glancing at some of the excellences of this particular version, I wish to examine some of the generic reasons why *Measure for Measure* seems almost to have been written for television.

Measure for Measure has been labeled a "problem play," a convenient category that critics have invented to solve their problems. The problem play is unlike a comedy such as *As You Like It* in that the problems it raises run deeper than the "folly" and myopia that get resolved at the end of the comedy. The problems of the problem play—in this case, illicit sexuality, radical abuse of political office, oathbreaking, attempted murder, and so on—are potentially tragic issues. Yet at the end of *Measure for Measure,* no Hamlet dies (*Hamlet* has been called a problem play, of course), no Othello kills himself, no Macbeth is struck down by Macduff, no Octavius gives orders for the funeral of Antony and Cleopatra. The Duke has power to save. The play ends "happily," with the multiple marriages endemic to the comic ending. Many feel, however, that nothing really has been solved beneath the imposition of Vincentio's politics, and that the "comic ending" is "coerced," rather than springing from new awarenesses within characters, insights that society is ready to incorporate within its widened frame. If society is a better place at the end of a Shakespearean comedy it is because most of the characters have learned something about themselves during the course of their dramatized careers. Is Vienna a better place as a result of all we have witnessed? Desmond Davis's BBC-TV production might answer with a craftily qualified yes. But one must be careful, for the production, like the script, invites the subjective response of the individual auditor, and *Measure for Meausre* finds itself high on the list of plays that evoke radically divergent views, along with *Hamlet* and *Henry V.*

The problem play tends toward melodrama, a mode that may

seem to raise profound issues but does not pretend to solve them. If it does pretend to solve them, the pretense shows through, as in the case of the celebrated *Equus* and, possibly, *Measure for Measure*. Television is a medium for melodrama, and the best shows are often the ones whose "solutions" are the most muted. It is true that the "situation comedy," a genre akin to farce, has been standard television fare for years. That means that *Love's Labours Lost* and *Taming of the Shrew* should be excellent on television. Our expectations for the medium form a large component of our response and also tell us something of the built-in limitations of the medium. It is a question, to paraphrase Robert Frost, of making the most of a diminished thing. Certainly television is not a medium for tragedy, nor is the "modern world." Nameless, faceless, sexless leaders, for all the world-shattering power at their fingertips, seem simply to have lost the stature of the Oedipus, King Lear, or Marc Antony whose fate is the world's fate. Perhaps that is a good thing. Derek Jacobi, a fine Hamlet at the Old Vic, is a very different Hamlet on television. Not only must he accommodate himself to microphone and camera, but we see a ten-inch figure mechanically reproduced within a frame. We are not inhabiting the space where *Hamlet* is happening. The distinction between mechanical reproduction and living space is less important when we talk of melodrama: first, because melodrama accommodates itself so neatly to the dimensions of television, and second, because there is something mechanical about melodrama anyway, as when Duke Vincentio assigns parts to everyone at the end of the play, even giving a tiny cameo role to the head of the dead pirate, Ragozine.

One of my favorite melodramas from many years back was "Father Knows Best," with Robert Young and Jane Wyatt. One of the Anderson children would get trapped in an emotional dilemma—invariably chaste and usually brought on by the sheer goodwill that welled within these three youngsters—and Robert Young would solve the problem with twinkly good humor during the final minute and a half of the show. The last scene of *Measure for Measure* consumes more than a minute and a half, but it is based on the "Father knows best" premise. Certainly that is the Duke's premise; whether it is Shakespeare's is debatable. But the problems the Duke solves are not just those of lukewarm youth or baffled adolescence. We have enormities here: the twin problems of sexuality and politics run amuck. We do not expect, in the United States at least, anything of this magnitude from television. We turn ourselves off as we flip it on. *Measure for Measure* gives us unusual intensity, but it is momentary, because all issues seem to be resolved by ducal fiat and manipulation. We can, if we wish, comfort ourselves with the belief that although things looked pretty bad there for awhile, it all turned out for the best.

Measure for Measure is super "soap." While soaps do not end, they are melodramatic and episodic. In *Measure for Measure* we experience a sequence of one-on-one confrontations that only at the end come to be what the Duke wants them to be, or not to be, depending upon how we take this play and its shadowy chief character. Whatever we make of the Duke, he is a strangely passive protagonist, a disguised eavesdropper—a good character for melodrama. We do not get in this play the kind of "linear" progression of a comedy such as *As You Like It*, where banished Rosalind discovers that (a) her male disguise is a bad thing ("Alas the day! What shall I do with my doublet and hose?": 3.2.231–32), and (b) her disguise is an excellent thing in a woman. We observe as she translates disguise into a dynamic device that sets most of her world into an androgynous harmony. Our participation in Rosalind's evolving awareness of her own vibrant ability allows us to experience the comedy from the inside, with the feeling of participation that the comic form of dramatic irony permits. We derive similar benefits from the French Ladies in *Love's Labours Lost* and Petruchio in *The Taming of the Shrew*. Viola's reversal of the process ("Disguise, I see, thou art a wickedness!" :3.2.28) neatly evokes our empathy for her. We can, however, only begin to second-guess Vincentio, and then only at the end of the play. Melodrama alienates us from the "participation mystique," except when we see a shadow looming behind the hero or hear footsteps as the heroine takes her shower. Melodrama makes us feel as helpless as Isabella feels after her second meeting with Angelo. Our response to melodrama, like our response to so much within our own lives, is primarily to hope that "things will work out." In melodrama, at least, they usually do. The Duke is there for a reason, even if only to force a happy ending on problems he himself has promoted. If the Duke is the moral focal point in this play, he is neither as attractive nor as seductive as, say, Rosalind or Hamlet. That Vincentio is not humanly appealing makes him useful, however, in this play.

Television is an excellent medium for the titillation that is the effect of melodrama. It can arrest us for its diagonal moment, but on a scale smaller than life, and the problem flees into the receding moon as the set clicks off. The space is ours again, the intruding picture now a blank window, the voices now silent. Whatever dissatisfaction we may have felt with "the ending" of the peculiar show is easily dissolved in the universal solvent, another beer. With television, we do not have even the transitional time it takes to walk from the cinema, locate our car keys, and drive home. One reason melodrama is suited to television, of course, is that it need not be discussed. All has been resolved by the time the credits waft across the foreground.

I am being unfair to *Measure for Measure*, not only one of my favorite plays but a superb stage play, as John Barton (RSC, 1970), Jonathan Miller (Greenwich, 1975), and Don Taylor (St. George's, 1977) have all shown—after the play had been neglected for years. Yet it seems almost to have been written for television. Not only is it melodramatic and episodic, but, as episodic narratives often are, it is a series of vivid one-on-one confrontations. Such scenes work very well within the limited space of a studio or a television screen. Contrast *Measure for Measure* with, say, the rich and ambiguous second scene of *Hamlet*, or the multifaceted and climactic first scene of *King Lear*. *Measure for Measure* may resemble *King Lear* thematically, in that a ruler absents himself from power, but Lear simply does not know what he is doing, and Vincentio, it would seem, does know. The jungle that Lear encourages ultimately swallows him. Vincentio, faced with something less than the explosion of Nature herself, is able to improvise his way toward the "happy ending" Lear intended to dictate in his first scene. Vincentio's big scene occurs at the end of his play, as he gathers all fragments together and labels them. We may not be satisfied with his labels—certainly Lucio is not—but they may be more satisfactory than fragments left to find their own destinations. Until the last scene of *Measure for Measure*, we witness confrontations between Lucio and Claudio, Lucio and Juliet, Lucio and Friar, and so on. Even the large final scene is staged within the confrontational model.

Having argued that *Measure for Measure* is generically suited to television, I wish to suggest why Desmond Davis's production is a fine fulfillment of platonic form. First, consider the face of Kate Nelligan, a face figuring itself out. Miss Nelligan plays an introverted and superficially self-possessed Isabella, at once ascetic and capable of that "prone and speechless dialect such as moves men." She makes believable both Angelo's and Vincentio's response to her. Penelope Wilton, Miller's Isabella at Greenwich (1975), was very like a nun, other dialects mute within her. Anna Carteret, Taylor's Isabella at St. George's (1977), was opulent and sensual. What aberration had gotten her to a nunnery? Had

Wilton accepted Joseph O'Conor's proposal at the end (she did not), we would have felt that she misunderstood her own sexuality or lack of same. Had Carteret rejected the same O'Conor in the later production (she did not), we would have felt that she misunderstood her own sexuality or abundance of same. Nelligan portrays ambivalence with a fine balance that Davis's camera explores effectively. At the end, aware of the pressure of the crowd that Vincentino has brought to bear on her, Nelligan's Isabella dismisses it as irrelevant, searches within herself for a response, finds that being a duchess feels right to her, and takes Vincentio's greatly relieved hand.

One feels the lack of a stage history behind this production—a point the Royal Shakespeare Company has driven home with a television version of its superb studio production of *Macbeth* (Thames, 1979). The relative stiffness of the two scenes between Angelo and Isabella, however, make a point. The ducal palace itself is a sober, almost Calvinistic zone of oaken furniture, inlaid flooring, and intricate leaded glass, a suitable setting for Tim Piggot-Smith's arrogant Angelo. But the arrogant facade soon melts in a flash of lust. The two scenes between Angelo and Isabella suggest profoundly how inner confusion can emerge as external absolutism, can become "that icy zealotry which is repressed passion," as Michael Long suggests of these two.[33]

Davis's camera is always alert to emotional nuance. Christopher Strauli's Claudio, with his weak and sensual mouth, agrees with the Friar's "Be absolute for death" (3.1.5) because it is polite so to do. His superficial acceptance prepares us for the deep panic of his plea to Isabella. Yolanda Palfrey's Juliet, very much with child, accepts the Friar's condemnation of her transgression but resents his remorseless emphasis on the point. Although American television has little or no feeling for nuance, the intimate effects achieved by Davis and his actors are nicely suited to the medium. Many of these grace notes would have been swallowed up by large amphitheaters like the Olivier or the RSC at Stratford. Davis's interpretation does not go as far, perhaps, as Long's indictment of Vincentio for believing "that the social world will be made beautiful if only nature can be stopped working."[34] Since some of the Friar's advice in the gaol does not really apply to the human issues involved—a young man facing beheading for premature consummation of his marriage, a young woman swelling with new life but about to deliver a Posthumus—Davis's focus on the receivers of the advice allows us to question the easy formulas.

Davis employs a technique in this production that might have been emulated by later BBC directors. Either sound from the upcoming scene comes in over the image of the scene just ending or the image of the upcoming scene superimposes itself upon the fading sound of the previous scene. What might seem like sloppy editing is actually a televisual version of Shakespearean staging, where exits and entrances coincide with each other so that spectators are never permitted to lapse into consciousness of themselves as a mere whim of creation. This overlapping creates a sense of the continuity of the script even as it brings us from street to convent to brothel to ducal chambers.

Certainly Davis gives us a "studio production" at the end of the play—the obviousness of the setting reminiscent of Olivier's intentional reminders of artificiality in *Henry V*. And much to the same purpose: the war in France is a production staged by Henry V, and the long final scene of *Measure for Measure* is certainly Vincentio's production. The overt theatricality of that scene, as Davis renders it, calls attention to its function as a kind of "play within the play." Thus, as in so many of Shakespeare's plays, we are placed at a distance from the "on stage" audience. Thus we are allowed to "judge" the Duke's production.

I have always found the Duke's manipulations distasteful. Davis allows, I believe, for that interpretation, showing us only that Vincentio's elaborate mechanism "works." But has the sociopolitical structure of Vienna's court widened to incorporate a vision of human possibility that it had formerly excluded? Or is the final scene merely an articulation of the Duke's ego needs? While Davis gives us an image-conscious Duke, the production does not necessarily condemn him for that. Perhaps image making is a necessity in politics, and perhaps Vincentio belongs in a triumvirate with Henry V and Octavius as Shakespeare's most successful public leaders. Davis's treatment probes the question of Vincentio effectively. The production does not coerce either script or spectator into any black-and-white interpretation. It treats spectators as Shakespeare did—as reasonably intelligent human beings.

Free of the "bright idea," the script is allowed to flow beyond the rigid demarcations Vincentio might have wished to impose on inchoate Vienna. And it is just that tension between individual energy and preconceived format that Davis captures, achieving a probing of viewers' own energies that the usual television show does not attempt. The issues have not resolved themselves for us, obviously, nor will they merely because a duke on television has dictated a comic ending to the tiny characters held within the colored rectangle.

The ending, then—no matter what we make of it—goes well beyond melodrama. The term "melodrama," in fact, is both inadequate for and unfair to *Measure for Measure*. The Duke may be a benevolent ruler, but with all Shakespearean rulers, including Prospero, ironies accrue. Angelo is hardly a conventional mustache-twisting villain; nor is he merely a typical hypocrite. Isabella is no Pearl Pureheart, roped to the railway tracks and awaiting rescue by Mighty Mouse. Melodrama gives us characters both conventional and predictable, and that cannot be said of *Measure for Measure*. The issue of the play is a continuing evaluation by its spectator of the issues seemingly resolved on stage.

Television has an opportunity, via Shakespeare, to deepen its function. Some have argued that television, with its fantasies and wishes come true, represents America's unconscious. Television, then, takes over the normal function of dreams, whether that function be to work off gastric upset in technicolor or recreate the previous few days' events. While I happen to believe that dreams are deeper than that, I find it interesting that television tends to reflect only the shallower versions of the psyche. Is such shallowness an absolute generic limitation of the medium—or is it merely a structural problem? Certainly such shallowness is a component of our crucially important expectation of what television will yield.

Suffice it to say that Davis's fine *Measure for Measure* opens our expectations for the medium to the deeper definitions of the unconscious. Davis was not consciously attempting to do this, of course, but a good director's instincts take him or her in directions that challenge the shallow one-dimensionality of a medium that *can* deal "in depth." This production proves the point. If our expectation of the medium incorporates only what it usually gives us, then we are as diminished as we would be were our expectations of our unconscious activity reduced only to the effects of those damned onions we had in the salad. Davis's production, based on a play already framed for a medium undreamt of in Shakespeare's philosophy, releases the meanings latent in this ambiguous script. That meaning is, simply put, "With what measure ye mete, it shall be measured to you again, measure still for measure."[35]

VII   The Stage as Studio

A television studio, with its limited size, creates a performing area similar to that of a stage. In the theater, however, we see what the director wants us to see, even if, theoretically, we have the entire stage in view, and even if we believe that we can look anywhere we want. Entrances and exits, variations in lighting, and carefully constructed lines of sight control our eyes. If Shylock is slumped downstage right on a raked stage and all the other characters form a kind of arrow, headed by Portia, and all are looking at Shylock, *we* look at Shylock. The stage is a frame for movement and detail. Tableau and spectacle may simulate a sense of painting on stage, but they will break up to components like character and conflict and, possibly, reassume their larger pictorial aspects at moments and at the end of the play. Meanwhile, the director is moving our eyes from place to place within the frame. Television has conditioned us to allow the camera to do the looking for us. Some of that conditioning comes from film. If we watch what amounts to a filmed play—the Evans-Anderson *Macbeth* or the Olivier *Othello*, for example—we know that while each may be a valid record of performance, each is dull as a film. In Olivier's Shepperton version of *Othello*, I kept yearning for a glimpse of Venice or the harbor of Cyprus, with the rack dislimning and the Turkish wreckage bobbing in the still-excited surf. In the dark and studio-bound BBC *Hamlet* a graveyard scene shot at the Church of the Holy Trinity at Stratford would have been brilliant, but it was not to be. When a television director employs a static camera, as Miller tends to do in the BBC *Taming of the Shrew* and *Othello*, the results are deadly. The camera, as transmitted to the small screen, does not become a surrogate for a spectator sitting in a theater. On television, the movement of the camera and the editing of three or more shots and camera angles must substitute for the way in which a stage director shifts our vision within the space of the stage.

On stage, Shakespeare presses us past obvious artifice and toward something far more deeply interfused, something that becomes reality for our psyches and imaginations. The issue of the stage script *is* our imaginations, and that is seldom an issue on television, which, for all of McLuhan's insistence that "it engages you. You have to be with it,"[36] lacks a theatrical sense of levels and depths. Furthermore, as William Worthen suggests:

Perhaps because TV performances are transmitted by the camera, across a visibly domestic space, TV acting rarely tests its fictive boundaries. *King Lear* constitutes a certain kind of role for the spectator by requiring a range of response from him, a response both to the drama and the acting of it. The TV camera requires different responses—

more "receiving" and less "doing" and so constitutes a rather different role for us, one that seems partly incompatible with the challenges of the play.

By protecting us from the particular kind of challenge that *Lear*—and perhaps any stage play—creates in performance, the camera constitutes an inadequate role for the TV viewer. The challenge to feeling remains, but the difficult challenge to presence, the challenge that the spectator shares with and experiences through the actor is simply not a part of the play [for the viewer of television].[37]

Television inhabits a middle ground. It cannot achieve the scale or special effects of film, nor can it simulate the living space within which theater occurs, the space that creates a special kind of energy. The energy for television comes from a plug in a socket behind the set. Most network television shows must wrap everything up within a strictly delimited time between commercials. On television, Isabella cannot refuse the Duke. Father knows best. That closure is even truer on a recorded version of the play, where the pealing of bells fills in for Isabella's silence. At the end of a television production, we do not engage in applause, a gathering of coats, and a pondering of what the play may have been all about. These are the rites of passage attendant upon theater. Assuming we have stayed awake enough to the end of a show, television sends us to bed. The hijinks of Papp's *Much Ado* and the drying oils of Miller's *Antony and Cleopatra* ultimately have the same numbing effect. The Nunn-Schoffield production and Davis's *Measure for Measure* remain happy exceptions proving that the rule should be broken more often.[38]

One version of "space for Shakespeare" is an actual stage, something a step beyond the studio that Bernice Kliman describes in her discussion of the 1980 BBC *Hamlet:* "the producers . . . have finally met the demands of Shakespeare-on-television by choosing a relatively bare set, conceding only a few richly detailed movable panels and props to shape key locales. By avoiding both location and realistic settings, they point up the natural affinity between Shakespeare's stage and the undisguised sound set. This starkness of setting admits poetry, heightened intensity."[39]

The wish to "get back to what Shakespeare did" was enunciated long ago by Poel in productions that look as dated to us in their "authenticity" as Shakespeare's would, had we not lost the negatives. Still, however, simplicity of setting is usually a virtue. That does not necessarily mean that the director's awareness that the studio and the stage are somehow analogous is always helpful.

The television version of a live stage production can simulate the energy field that develops in the space of live performance that is in a sense continually developing on the tape that the camera has made. A simulated stage, as in the Bard productions, is not a substitute because there is no energy field. The effect is often flat, or worse. If the acting is not superb—micro-acting tailoring its nuances to the close up camera—the results can be disastrous. A live production, even on television, can get away with some inept acting. It may be that our placement "within" a live audience makes us more tolerant. We know we are involved in a fictional transaction, and our disbelief (even in the skill of the actors!) is a component of our response and evaluation. We do not disbelieve as we watch television, even though it asks that we believe little. But we will not forgive the exaggerated verbal and gestural acting that might escape without censure if the identical acting space opened out to a live audience.

I wish to deal briefly with four examples of "stage as studio": Joseph Papp's live production of *A Midsummer Night's Dream* (New York Shakespeare Festival, Delacorte Theatre, 1982; televised in 1982 by ABC), the Bard *Macbeth* (1981) and *Othello* (1984), and the Renaissance Theatre *Twelfth Night* (televised in Great Britain on 31 December 1988).

Papp's *Dream* begins with wildflowers, musicians, and a splendid "establishing shot" in which the camera roves across the settling audience towards the stage.

While the audience is seen a few more times (behind Egeus's angry entrance, for example), it is mostly merely heard now and then as the play progresses. Since *Dream* is as metadramatic as *Shrew*, the erasure of the outer audience—the god to whom Prospero prays at the end of *Tempest*—is disappointing. Some way must exist to employ all those people watching a play, even when we see them watching a play on television. They represent an energy beyond that of the canned laughter to which they tend to be reduced here.

The setting is superb. A bronze Cupid rises above a pool. A mossy old tennis court creates a central platform. Birch trees bend to left and right against the straighter lines of New York City. The set alone makes this production a joy to watch. It can be usefully compared with Moshinsky's "homage to Max Reinhardt" for BBC-TV, but it is really a stage set, like that one encounters at London's Regent's Park. This one is as enchanting in its way as was the beautiful set for John Barton's RSC *Dream* (Aldwych, 1978), based on the illustrations of Arthur Rackham.

The weaknesses of this production, however, are glaring. The costumes are eclectic, either bizarre or drab, and contribute nothing to the texture of the production. The artisans are a group of types apparently instantly recognizable to the audience but in no way coherently blended in with whoever the other groupings are supposed to be. "Pyramus and Thisbe," however, is done in a quasi-Elizabethan mode which does make some sense. Any play done in relatively modern dress that has a play-within can do some stunning things when the play-within is "Elizabethan" as was "Gonzago" in the Prussian Ciulei *Hamlet* at the Arena in 1978.

Marcel Rosenblatt's Puck is awful. She is allowed to upstage Quince's rehearsal, to bray stage laughter against the delicate sway of leaves in a summer night's breeze and, in sum, to destroy those moments in which she participates. For this the director is to blame. Bottom's head is a huge set of ear muffs and a smudge on the nose. All that stuff about transformation and monstrosity is simply ludicrous. There is Bottom all along! The lighting has not been adapted to the close vision of the television cameras and is often blatant. The exception is the moment when a spot switches off as Oberon says, "I am invisible." That earns its laughter. Film actor William Hurt's Oberon is not helped by his "son of Sitting Bull" outfit, but he wrecks a rich role by running past signals in Oberon's poetry and, perversely, by pausing to sing out irrelevant vowel sounds. He does get music behind "I know a bank . . ." and he probably laughs all the way to it. Michele Shay gets a sense of vicarious pregnancy into her description of the changeling's origin but otherwise concentrates on looking beautiful. In that she succeeds.

The cutting is standard—Theseus's lecture on magnanimity is gone, as is much of the raillery during "Pyramus and Thisbe." One sequence, however, may disturb those who know the script. While Puck leads Demetrius and Lysander through the fog, Oberon is rebuffed at the edge of Titania's grotto. She, feeling guilty it seems and doing the only thing she can, slips out with her Indian boy. Finding Oberon prostrate in pretended grief, she places the boy in his arms. Oberon reports to Puck, "While I in this affair did thee employ, / I've been to my Queen to beg her Indian boy." His later speech cuts from "Her dotage now I do begin to pity" to "And now I have the boy again." This editing does not alter the masculine control Oberon asserts over Titania but it does qualify sympathy for her distress within a bad dream she knows she is having. I leave it to other auditors to assess the impact of a changing of the script seemingly dictated by the values the production is finding within its setting.

While Deborah Rush's Hermia has a baby voice just this side of

Helen Kane's, Christine Baranski's Helena has an aristocratic and self-mocking tonality that wonderfully fulfills one of the great roles in the canon. Baranski's pulling on her gloves—à la Oscar Wilde—as she chooses to leave an unsatisfactory social scene in the forest is hilarious.

Another good moment occurs when Bottom, preparing for Pyramus's elongated death, spies Titania tripping past the storm-soak of an oak bole. Pyramus's final words press their silliness toward the quality of the lines they parody—Romeo's in the tomb. Pyramus's lines will not support tragedy, of course, but it is a brilliant directorial touch to have Bottom reminded of his love in the middle of his equally fictional love affair with Thisbe. Bottom's "what I had" alludes not to his ears but to where he has had Titania. He recognizes at the end of the play-within that his woodland experience has been more than a dream. We recognize that something exists that is deeper than and prior to the painted backdrops of our "reality."

For all the unevenness and remarkable lapses of taste of this production ("Ay, that left Papp!"), this one is worth watching.

The Bard productions are taped on a platform in front of pseudo-Tudor facades of plaster and timber. I have trouble accepting this background as a setting for *The Tempest*, particularly when the lighting is unimaginative, even unvaried. While the primary problem of the Bard productions is that of a stage without an audience, the results are mixed. When they are good, they are very good, but when they are bad. . . .

The Bard *Macbeth* is a deed without a name. It represents the nadir of American Shakespeare. It would, were it to achieve any speculation in the eyes of our students, fulfill the curse that seems to have fallen upon the Scottish Play from the beginning. Jay Robinson's Porter and Michael Augenstein's Donalbain are worth preserving as workmanlike efforts. The rest should be erased.

Jeremy Brett's Macbeth, haggard and gaunt, is better at times than Nicol Williamson. But, like Williamson, Brett leaps into the sudden bellow, and leans toward this technique known as "wringing new meanings out of the lines," also known as "I haven't a clue about the meaning of the words, so I shall confuse everyone else to hide my own confusion." Brett hits a brief effective stride between "whose howls his watch" and "to heaven or to hell," but the rest is mishmash. He begins "To be thus is nothing" with a huge and happy "whoop!" Suffering from something called the "glugs," Brett's Macbeth delivers his lines to the Doctor about a "mind diseas'd" as if it were a final, fevered deathbed confession.

One is surprised to find Macbeth rising to strike Seyton down, then stroking his henchman's fanny during the "Tomorrow" speech, as if seeking the tail of an idiot. At the end, Brett lays down his cardboard as he says, "Before my body I lay my warlike shield"—an even grosser misreading of the text than in the bad BBC version. Macbeth is kidding!—he rises and drop-kicks Macduff in the groin. "Let fall thy blade on vulnerable crests," he mocks. No crests can have been tame enough for Macduff's blade at that point, but he rises manfully and tells Macbeth that he—Macduff, that is—has been from his mother's womb "untimely whipped." Macbeth has at least accomplished the orientalization of this Macduff with his timely kick in the groin. Macbeth himself gets it in the same place and gets out his last lines thus impaled, or, given the weaponry here, impailed.

To say that the rotund Piper of Laurie dominates the stage is to indict the size of the stage. Let her retire and, as Octavius says, feed and sleep. Laurie went to school to Jeanette Nolan, a worse Lady Macbeth than Francesca Annis or Jean Lapotaire. "If we flunk we flunk," as Lady Macbeth says. Laurie does, and gives poor Jeannette a well-deserved second-to-last place in the canon.

One must admit that Brett's Macbeth was rotten to begin with—no internal debate here: "my own words are merely the cursory cross-examination to my intention." While Brett's desires merely awaited the ratification of Laurie's Lady, he should have been turned off and not seduced. That is, in spite of his draculean desire to get his incisors into her throat. Would that he had. She should have died immediately. She provided a new link to Macbeth's later line, "her former tooth!" which Brett delivered with seeming envy for the king's original dentures. Brett gives this line a left-handed imitation of a dentist's drill that has to be seen to be disbelieved.

Laurie gives her all to the word "screw" by jumping on Brett (who could hardly jump what life there was to come). But Brett revenges himself by shaking her on "Be thou jocund." Piper quivers like a bowl full of jelly and does not savor the sansation. Her expression is that of a 1950s teen queen just goosed by a turkey.

The banquet scene hits a low, however. Banquo's Ghost is announced by the squeak of a $29.95 keyboard instrument. Brett introduces that technique popular among good young actors of being scarcely able to withhold his tendency to barf between lines. Laurie perches between her cleavage and delivers lines so soft that even the microphone can't pick them up. Brett develops an oddly Strangelovian movement of the arm that we recognize as his effort to hitchhike out of the scene on the wrong side of the road. It is, one has to admit, the most dignified exit available. One of Laurie's wonderful misreadings deals with the invitation Macbeth had sent to Macduff: "Did you send to *him*, sir?" This translates to—Don't you know, he never RSVPs!

It would be unkind to mention other elements of this production, like the beardless Weird Sisters (although Banquo on their beards is left in), and the lascivious chimpanzees who keep molesting the girls. Why are these young women seeking anything beyond lucrative one-nighters? I won't mention the silly sexuality in which Brett and the ponderous Laurie engage, with its passionless nipping at necks and ears. I refuse to point out that Lennox's "by a hand accurs'd" (as opposed to "under") reverses the meaning of the line. I will not suggest why Ross visits Fife (it is to see young Macduff!). I will not deal with a Macduff who muffs most of his lines, like "I cannot but remember such things were / That were most precious to me." It is a performance geared to some sublinguistic level—a performance made, one assumes, for television. I refuse to question the literal stake to which Macbeth allows himself to be strapped before his final battle. One assumes it captures the spectrum between a baited bear and Christ on the Cross. I must admit that Ross's sudden whisper—"Where is Duncan's body?"—raised my expectations for an exploration of this "mystery of the missing corpse." That hope is dashed by Macduff's specific answer in the next line. I will not describe Lady Macbeth's final exit, howling like a dog with a thorn in its poor paw and seeking some stream to dam up, unlike the slender Ophelia, who had the grace to sink.

At the end, the Weird Sisters, who had popped up inconveniently at odd moments throughout this descent into hell, weave their way among the victors, pursued by a fan-blown trail of dry ice. I mention this detail only to prove that I did not cry Hold—enough! sooner. If this is the best that America can do, I understand why the BBC-TV version has been so highly praised. Next to the Bard production, the BBC-TV version, bad as it is, really looks mediocre.

Of the five Bard productions I have seen the *Othello* is easily the best. In fact, it is at least the equal of the two other available versions. The Olivier, although a film produced at Shepperton, scales down to the shallow depth-field of television and is a dull production, though it was exciting on stage. Jacobi's brilliant Cassio comes through in the film, however. The BBC-TV version

employs static camera angles that negate what a well-edited production can do for Shakespeare. The Bard version employs a
stage setting but is neither as silly in its staginess as the *Macbeth*
nor as cramped by its set as the *Richard II*. *Othello*, as domestic
tragedy, clenches in, as Bradley says, to "a close-shut murderous
room."[40] The one-on-one confrontations are suited to the dimensions of television, as one notices by contrast in the somewhat
awkward scenes from Cyprus Harbor and in the scene following
the discovery of Desdemona's death—often difficult as everyone
crowds into the chamber. Here, it is not only tedious but anti-
climactic after the very moving scene in which Desdemona dies
has pulled most of the emotion out of us. It is not that William
Marshall throws Othello's finale away, as had James Earl Jones in
the 1982 Winter Garden production, but that we feel that Othello
deserves what he is going to give himself and wish he would be a
bit more laconic in his leavetaking. On the whole, however, and
with a few exceptions to be further noted, this production works
superbly within its various spaces, evoking the nocturnal scenes
convincingly via the flicker of torch and candle, and creating vivid
visual moments with its rich costumes—blues, reds and golds,
pinks and purples. A lot can be said for an opulent foreground in
a medium that can provide little or no background. The production is free of the self-conscious "old master" technique that can
work well in a film (like *Romeo and Juliet*) but that can trap a
television production under old paint (as in Miller's *Antony and
Cleopatra*).

Marshall gives us the basso Othello to which Robeson conditioned us in the Margaret Webster Production of the 1940s. But
Marshall is more in control of verse rhythm than Robeson and
brings anguish to the role as Jones did not. Marshall's is an
understated performance, appropriate for television, but at times
he seems too "laid-back," as in his unemphatic "Naked in bed,
Iago, and not mean harm?" He peaks in his "when we shall meet
at compt" speech, which is about as late as an actor can choose to
peak (Jones chose not to do so at all), but what we get is a
restrained and quietly moving performance. Marshall's "her father lov'd me" is said, in some sorrow, right to Brabantio. On "a
friend that lov'd her," Marshall puts his arm around Cassio, a nice
foreshadowing of what Othello will come to believe.

Jenny Agutter's Desdemona is a bit beyond the first bloom of
youth, but not yet the sophisticated woman, a few years from
spinsterhood, of Maggie Smith. Agutter really does seem to be
the daughter of the gentle, merely saddened Brabantio of Peter

MacLean. Human and humane, he has encouraged in Desdemona the qualities that allow her to endure convincingly the terrors Othello is to inflict upon her. Agutter is convincingly womanly *and* innocent. One can share Othello's sadness in having to kill her and understand why this script has such a record of audience intervention. The murder scene is powerful, so much so that it pretty well erases what is to follow. What is to come is almost superfluous, and the production should have ended with alacrity.

Moody's Iago is not a NCO up from the ranks but a fallen aristocrat to whom lack of promotion is motivation enough. Moody's social status makes sense of his "relationship" with Joel Asher's Roderigo, who is Brabantio's best example of a "wealthy, curl'd darling" of Venice, and an embarrassing example who allows Brabantio almost to understand Desdemona's choice of the Moor. Moody's bald head is a space to be drummed as he asks "How? How?" A superb moment comes when Moody turns with a half-smile to the camera on " 'till us'd." Since the "talking head" approach is used sparingly in this production, its brief employment is potent here. Iago with Roderigo is splendid, but he is even more convincing with Othello. The hinge on which Iago swings Othello here is the latter's sense that he has been a winner over the Brabantio, who is, in a sense, a rival for Desdemona. Othello's arrogance, though mildly expressed, allows Iago to give more weight to Desdemona's deceiving of Brabantio than, obviously, it should have, and helps Iago push Othello into the Brabantio "position," which includes a declination into the vale of years. Thus this production shows Othello carrying out Brabantio's revenge upon Desdemona, unconsciously, of course, but brilliantly, as the initial gravamen is reiterated by Iago as Othello's mission.

A few sour grapes: one seldom realizes the importance of a small role until it is badly done, as is Leslie Paxton's Emilia, hardly an effective foil for her gentle mistress. When the Duke tells Othello that he "must stay tonight," Desdemona's dismay shows that she has had other plans. That instant nicely touches upon the matter of consummation of the marriage. But, later at Cyprus, Iago is robbed of his description of "bride and groom / Devesting them for bed"—that "innocent" simile which thrusts at Othello's possible sexual insecurity and describes what he and Desdemona have presumably just been doing. So—the earlier suggestion is, inexplicably, allowed to drop, as are Othello's lines about his "gentle love" being "raised up." Gone also is Iago's "Ha—I like not that!" Yet Othello alludes to the line a moment later.

While the editing leaves a lot to be desired, the brief scene in which Othello visits the fortifications of Cyprus (3.2) is retained. It gets Othello out of the way while Cassio visits Desdemona and shows us Shakespeare at work on thematics even while engaging in essential dramaturgy. External fortifications are rapidly becoming irrelevant as Iago's pestilence penetrates Othello's soul.[41]

The Renaissance Theatre *Twelfth Night* is a television version of a stage production directed by Kenneth Branagh. It appeared originally on New Year's Eve, 1988, on Great Britain's Channel Four. The television version is directed by Paul Kafno. The play is seldom translated to television, perhaps because the identical twin convention does not play on a medium that asks us to suspend disbelief only for cartoons and political speeches. Another *Twelfth Night* is most welcome.

Paul Kafno scales the stage version effectively to the diminished diagonal of the small screen, although Frances Barber's Viola is almost too muted even for television. This virtually complete version of the script becomes a series of conversations appropriate for the medium.

Yet the twins are troubling. Kafno does not permit us to see them together. If anything, Christopher Hollis's Sebastian is prettier than Barber's Viola. The Renaissance Theatre production shows us again why the play seems to work only on stage, where the twin convention is acceptable.

Kafno and Branagh employ a unit set and cameras that keep us in the role of "audience" facing the set, as opposed to omniscient observers of inner and outer dialogue. The action occurs between the door to Olivia's house (stage right) and the gate to her courtyard (stage left). The set holds the memorial to Olivia's brother, the crypt in which Malvolio is buried alive and left to rot, a mouldy divan, and a stopped clock apparently overlooked by the dustman. Fortunately, the acting atones for the director's pusillanimity in failing to reach for real surrealism. The time is late Victorian, but the set's iron gate is borrowed from Andrew Marvell—a grateful grace note to coy mistresses. The tonality is often black and white, with snow sieving down atop a bleak midwinter. Canvas mountains suggest the depth that television's field cannot convey.

One can understand the infatuation that the senescent Orsino (Christopher Ravenscroft) harbors for Caroline Langrishe's Olivia. She is luminous in a way television seldom permits.

Richard Briers's Malvolio is middle-aged and indeed, "notoriously abused." He may be serious about his imperious command that the Toby he apostrophizes bend to his right hand, but we recognize his motion as a borrowing from Olivier's Richard III. At the end, he feels more pain than anger, as opposed to Alec McCowen's rage at the end of the 1980 BBC production. McCowen feels himself still to be superior. Briers has been broken. Briers's off-camera cry for revenge freezes the onstage actors, much as Olivier's howl as Shylock shakes the victors of Venice in the 1974 *Merchant*. Briers's response to his own mistreatment obliterates any sense of "festive comedy." The possible flaw in Briers's conception of the role is that this Malvolio—unlike McCowen's—seems unlikely to talk himself into the trap he sets before he picks up Maria's letter.

The festive encoding is further smudged by Anton Lesser's Feste. He is a Victorian vagabond, yearning to be incorporate with the world he satirizes, a Hamlet who, like Hamlet, has wandered into the wrong script. His carpe diem "O, Mistress Mine" is spoiled by tears he can scarcely hold back. What is Hecuba to him? Lesser is splendid, though, as he plays palm-reader to Orsino's meaningless hand.

At the end, Feste's song sends Andrew, the honorary hussar, off, blood caked on his face. The Captain, birthmark vivid on his face, is unhandcuffed. Snow falls. Feste goes out through the iron gate and looks back, a prisoner to his outer world, as Malvolio is to his inward hubris. The two are as consciousness is to shadow.

This production should be made available in the United States and Canada.[42]

VIII   Trevor Nunn's *Othello*

A production that will appear on television and perhaps has done so by now is Trevor Nunn's *Othello*, which I was fortunate enough to see at The Other Place in Stratford, thanks to Christopher Millard of RSC. Although I write of it in the past tense, I watched it in anticipation of its being translated to television. It seems that directors are designing productions with more than one medium in mind, choosing dimensions perhaps ultimately designed for the cassette. Format and marketplace seem increasingly to dictate production scale. Bernice Kliman, for example, says of Kenneth Branagh's *Henry V* that he makes "choices more suggestive of tv than of film."[43]

Nunn's was a minimalist production precisely framed for its limited playing area, the smaller-than-life space of the tube. But Nunn created "a strong presence of actors and a strong presence of spectators [that produced] a circle of unique intensity in which barriers can be broken and the invisible become real."[44] Although it was hot in the balcony—my sweat sizzled on the light casing below me—running time was more than four hours (with one interval), I was tired (having been up all day), and this was a preview (virtually a dress rehearsal), I did not nod.

Nunn's decisions were made with the cathode ray tube in mind. This approach created a pressure equal to that generated by his *Macbeth*, which ran for two hours and fifteen minutes sans interval and which I saw years ago at the Warehouse. That production became one of the best television versions of Shakespeare ever. And so will this *Othello*, which, with its centripetal energy, narrows down that "close-shut murderous room."

Nunn will have to do some cutting, I think, even as the production loses a "natural" half hour as it gains confidence in front of live audiences. The scene where Iago is profane and Desdemona tries to be merry as all wait for Othello to emerge from "the high-wrought flood" (2.1) reached a wonderful silence on stage. "We have run out of language to toss into vacancy." I doubt that the scene will play on television, with its radio ancestry, where silence calls for a "Do not adjust your set" notice. The BOQ scene, where Iago tested his barracks punch with a finger, then added more brandy, was splendid on stage, but will have to quicken to accommodate the ever-eager television cameras. The letters and confessions that Lodovico mentions at the end are extraneous and can go. The story has almost been told. It is our understanding of it that will become the issue in just a moment.

One problem with this script is that the actors playing Iago and Othello can compete with each other, as Jones and Plummer did in the notorious Winter Garden production of 1982. Jones was an Othello deflated in advance. Plummer was permitted to caper about in a "freeze frame" that held the other characters motionless. In Nunn's production, Ian McKellan as Iago had the upper hand. A "cool medium" in which Iago fills in the sensory detail is an Iago medium. Othello is grand opera—Verdi, not twenty inches measured diagonally. Willard White's muted Moor, however, seemed precisely scaled for the economy of the tube. White's underplayed reception of Iago's initial insinuations in 3.3 was not only calibrated for television but also avoided the danger of the actor "peaking" too soon, leaving no place to go with voice and gesture.

I was not persuaded that Iago had done enough to convince Othello of Desdemona's infidelity. Nunn set his interval some 290 lines into 3.3, so that as we cooled in the breezes flowing from Avon, we were meant to percolate Othello's increasing heat through the filters of our disbelief. We began, after the interval, with Emilia's discovery and Iago's capture of the handkerchief. It will be interesting to see how this central pivot of the play works on television.

Several people with whom I spoke felt that Clive Swift's Brabantio was not upset enough about Desdemona's elopement. Swift, a shrewd television actor, will be upset in precise proportion to television's demand when the show airs.

McKellan is there already with that lime-dry, back-of-the-throat voice and remarkable detachment that lends such intensity to his performances. I have seen him as Hamlet, Romeo, Macbeth, and Coriolanus, but he has been Iago all along. He was the chief beneficiary of Nunn's decision for a post–American Civil War setting. Iago was an overaged junior officer, playing the saluting automaton with ironic perfection even as he sneered inwardly at his superiors. He worked the inflexible military structure to his own advantage, exploiting its fissures and cracks even as he observed its form with parodies that perhaps only former junior officers would recognize. At the end of 1.3, after the big guns had left and after Iago had dealt with Roderigo, McKellan savored Napoleon Brandy and filched one of the Duke's cigars. Iago knew that he deserved these finer things! McKellan's soliloquies were to the audience around him, perhaps suggesting that this production should be televised before a live audience. As he said "How, how—Let's see" during his first soliloquy, he seemed to listen to some malign god who told him "to abuse Othello's ear." Whatever Iago's motivation, his motive-hunting and pondering of scenarios will play superbly on television, a close-up medium that trades the supernatural for the psychological. We got a hint of motive, perhaps, in his "Look you pale?" to a black Bianca (Marsha Hunt)—her name and casting a wry glance at a "White" Othello. Iago's question—repeated, of course—could only be viciously racist here.

Nunn had Imogen Stubbs play a young and love-at-first-sight Desdemona, as opposed to the older, almost spinsterish Desdemona of, for example, Maggie Smith, who had been too long among the curled darlings of Venice. Othello's smothering of Stubbs exuded the perverse sexuality the scene demands, a first and final *coitus quietus*. One advantage of a complete script was that Iago's thrust—"like bride and groom / Devesting them for bed" (2.3.170–71)—found its ironic fulfillment at play's end.

Nunn paid attention to Desdemona, as some directors do not. Just before the interval, she remembered that she had left something behind. Was it the handkerchief? When she was Othello's "soul's joy," she was placed on a pedestal—a quayside trunk. When *he* became "a fixed figure for the time of scorn," she was placed atop a chair, the nearest scaffold available. Idealization leads to degradation, a lesson learned in the comedies, but too late by Othello. Here, Desdemona's final lines were delivered to Zoe Wanamaker's Emilia, who repeated them via effective "voice-over." The moment echoed Iago's cradling of Desdemona when she pleads for his help in 4.2. It was—and will be—a powerful visual parallel.

At the end, Iago stood in front of the bed without expression. He pondered his own absence from an event that appalled all other survivors. He left us with the mystery of human evil resonating out from his silence.

IX "Now might I do it" in Production

Any discussion of a space for Shakespeare must account for the space in which he worked. Modern filmic and televisual techniques seldom try to simulate Shakespeare's staging, except where an Olivier uses London and the Globe as an entrance to the History of King Henry the Fifth. Even there the zoom-in camera and the cuts to backstage preparations are film techniques. It may be that the camera actually reverses the viewpoint of the spectator, bringing him or her closer to what would be distanced on Shakespeare's stage, and vice versa. Hamlet's soliloquy near the kneeling Claudius represents a potentially interesting example of the use of space and the consequent manipulation of viewpoint.

The soliloquy wherein Hamlet decides not to kill Claudius just yet is—like almost everything else in *Hamlet*—subject to a wide range of interpretations. Dr. Johnson called Hamlet's words "too horrible to be read or to be uttered."[45] Coleridge was forced, naturally enough, to rationalize: "The determination to allow the guilty King to escape at such a moment is only part of the indecision and irresoluteness of the hero."[46] Roy Battenhouse avoids what the words say and claims that the speech does not demonstrate "a directly willed malice. . . . There is enough humanity in [Hamlet] to balk at an act of open murder."[47] What Hamlet seems to be saying, however, is that revenge is not revenge unless the victim's soul goes to hell. The words convey more than some sullen menacing vibration. Revenge is projected into the context of the eternity that surrounds and invades Elsinore.

The available versions of the scene include the Olivier black-and-white film of 1948; the Franz Peter Wirth made-for-television film of 1960, with Maximilian Schell; the NBC Hallmark Hall of Fame production of 1970, with Richard Chamberlain; the BBC-TV production of 1980, with Derek Jacobi; and the Ragnar Lyth Swedish production of 1985. Tony Richardson's film of 1970 gives Claudius his soliloquy at a point much later than that which Shakespeare's script indicates. The Kozintsev film does not include the scene.[48]

I assume that on Shakespeare's stage, Hamlet would have entered from one of the doors (probably stage left), discovered Claudius kneeling in the study, delivered his soliloquy downstage of Claudius, then exited through the other door, stage right. Claudius's conclusion and Polonius's admonition of Gertrude covered Hamlet's climb to the upper stage and Gertrude's closet. Modern productions—like Olivier's, in that film so full of staircases—often show Hamlet climbing steps to Gertrude's chamber, not necessarily to pursue the line of Shakespeare's stagecraft but because great people usually live on the floor above the ceremonial chambers.

The Globe stage would have shown us the entire picture— Claudius on his knees, Hamlet drawing his sword and gesturing with it. As Claudius exited, or as the curtains closed upon the study, the curtains would have opened upon Polonius and Gertrude above. The rationale of Shakespeare's stage was demonstrated, in absentia, by the 1985 RSC production, in which Roger Rees delivered Hamlet's soliloquy from directly behind a downstage Claudius. This format strained an audience's suspension of disbelief.

Olivier has Basil Sydney's Claudius slumped before a statue of a bearded Christ. Hamlet has climbed some steps and is walking down a corridor toward a further set of steps leading to his mother's closet, when he spots Claudius. Hamlet's soliloquy is voice-over. As he raises his dagger to strike Claudius in the back, Hamlet's eyes come up to the icon (on "and so he goes to heaven"). Christ has dissuaded Hamlet from murder. But the camera shifts to show the icon in relationship to Hamlet as he delivers the rest of the speech. Claudius has fallen below camera range. The surprising effect is that Christ seems to be endorsing Hamlet's "dark intent." Olivier has substituted this phrase for Shakespeare's "horrid hent," a decision that shows that it is

Hamlet's intent to damn Claudius. It is this intent that the icon blesses. While damnation does occur with divine sanction, the theology here is dubious. Heaven is ordinant only if the revenger remains untainted. But this film depicts Hamlet as hero—one ordained both by the will of God and the will of the director, Olivier. The scene is consistent with this vision. Regardless of the words he speaks, Hamlet's alignment with Christ makes the former look good, even if the latter can only stand there in iconographic muteness.

The 1960 Austrian production employs a simple cross consistent with the solid-block construction of the set. Schell appears as Claudius says "white as snow," and this is a Hamlet as Snow White and Prince Charming. Schell draws his dagger on "now I'll do it," and Claudius grasps the base of the cross in both hands. Hamlet's hand appears from behind a column, followed by the rest of him on tiptoe. Again, the soliloquy is voice-over. Spurred on by his own rhetoric about "the incestuous pleasure of [Claudius's] bed," Hamlet, framed in close-up, smiles and mouths a word or two of the soliloquy's final lines. The editing shows that Hamlet is not concerned about his father's heavy fate but with Claudius's damnation. Schell seems satisfied with the taste of "damned and black" on his tongue and tip-toes off to Gertrude with his dagger in his right hand. When he says "as kill a king," Hamlet is still arras-side, holding Polonius on dagger-point. Gertrude (Wanda Rotha) seems stricken by a sudden glimpse of the truth and kneels by her own simple cross. It is her effort at prayer that becomes "wringing of the hands." Hamlet accuses her of that, though she might be making a sincere effort from the audience's point of view. Hamlet had not recognized Claudius's wingless words a moment before. The two scenes are neatly linked. "The rood" is an object before which hypocrites pose.

The Austrian production, like the Olivier, is a product of the *zeitgeist* that made Hamlet a "sweet prince." One of the attractive sides of Schell's Hamlet is that he can articulate the evil within himself, as the venom of revenge momentarily tinges his essential winsomeness.

Richardson's film renders Claudius's soliloquy after Hamlet has been sent to England. This placement makes little sense, since the effort at repentance emerges right after Claudius (Anthony Hopkins) has apostrophized England to "contrive the present death of Hamlet." This approach might have worked had Hopkins caught an earlier glimpse of the lifelike ribs and slumped head of the crucifix to which he suddenly decides to try to pray. As it is, the icon is an object along the way, a prop that provides no rationale for its sudden magnetism. We only see the front of the icon toward the end of Hopkins's recitation. Were we to see it earlier, accompanied by some subtle interplay between it and the eye of Claudius, we might believe that it was enough to recall the King from his desperate politics of improvisation and to remind him that he is mortal and a murderer. Then the cut to Fortinbras that follows might make some ironic point. The speech becomes undramatic without Hamlet lurking nearby.

The NBC production shows Chamberlain suddenly focused in a rack-shot as Richard Johnson's Claudius drops before an icon of Virgin and Child. As happens so often, and as perhaps is consistent with the emotional tone of the scene, Hamlet is a background figure, as opposed to the foreground figure Shakespeare's stage would have made of him. Chamberlain uses his sword to suggest the upstairs-downstairs destination of the soul. He may give some hint of Coleridge's "indecision and irresoluteness of the hero." This Hamlet seems to say, I would rather play metaphysical word-games than kill the King. Revenge is only revenge if Hamlet can dictate the world around and beyond the act. Chamberlain also seems involved in Claudius's "incestuous pleasure." It seems to be Hamlet's pleasure as well and therefore not to be denied. So—up the steps!

The transition to the next scene is superb. From Virgin and Child, the camera cuts to Gertrude looking into a mirror. The contrast between Mary and Jesus and Gertrude and Hamlet is nicely anticipated. The contrast between virginity and vanity— "paintings" and "this favor"—hints at the question of Ophelia, trapped within the virgin-whore dichotomy constructed by the male imaginations that shape the script.

The best version of these several beats is that of Derek Jacobi in the 1980 BBC production. Here is no sweet prince but a creature of "feline hostility," as Kenneth Rothwell notes.[49] After Patrick Stewart's Claudius has ruthlessly cross-examined himself—an offender in the hands of an angry conscience—Jacobi delivers his soliloquy via medium close-up. Here is hatred articulate. Jacobi does not permit his Hamlet to emerge from this rage until, moments later, he looks down upon his sword and realizes he has drawn it upon his mother. Almost immediately, he is stabbing wildly through the arras in search of another target. Jacobi takes the words at face value—as Johnson did. And Jacobi utters them.

Lyth's 1985 made-for-television film does not allow Hamlet to speak his piece. Claudius (Ferj Lindquist) is momentarily abashed beneath a superb crucifix, emblematic of a production located in the abandoned Nobel dynamite factory. This icon is a tragic mask sunk below the shoulder blades, with despairing eyes having died looking up at emptiness as stomach muscles strain against the downward crush of lungs. Stellan Skarsgaard's Hamlet can produce brilliant extemporaneous anger, but he is a spoiled tennis star, incapable of calculation. Furthermore, while Lyth shows us the political sector of the script incisively, his work does not finger cosmic perimeters. This is an apparitionless *Hamlet*, clenching in on what people do to each other. Here, Claudius offers to let Hamlet kill him. Hamlet remembers his sudden need to visit his mother. We notice in this version the interpolations that film permits and that Shakespeare's stage did not. As Claudius struggles before the grotesque icon, Polonius briefs Gertrude, and Hamlet and Horatio watch the players depart to the lascivious whistling of a pipe. The Lyth version makes filmic sense of a sequence that makes a different sense on stage.

The play *Hamlet* and the character Hamlet show us that revenge is often a fantasy activity in which we become pretty gods of our own creation, free to delectate in the mortification and agony we can inflict upon the waxen image of our victim. When we face the victim's flesh and blood we usually back away. A look of terror might well melt the icy vein of our hatred even as we wall up our Fortunato. Hamlet means what he says as he stands, sword drawn, over Claudius, but he means it in that special theater of the mind, where heaven and hell actually do exist. As usual, Hamlet escapes to his imagination, at once hospitable and alien to his conscious intent. At this moment, when Hamlet might do it, his Jungian shadow flows out to darken his consciousness and his conscience—two words that meant the same thing to Elizabethans. The shadow, a male of "dark intent," is a comforting companion, for the male can choose to seek no other but the shallow confirmation of his own ego. This moment in the play and the man occurs precisely as Claudius is pulled back into his own personal agenda—crown, ambition, and queen. Claudius's conscience falls under the shadow cast by the cross before which he kneels. In playing at God, Hamlet reveals his worst to us. It may be that Hamlet merely *says* the worst things he can think of in preference to doing them—in preference to doing anything other than speaking daggers to his mother. The actor playing the role, however, should be permitted to spit out his hatred here. Spectators need some background against which to measure what is good in Hamlet.[50]

X   Shakespeare and Special Effects

Alan Dessen's article in the December 1986 issue of *Shakespeare on Film Newsletter* is a splendid step toward an understanding of why "the supernatural" does not work on television. Television directors, Dessen argues, tend to avoid "anything smacking of things beyond man." The "emphasis" falls "upon the psychological rather than the otherworldly," an approach that "suits prevailing interpretations . . . and sidesteps effects that may strike television viewers as questionable, even laughable."[51]

I wish to add a few tentative generalizations that may keep the discussion going. The "conditions of performance" include the expectations of the spectator and dictate what can occur within the mimetic frame. Dessen accurately defines television's "naturalism." If television has a theatrical equivalent, it is the "fourth wall," proscenium format whereby the audience looks in on "reality" (a wall having been removed as a convenience to those of us who have bought the tickets). Here the actors are "characters," unaware of an audience. Television works an occasional variation on that concept, with "All in the Family" taped before a live audience and "Buffalo Bill" conducting a fictional talk show before a "studio audience" made up of equity actors.

Shakespeare's stage acknowledges an audience, indeed demands that it "piece out" the "imperfections" of the Globe stage with "imaginary puissance." We are asked not merely to suspend our disbelief, but to provide the energy of our imaginations in the face of an inadequate "wooden O." The opening Chorus of *Henry V* invites us to observe the convincing imitation of kingship that Henry creates for the inner English and French spectators. Shakespeare gives us the advantage—even today—of assuming the ironic stance of detachment essential to our making what we will out of his fictions, and those of a Henry V. We become a part of the "swelling scene," rendering its artifice and the illusions its characters would pull over our eyes "real." Our meager existential formats are challenged into the transcendence of mere ego that good theater can engender.

Television is already "real," all by itself. It needs no help from us. We are reduced to passivity by a medium that specializes in reduction. The exceptions to television's version of "reality" are themselves normative—M/TV, Saturday morning cartoons, and television's rare successful venture into fantasy, the presidential news conference. A play on television has already been recorded by a camera on tape. The event is already in the past. We do not participate in a sequence of moments created by and for us within that intensity known as the present. A "television play" is an oxymoron. Television's fourth wall is permeable only by ratings.

As Dessen says, television denies the possibility of agencies larger than man. To render the unknown as psychological is to reduce the unknown to the space of a single brainpan and to enclose "meaning" within the narrow mode of "realism." I do not mean to demean the concept of "mind," which, as Hopkins says, "has mountains." I do suggest that television's narrowing and conventionalizing tendency is inevitable, given a fourth wall that blocks out more than it can include within its frame.

One irony pertaining to this medium that controls us is that we, ostensibly, control it. Television claims to give us what *we* want. And we, the humanoids reclining in our self-propelled loungers, can summon strength to press a thumb against a channel-changer. (Television is designed to tire and frustrate us—for reasons best known to that oxymoron known as the corporate mind). Television does not confront us as theater does. It is surrounded by what we have placed near our Zenith or Nadir.

The scale of television involves, obviously, a diminution of the image and an erasure of "background." When the television image is enlarged to the size of even a small movie screen, the picture is distorted, not enhanced. Film, on the one hand, provides the dimensions essential to fantasy. One of film's greatest eras displayed opulence to a radically depressed world. The two hours traffic of the flick was often larger than life in the 1930s. Although film brought us quasi-documentaries like the Joad story and monochromatic Kansas, more often it tended to waft us to Oz or down to Rio. It placed Hepburn, Grant, and Stewart within the same fantasized Philadelphia. On television, Fred and Ginger shrink and the Wicked Witch of the West is scarcely a threat.

Film's larger frame can incorporate special effects. Often it must do so, if Atlanta is to burn convincingly within the huge, darkened space where we sit, or if we are to believe in those twisters that churn toward Dorothy as she beats against the storm door, or if we are to be impressed by all those icons exploding at us from *Raiders of the Lost Ark*. On television, the twisters in *Wizard* look like a documentary on tornadoes. Television's naturalism is admirably suited to the documentary, but Arnold Gillespie had more than a documentary in mind when he designed ominous background and swirling foreground for his large screen. The effects of *Raiders* are abjectly trivialized when they pop and crackle from nineteen diagonal inches of tube into the domestic and domesticated space of our living rooms. In the spaces we inhabit, imagination, if it functions at all, is a product of panic. Television is Disney World. We need provide no imaginary puissance. The experiencing is done for us.

One of the sources of energy in Shakespeare's theater comes from the audience as it contributes to the continuum that flows between spectator and stage. At the cinema, of course, we experience a mechanically reproduced sequences of images. We are *within* the experience in one sense, however, as we learn when we turn toward the projector and see the white light cutting through a billion motes of dust a millisecond before the light becomes a moving picture on a screen. The source of power for television is a plug in a wall behind the set. The zone between viewer and cathode-ray tube is itself a vacuum.

Those who took their picnics out to enjoy Bull Run on 21 July 1861 fled back to Washington in terror, their mimetic frame splashed by the acid of reality. The Shakespearean stage attacks into our imaginations and psyches and can excite our archetypes personal and collective, into glimmering outline. Film can overpower us into terror, giving us an intimation of what sudden death must feel like to the final flicker of mind. Television, in spite of its scale and status as subgenre and in spite of our diminished expectations for it, can deal with segments of Shakespeare superbly. The tiny one-on-one scenes that can be awkward on stage are often splendid on television. And, to cite an exception many critics have noted, Jane Howell showed that special effects can work on television if held within the limits of televisual scale and if conceived within a production style that educates its audience toward some suspension of disbelief. The Margorie Jourdain and Jack Cade scenes in *II Henry IV* are precisely calibrated to the medium.

By definition, however, television is seldom a medium where special effects are other than "questionable, even laughable," as Dessen says. Directors of those Shakespearean scripts that do incorporate the supernatural are likely to be defeated as they attempt to scale the material to television. The tendency to make the supernatural merely psychological signals the necessities dictated by television: "to make the most of a diminished thing." I hope that directors with the imagination and daring of a Jane Howell will prove me wrong. Their thoughts must piece out the imperfections of my own vision, and the limitations seemingly inherent in television.[52]

10

The Tempest on Television

I wish to end with a set of specific applications that draw on what has gone before: to deal with the problem of *The Tempest* on television. This is a negative example, no doubt, but the script launches a challenge—as in different ways does *Twelfth Night*. Can *The Tempest* be translated successfully to television? We pause for a reply.

Three television versions of *The Tempest* exist: the Maurice Evans production of 1960, directed by Peter Schaefer; the BBC production of 1980, directed by John Gorrie; and the 1983 Bard version, directed by William Woodman. We get a glimpse of the 1982 Stratford, Canada, production via a half-hour "Page to Stage" cassette. None of the "complete" versions is particularly successful. The reasons lie within the productions, of course, but more deeply in the nature of the medium. Television has not proved a good vehicle for this script.[1]

The Schaefer production is pleasant but lightweight. Jack Gould accurately notes that the play "poses a severe traffic problem" for the small screen and goes on to say that close-ups are not helpful in a play that "requires reporting that is fanciful, not factual."[2] In other words, television lacks the scope for the play's larger effects even as its capacity for intimacy proves to be no advantage. Close-ups tend to invite the viewer to make psychological interpretations that are probably less appropriate for this script than for others.[3]

It follows that the most "physical" of the plots, that of Caliban, Stephano, and Trinculo, should work well. It does. The farcical byplay among the three (abetted in this production by an Ariel voluntarily concealed in a tree) is nicely framed for television, as is their descent via wine into the stereotypes of paranoia, megalomania, and compulsiveness. Tom Poston's vulnerable Trinculo, Ronald Radd's queasy and cowardly Stephano, and Richard Burton's sonorous Caliban, replete with finlike ears, armadillo shoulders, and a brush of tail, work well together—"obviously having a good time," as Virginia Vaughan observes.[4] Here, Burton reprises his 1954 Old Vic performance.

The play is shaped, shortened, and simplified for commercial television and its presumed audience. The opening storm is unconvincing and brief (one minute) and narrated. We are introduced to characters who rock and roll "near a mysterious and uninhabited island." But Prospero and Ariel are there! Their discussion is placed before Miranda's plea and Prospero's story, perhaps to keep the action boiling. Prospero's narrative is accompanied by a crystal ball in which the disembodied characters swim. The Caliban-Stephano-Trinculo meeting precedes the Antonio-Sebastian conspiracy, a transposition intended to get Burton et al to hold the audience. Antonio is a pot-bellied villain, while Sebastian is a fop in peach, pink, and pearl. Claribel is eliminated. Sebastian doesn't realize that he is heir of Naples until Antonio points it out to him. The "living drollery" are squat and dancing rocks. No banquet appears or disappears. Ariel does appear and gets one of his harpy wings tangled in a bush. The wedding masque is miniaturized and lasts for one minute. Prospero's "No more!" expresses disapproval, not merely dismissal.

Evan's Prospero is of the crinkly, "father knows best" model. The role suits Evan's tendency toward recitation. McDowall's Ariel has stiff, sticklike spangles gleaming from his head, as if he has just emerged from the frost-baked earth. Ariel admires Lee Remick's dewy Miranda and wishes he *were* human. Having an experiential sense of what punishment is, he pities Caliban. McDowall makes one hilarious entrance from above to harry Trinculo and Stephano. Released too soon, he seems lucky to escape a broken leg. Another moment that one misses in these days of productions "in the can" occurs when Alonso's ornate collar brushes a camera lens in the last scene.

The production ends, à la Margaret Webster, with the "Revels" speech. Evans moves forward as the camera dollies back. The rest of the characters become indistinct on a diminishing promontory.

This is a good production for 1960, but except for the Caliban underplot and a few moments in the Antonio-Sebastian conspiracy, the effect is bland, as television usually is.

The Bard production begins as Prospero's head dreams up the storm. Or—are we to take the entire play as Prospero's dream? The production is set on a Globe-like stage, with Tudor facades on the sides, a long balcony between, and a long inner stage below the balcony. The ship is on the balcony, an arrangement that gives the storm a strangely linear quality. Two long, blue streamers pulled up and down by spirits stimulate wave and wind. The problems with having Prospero in command from the outset are that the storm lacks even a theatrical sense of danger and that his subsequent explanation to Miranda is irrelevantly *ex post facto*.

Ephrem Zimbalist, Jr., is a naturalistic television actor, magus of a different island. His mild ingratiation finally begins to work toward play's end, but it is an attitude that should by then represent modulation. Here, it is bland consistency. J. E. Taylor's Miranda is not helped by a pulled-back hair style that emphasizes her severe bone structure. Prospero's luxuriant mane would have looked better on Taylor. William Hootkins's Caliban plays sullen rejection and renders the role with understated precision. He points at Trinculo on "and thy dog," thus motivating the latter's resentment. The scene between Caliban, Stephano, Trinculo, and the hidden Ariel is, as usual on television, very good. Duane Black's Ariel, a lithe dancer, would have been excellent in live performance.

The tudor facade is too often in the background. It forces us to unsuspend whatever disbelief the stagelike setting and the consistently front-on camera might have encouraged. And it begs the question of the nature-nurture, savage-civilized tension by its very presence. Woodman keeps the same lights on all the time, although they brighten as the conspirators awaken on "All torment." For this set and lack of lighting technique to work, the production needs a live audience, like that of the opening of Olivier's *Henry V* film. As it is, the lack of contrasting tonalities makes the production duller than it needs to be.

Woodman employs one effective technique by having events occur off-camera. The banquet is replaced by skulls, but we do not witness the substitution. The table disappears as the camera concentrates on Prospero as later (blessedly!) does the masque. Thus, staging problems are no problem here.

The "living drollery" become the dog-faced creatures that chase Caliban and company. This "doubling" gives us a brief glimpse of the metamorphic nature of both Prospero's and Shakespeare's "bare island."

The "Page to Stage" cassette mixes some old-fashioned thematic criticism with a "plot summary" provided by the 1982 Stratford, Canada, production. Narrator Nicholas Pennell tells us that the script "distills the imagery of [Shakespeare's] life's work." That, I believe, is accurate, but is it helpful to ask, "Is it possible that Prospero's desire for revenge motivates him towards positive action because he is himself an innately good person"? Is it accurate to claim that, at the end of *The Tempest*, "justice prevails and the natural order is restored"?

From what we see of the production, one of the high points is Pennell's Stephano, "a masterly miniature," as Ralph Berry says, with the "brutality of sentiment and language" of Iago.[5] Indeed, it seems that Pennell is creating a parody of Ian McKellan's Macbeth.

Caliban, however, is incredibly grotesque, a creature incapable, one has to assume, of copulating with Miranda. It is a gray and weed-bearded thing covered with rocks and shells that has emerged from the bottom of a tidal pool.

The production employs the large and multitiered Stratford main stage splendidly. The storm scene finds the boatswain on the upper stage, wrestling with a huge wheel. Antonio enters from a trap in the main platform. The audience, then, has a full-scale storm in front of it, one that we can appreciate, if not experience, on television. This staging does, as Berry says, "cost some of the lines." Berry calls the wedding masque "dazzling."[6] It seems to be an actual wedding, Miranda in bridal attire, Juno presiding from the upper stage.

Like other Stratford productions—the 1981 *Taming of the Shrew*, for example—this one shows how a quasi-Shakespearean stage can recreate the remarkable integration that Shakespeare achieved between script and stage, an aspect lost on other stages and certainly on television. Some would argue that the best television versions of Shakespeare are productions done before a live and responding audience and adapted to television. These productions can work well when viewers are given a "frame," like the audience settling in before the beginning of the Joseph Papp *A Midsummer Night's Dream*. While the production was not as good as the frame, viewers were granted an imitation of going to theater that had the potentiality of exciting energies seldom elicited by television.

The weaknesses of the Stratford *Tempest* seem to reside in Sharry Flett's Miranda, who sought not for Ferdinand but for Congreve or Sheridan, and Len Cariou's Prospero. His "Revels" speech is read in panic, an acceptable interpretation, perhaps, but badly overdone here. Cariou's delivery is often sing-songy, disinterested, and oddly stressed ("As you from *crimes* would pardon'd be"). He gives his fellow actors nothing on stage while carrying on an unrequited love affair with his audience. Yes, you *can* bring in a wall.

This tape gives us a glimpse of what *spectacle* might have been for Shakespeare's audience—the grand effect for which the modern dramatic stage seldom reaches and television never does. Like many Stratford productions, however, and like many stage productions taped for television, this one tends to reach into the large auditorium. It is not scaled to the intimacy of the television camera and microphone.

The BBC version has merit in spite of its hostile reception: "Everything goes wrong here";[7] "Horrendous . . . a lead footed production";[8] "Stiff. Aimed at the archives, and one can certainly see it gathering a lot of dust there in the years to come."[9]

Certainly, the critics have something to complain about. The opening scene is filmed yet presents no sense of emergency. Masts and sheets appear under the opening credits while the rain falls straight down, as if the King's ship were safely moored in harbor. Film, if carefully scaled, works on television. BBC wastes four minutes and forty seconds of film on this sequence.

The production tends to fall between stage, which can incorporate long speeches, and film, which demands visual equivalents for the language. Even in a basically verbal medium like television, Michael Hordern's expositions are tedious, though Pippa Guard does what she can as listener and is given the "Abhorred slave" speech, one that surprises and frightens Prospero. I had seen Hordern in Clifford Williams's tame 1978 RSC production and thought that the muted Prospero might work well on television, which can reward underplaying. But Hordern pulls his performance further back for television. "What has been very interesting," Hordern says, "is that, instead of trying to reach the back of the gallery with your innermost thoughts, you have only to cover the distance between you and the camera, which may be only eighteen inches away."[10] What we get is the irascible schoolmaster model, a "droningly grandfatherish" Mr. Badger,[11] only warmed by the mild affection he feels for his daughter.

Caliban's is the complaint of the aborigine, who, having instructed the colonist on the local environment, is consigned to its slums. This is a pot-bellied bum awaiting his introduction to his first six-pack. Warren Clarke's shaggy Caliban contrasts with David Dixon's frail, androgynous Ariel, with his boy-soprano voice. Each, of course, contrasts with Christopher Guard's tall, dark, and virile Ferdinand.

Director John Gorrie's concentration on body types runs into disaster with a group of virtually naked men who form the "living drollery" of the banquet scene, prancing to the lascivious pleasings of a pipe. It is, as Cecil Smith notes, "quite embarrassing in a professional production."[12] Almost as embarrassing is the masque, meant to resemble an English Morris Dance.[13] It is all remarkably awkward. Spirits step on other spirits' lines. Spirits cast heavy shadows, and those naked boys return as pale sicklemen bent on an orgy with nymphs peeled from a Victorian mural. The boys return, dog-visaged, their concupiscent purpose delayed but not forgotten, to leap upon Caliban, Stephano, and Trinculo.

For all the lapses in taste that make students laugh and teachers cringe, the production is effective at times. Its "staging" is often good. As Miranda and Ferdinand exchange the sight of first love, Prospero, downstage left, tells us that he must prevent "too light winning." Antonio and Sebastian plot downstage, framing Alonso and party. Trinculo's lines about Caliban (2.2.148 ff.) are delivered as sour asides. This technique grants the jester surprising "interiority." The main plot and the subplot conspiracies are splendidly orchestrated. Nigel Hawthorne's Stephano is particularly good as he attempts to press his concentration on Caliban through his stupor. Clarke's "Be not afeard" is fine, as Caliban expresses a sense of selfhood symbiotically interfused with his island. Since the banquet disappears beneath Ariel's enclosing wings, Prospero's "A grace it had devouring" has a visual antecedent. At the end, Miranda's "how beauteous mankind is" is directed at Antonio. It is a wonderfully ironic instant.

While television productions of Shakespeare can incorporate splendid "spots of time," the good moments tend to be unintegrated. Television cannot give us an incorporating frame as stage can, a sense of the total space within which the large and small, the spectacle and the soliloquy will occur. An occasional exception—Trevor Nunn's superbly scaled and neatly stylized *Antony and Cleopatra*, the heightened "soap opera" of Desmond Davis's *Measure for Measure*, the unit set and the theatricality of Jane Howell's *Henry VI*, particularly Part II—tend to prove the point. Why BBC refused to learn from Nunn's 1974 production remains a mystery. To use Doré as a model for television settings, as Gorrie did for the BBC *Tempest*,[14] is to create a somber background that must pull much of the production back into it, particularly given so much dark costuming.

Something else that television cannot do and something essential to this script as electronic vehicle are special effects. The Bard version, a stillborn stage rendering, suffers from its director's unwillingness to vary his lighting. The same set can be remarkably protean through lighting alone, as Jane Howell shows in her

II Henry VI, and, for that matter, as Bard shows in its *Othello*. Schaefer's special effects are better than for his 1954 *Macbeth*, but they are still silly, particularly for the latter-day audience that knows that television doesn't try to do such things. At one point, Prospero attempts to help Ariel waft from the former's arm. But the timing is off. Ariel leaves too late, and Prospero seems to be fending off an irritating insect. Gorrie tends to eschew special effects. "We felt," says his producer, Cedric Messina, "it wasn't fair to the play to do too much. If you make it an electronic night's dream, you are asking for trouble."[15] A wise decision, but it leaves Gorrie with his heavy Doré set and the blank wash of studio-land, not "a real place where magic things happen."[16]

It might be said that Shakespeare is a magic place where real things happen. So far, however, television seems to have blocked the magic of this script.

Notes

Introduction

1. Henry Fielding, *Tom Jones* (New York: Random House, 1950), 758–59.
2. Ibid. 758.
3. Ibid. 759.
4. See Barbara A. Mowat, *The Dramaturgy of Shakespeare's Romances* (Athens: University of Georgia Press, 1980), Appendix, for a discussion of the aesthetic distance of a theater audience. See also Theodore Shank, *The Art of the Dramatic Art* (New York: Delta-Dell, 1969).
5. Michael Goldman, *Acting and Action in Shakespearean Tragedy* (Princeton: Princeton University Press, 1985), 3–16.
6. Peter Brook, *The Shifting Point* (New York: Harper & Row, 1987), 41.
7. Richard Levin, "Performance-Critics vs. Close Readers in the Study of English Renaissance Drama," *Modern Language Review* 81, no. 3 (July 1986): 547.
8. Levin, "Performance-Critics vs. Close Readers," 548.
9. William Worthen, "Deeper Meanings and Theatrical Technique: The Rhetoric of Performance Criticism," *Shakespeare Quarterly* 40, no. 4 (Winter 1989): 453.
10. See Levin, "Performance-Critics vs. Close Readers," for the mixed evidence that the sixteenth and early seventeenth century provide on the issue.
11. Ann Thompson, *King Lear* (Atlantic Highlands, N.J.: Humanities Press International, 1988), 81.
12. John Dover Wilson, *What Happens in Hamlet* (Cambridge: Cambridge University Press, 1935), 94.
13. John L. Styan, "Psychology in the Study of Drama: the Negative and the Positive," *College Literature* 5 (1978): 92.
14. Miriam Gilbert, "Re-viewing the Play," *Shakesperae Quarterly* 36, no. 5 (1985): 609–17.
15. Thomas Clayton, "'Should Brutus Never Taste of Portia's Death But Once?': Text and Performance in *Julius Caesar*," *Studies in English Literature* 23 (1983): 254–55.
16. Albert Camus, "Reflections on the Guillotine," *Resistance, Rebellion, and Death* (New York: Alfred A. Knopf, 1951), 184–85.
17. On Polanski's *Macbeth*, see Jack J. Jorgens, *Shakespeare on Film* (Bloomington: Indiana University Press, 1977), and my "Polanski's *Macbeth*: A Dissent," *The University of Dayton Review* 14, no. 1 (Winter 1979–80): 95–97. In the same issue, see also Virginia Wright Wexman, "Macbeth and Polanski's Theme of Regression," 85–88; and David Middleton, "The Self-Reflexive Nature of Roman Polanski's *Macbeth*," 89–94. See also Normand Berlin, "*Macbeth*: Polanski and Shakespere," and Michael Mullin, "*Macbeth* on Film," both in *Literature/Film Quarterly* 1, no. 4 (Fall 1973): 291–98, 332–42; Kenneth Rothwell, "Roman Polanski's *Macbeth*: Golgotha Triumphant," *Literature/Film Quarterly* 1 no. 1 (January

1973): 71–75; Bruna Gushust, "Polanski's Determining of Power in *Macbeth*," *Shakespeare on Film Newsletter* 13, no. 2 (April 1989): 7; Pauline Kael, "The Current Cinema," *The New Yorker*, 5 February 1972, 76; and Stanley Kauffmann, *The New Republic*, 1 January 1972, 32.

18. The moment is visually powerful. Cf. Wexman ("Macbeth and Polanski's Theme of Regression"): "Finally decapitated, [Macbeth] is literally reduced to a head, and in this state he is swept through a jeering crowd on the end of a stick" (87). Jorgens *(Shakespeare on Film)* remarks on "the remarkable silent, fast motion, point of view shots of jeering soldiers as Macbeth's head is rushed towards the ramparts" (172).

19. Jorgens, *Shakespeare on Film*, 168.

20. Ibid., 166. The film is, as I will argue, for better or for worse, a precise working out of the thesis enunciated by Harry Berger, Jr., in "Text Against Performance: The Example of *Macbeth*," *Genre* 15, nos. 1–2 (Spring–Summer 1982): 49–79.

Chapter 1. Preliminaries

1. Malcolm Evans, *Signifying Nothing* (Athens: University of Georgia Press, 1986), 252.

2. Richard Levin, "Refuting Shakespeare's Endings," parts 1, 2, *Modern Philology* 72, no. 4, and 75, no. 2 (May 1975, November 1977): 337–49, 132–58; *New Readings vs. Old Plays: Recent Trends in the Reinterpretation of Renaissance Drama* (Chicago: University of Chicago Press, 1979).

3. Levin, "Refuting Shakespeare's Endings," part 2, 157.

4. Barbara Hodgdon, "Parallel Practices, or the *Un*-necessary Difference," *Kenyon Review* 7, no. 3 (Summer 1985): 65.

5. Levin, "Refuting Shakespeare's Endings," part 1, 341. For an implicit response to Levin's interpretation of *Measure for Measure*, see Jane Williamson, "The Duke and Isabella on the Modern Stage," in *The Triple Bond*, ed. Joseph Price (University Park: Pennsylvania State University Press, 1975), 149–69.

6. For an extension of this argument regarding *Love's Labours Lost*, see my "*Love's Labours Lost* and the Comic Truth," *Papers on Language and Literature* 6, no. 3 (1970): 316–22.

7. Levin, "Refuting Shakespeare's Endings," part 1, 341, n. 3. See also "Directing the Problem Plays: John Barton talks to Gareth Lloyd Evans," *Shakespeare Studies* 25 (1972): 66.

8. Lillian Wilds, "Shakespeare in Southern California," *Shakespeare Quarterly* 33 (1982): 385.

9. Jeanette Knapp, "Virginia Shakespeare Festival," *Shakespeare Quarterly* 35 (1984): 473.

10. Wolfgang Reihle, "Shakespeare in Austria," *Shakespeare Quarterly* 33 (1982): 507.

11. Josef de Vos, "Shakespeare in Belgium," *Shakespeare Quarterly* 33 (1982): 521.

12. On this issue, see Sally Beauman, *The Royal Shakespeare Company's Production of "Henry V"* (Oxford: Pergamon Press, 1976); Joseph G. Prince, ed., *The Triple Bond: Plays Mainly Shakespearean, in Performance* (University Park: Pennsylvania State University Press, 1975); and Stanley Wells, *Furman Studies: Royal Shakespeare* (Greenville, S.C.: Furman University Press 1976).

13. Michael Goldman, *The Actor's Freedom* (New York: Viking, 1975); John Russell Brown, *Free Shakespeare* (London: Heineman, 1974).

14. Bertrand Evans, "Afterword to *A Midsummer Night's Dream*," in *The College Shakespeare* (New York: Macmillan, 1973), 51–52.

15. From H. R. Coursen, "Two D.C. Comedies," *Marlowe Society of America Newsletter* 6 (1986): 8.

16. From H. R. Coursen, "Shakespeare's Scripts and British Directors," *Shakespeare Bulletin* 5–6 (1987–88): 34.

17. Frank Rich, "Kelly McGillis Stars in *Twelfth Night*," *New York Times*, 4 October 1989, C17.

18. Joe Brown, "Transporting 'Twelfth': At Folger, a Pleasing Move for the Bard," *Washington Post*, 26 September 1989, D10.

19. Rich, "Kelly McGillis Stars in *Twelfth Night*," C17.

20. Cf. Mel Gussow, "A *Hamlet* Stamped with a Bergman Seal," *New York Times*, 10 June 1988. Gussow rightly calls the conclusion "aberrant."

21. See, for example, David Ansen, "Scaling the Bard," *Newsweek*, 24 April 1978, 108.

22. Quoted in Henry Fenwick, "The Production," in *Hamlet* (New York: Mayflower Books, 1982), 20.

23. For a discussion of this aspect of the production and other contemporary critical comments, see John A. Mills, *Hamlet on Stage: The Great Tradition* (Westport, Conn.: Greenwood Press, 1985), 252–61. For a discussion of the production as it developed, see Richard L. Sterne, *John Gielgud Directs Richard Burton in "Hamlet"* (New York: Random House, 1967).

24. Cf. Charles R. Forker, "Shakespeare's Theatrical Symbolism and its Function in *Hamlet*," *Shakespeare Quarterly* 14, no. 3 (Summer 1963): 215–29; and J. Scott Colley, "Drama, Fortune, and Providence in *Hamlet*," *College Literature* 5, no. 1 (Winter 1978): 48–56.

25. Iris Murdoch, *The Black Prince* (London: Penguin Books, 1975), 200.

26. Michael Pennington, "Hamlet," in *Players of Shakespeare*, ed. Philip Brockbank (Cambridge: Cambridge University Press, 1985), 119.

27. From H. R. Coursen, "The Decisions a Director Makes," *Shakespeare Bulletin* 8 (1989), 26–29.

28. Harry Berger, Jr., "Text Against Performance in Shakespeare," 51.

29. Ibid., 51. Phillip McGuire accounts for the freedom of directors and actors to interpret the "playtext" without violating the text's integrity in *Speechless Dialect* (Berkeley: University of California Press, 1985), 122–50. McGuire's is a strong refutation of Berger's thesis. See also *Shakespeare and the Sense of Performance*. Marvin and Ruth Thompson, ed. (Newark: University of Delaware Press, 1989), for a splendid collection of essays that approach performance from a variety of viewpoints, contemporary and historical.

30. Ibid., 61. The Sheldon Zitner article is "Aumerle's Conspiracy," *SEL* 14 (1974): 254–55.

31. Ibid., 62. The Alvin Kerman quotation comes from *The Playwright as Magician* (New Haven: Yale University Press, 1979), 118.

32. Kernan (*The Playwright as Magician*, 119–22) makes precisely this point in discussing the "morality plays" presented to Othello and Gloucester by Iago and Edgar.

33. Berger, "Text Against Performance," 50. See also John Barton, "Rehearsing the Text," LD 259, R.S.C. Performing Shakespeare Series, no. 4, (Films for the Humanities).

34. See H. R. Coursen, "Theories of History in *Richard II*," *The Upstart Crow* 8 (1988): 42–53.

35. Berger, "Text Against Performance," 76.

36. Ibid., 56. See Louis Montrose, "The Purpose of Playing: Reflections on a Shakespearean Anthropology," *Helios* 7 (1980): 60–64.

37. Berger, "Text Against Performance," 59.

38. Ibid.

39. Ibid., 60.

40. Cf. Mark Crispin Miller, "The Shakespeare Plays," *The Nation*, 12 July 1980.

41. Madelon Gohlke (Sprengnether), " 'I Wooed Thee with my Sword': Shakespeare's Tragic Paradigms," in *Representing Shakespeare: New Psychoanalytic Essays*, ed. Murray Schwartz and Coppélia Kahn (Baltimore, Johns Hopkins University Press, 1980), 177.

42. See H. R. Coursen, *The Compensatory Psyche: A Jungian Approach to Shakespeare* (Washington: University Press of America, 1986), 151–77.

43. Berger, "Text Against Performance," 65.

44. Ibid., 75.

45. Ibid., 73.

46. Ibid., 76–77. See Stephen Greenblatt, *Renaissance Self Fashioning: From More to Shakespeare* (Chicago: University of Chicago Press, 1980).

47. Berger, "Text Against Performance," 77.

48. Worthen, "Deeper Meanings and Theatrical Technique," 455.

49. June Schlueter, Review, *Choice* (March 1990): 1138.

50. Harry Berger, Jr., *Imaginary Auditions: Shakespeare on Stage and Page* (Berkeley: University of California Press, 1989).

51. Ibid., xiii.

52. Ibid., xiii.

53. Ibid., xiv.

54. Barbara Hodgdon, "Parallel Practices, or the *Un*-necessary Difference," *Kenyon Review* 7, no. 3 (Summer 1985), 65.

55. Ibid.

56. Nina Auerbach, *Romantic Imprisonment: Women and Other Glorified Outcasts* (New York: Columbia University Press, 1986), xix.

57. See Mills, *Hamlet on Stage*; and Michael Cohen, *Hamlet: In My Mind's Eye*, (Athens: University of Georgia, 1989).

Chapter 2. Kate and Consensus

1. Levin, "Feminist Thematics and Shakespearean Tragedy," *PMLA* 103 (1988): 127–28. In fairness to Mr. Levin, I should note that he isolates what he considers a representative group of feminist critics who demonstrate representative tendencies. He admits the diversity of the approach as it is employed by individual critics. In fairness to the feminist critical mode, I must say that several of its practitioners recognize what I call the "gender fallacy." Cf. Jonathan Goldberg, "Shakespearean Inscriptions: The Voicing of Power," in *Shakespeare and the Question of Theory*, ed. Patricia Parker and Geoffrey Hartman (New York: Methuen, 1985), 116–37; and Judith Newton and Deborah Rosenfelt's Introduction to *Feminist Criticism and Social Change* (New York: Methuen, 1985), which, as Peter Erickson says, "provides a useful contrast [to Goldberg] because they object to the polarization of the terms male and female as Goldberg does, but without

thereby implying that gender differences do not obtain or that differentiated gender categories can be eliminated." ("Review of *Shakespeare and the Question of Theory* and *Alternative Shakespeares*," *Shakespeare Quarterly* 37 [1986]: 518). One brilliant response to the debate is that of Catherine Belsey, who says of Viola/ Cesario: "who tells the blank history of Viola's father's pining daughter? The answer is neither Viola nor Cesario, but a speaker who at the moment occupies a place which is not precisely masculine or feminine where the notion of identity itself is disrupted to display a difference within subjectivity, and the singularity which resides in *this* difference. . . . The point is not to create some third, unified androgynous identity which eliminates all distinctions. Nor indeed is it to the internalization of difference a plurality of places, of possible beings, for each person in the margins of sexual difference, those margins which a metaphysical sexual polarity obliterates" ("Disrupting Sexual Difference: Meaning and Gender in the Comedies," *Alternative Shakespeares*, ed. John Drakakis [London: Methuen, 1985], 187, 189).

2. Quoted in Martin Banham, "BBC's Dull Shakespeares," *Critical Quarterly* 22 (1980), 36.

3. Coppélia Kahn, *Man's Estate* (Berkeley: University of California Press, 1981), 104.

4. Ibid., 118.

5. Ibid., 118.

6. Berners Jackson, "Shakespeare at Stratford, Ontario, 1973," *Shakespeare Quarterly* 24 (1973): 407.

7. Ibid.

8. D'Orsay Pearson, letter to author, 20 December 1987.

9. Joel Fineman, "The Turn of the Shrew," *Shakespeare and the Question of Theory*, ed. Patricia Parker and Geoffrey Hartman (New York: Methuen), 1985, 155–56.

10. Jeanne Roberts, "Metamorphoses in *The Taming of the Shrew*," *Shakespeare Quarterly* 34 (1983): 171. Cf. Marianne Novy, "Patriarchy and Play in *The Taming of the Shrew*," *English Literary Renaissance* 9 (1979): 264–80.

11. Jonathan Miller, "Interview with Tim Hallinan," *Shakespeare Quarterly* 32 (1981): 140. In commenting on a 1980 production in Berlin, Eva and Gunter Walch say that the final speech reflected "an image of the times in which such attitudes and convictions were held. The overall effect of [such] distancing did not, however, help us to understand Kate any better" ("Shakespeare in the German Democratic Republic," *Shakespeare Quarterly* 32 [1981]: 381).

12. Miller, "Interview with Tim Hallinan," 140–41.

13. Kenneth Rothwell, "The Shakespeare Plays," *Shakespeare Quarterly* 32 (1981): 397.

14. Irene Dash, "The Shakepeare Plays on TV," *Shakespeare on Film Newsletter* 6 (1982): 6, 10.

15. Cf. G. R. Hibbard on 4.5.18–20: "She has taken his measure, and, understanding his games, is ready to join in them, which is what she does for the rest of the play" (Introduction, *The Taming of the Shrew* [New York: Penguin; 1968], 123).

16. Graham Holderness, "Boxing the Bard: Shakespeare and Television," in *Shakespeare on Television*, ed. James Bulman and H. R. Coursen (Hanover, N.H.: University Press of New England, 1988).

17. Ralph Berry, "Stratford Festival: Canada," *Shakespeare Quarterly* 33 (1982): 200.

18. Roger Boxill, "Shakespeare in New York City," *Shakespeare Quarterly* 37 (1986): 511.

19. H. R. Coursen, "Shakespeare in Maine," *Shakespeare Quarterly* 25 (1974): 431.

20. Elizabeth Hageman, "Shakespeare in Massachusetts: 1983," *Shakespeare Quarterly* 35 (1984): 223.

21. Sears Jayne, "The Dreaming of the *Shrew*," *Shakespeare Quarterly* 18 (1966): 55.

22. John H. Maguire, "Idaho Shakespeare Festival," *Shakespeare Quarterly* 32 (1981): 248.

23. Elizabeth Hageman, "Shakespeare in Boston and Cambridge," *Shakespeare Quarterly* 32 (1981): 191.

24. Albert C. Labriola, "Shakespeare in Pittsburgh," *Shakespeare Quarterly* 32 (1981): 205.

25. Joseph H. Stodder and Lillian Wilds, "Shakespeare in Southern California and Visalia," *Shakespeare Quarterly* 31 (1980): 257.

26. Nicholas Shrimpton, "Shakespeare in Performance: 1985–86," *Shakespeare Survey* 40 (1988): 172–73.

27. Robert-H. Leek, "A Centenary Unobserved," *Shakespeare Quarterly* 31 (1980): 420.

28. Jeanne Roberts, "Shakespeare in the Nation's Capitol," *Shakespeare Quarterly* 32 (1981): 207.

29. Ibid.

30. Virginia M. Carr, "Boston Shakespeare Company," *Shakespeare Quarterly* 29 (1978): 231.

31. Lester E. Barber, "Great Lakes Shakespeare Festival," *Shakespeare Quarterly* 29 (1978): 247.

32. Ibid.

33. A. L. Braunmuller, "Shakespeare in Los Angeles," *Shakespeare Quarterly* 29 (1978): 264.

34. John A. Mills, "Shakespeare in Utah," *Shakespeare Quarterly* 29 (1978): 254.

35. Charles Frey, "Shakespeare in Seattle," *Shakespeare Quarterly* 32 (1981): 275.

36. Balz Engler, "Shakespeare in Switzerland," *Shakespeare Quarterly* 30 (1979): 303.

37. Robert J. Fehranbach, "Virginia Shakespeare Festival," *Shakespeare Quarterly* 30 (1979): 197.

38. W. L. Godshalk, "The Shakespeare Festival of Cincinnati," *Shakespeare Quarterly* 30 (1979): 210–11.

39. Gunnar Sorelius, "Shakespeare in Sweden," *Shakespeare Quarterly* 32 (1981): 370.

40. James Lusardi and June Schlueter, "New Jersey Shakespeare Festival," *Shakespeare Bulletin* 5–6 (1987–88): 26.

41. Andrew Kennedy, "Shakespeare in Bergen," *Shakespeare Quarterly* 31 (1980): 436.

42. J. C. Trewin, *Going to Shakespeare* (London: George Allen & Unwin, 1978), 57.

43. Wilds, "Shakespeare in Southern California," 259.

44. Ibid.

45. Leek, "A Centenary Unobserved," 420.

46. Quoted in Carol Rutter, *Clamorous Voices: Shakespeare's Women Today* (London: Woman's Press, 1989), 20.

47. Ibid., 22.

48. Ibid., 23.

49. Ibid.

50. Cf. G. R. Hibbard's excellent introduction: Sly "is thrown out of the only heaven he had known hitherto, the tavern, goes to sleep on the cold ground, and awakens to find himself in a heaven on earth, where the drink is free and plentiful. . . . The brief yet vigorous altercation between Sly and the Hostess . . . is a little curtain raiser for the struggle between Petruchio and Katherina" (*The Taming of the Shrew* [New York: Penguin, 1968], 13, 14).

51. Ibid., 44.

52. H. J. Oliver, ed., *The Taming of the Shrew* (Oxford: Oxford University Press, 1984), 43.

53. Ibid.

54. Curt Perrin, "The Metadrama of *The Shrew,*" Unpublished paper. Bowdoin College, 20 November 1989.

55. Jack Oruch, "Shakespeare for the Millions: 'Kiss Me, Petruchio,'" *Shakespeare on Film Newsletter* 11, no. 2 (April 1987): 5.

56. See also Tori Haring-Smith, *From Farce to Melodrama: A Stage History of the "Taming of the Shrew": 1594–1983*, Contributions in Drama and Theatre Studies, no. 16 (Westport, Conn.: Greenwood Press, 1985); and Bernice Kliman's review, *Shakespeare Bulletin* 5, (September-October 1987): 23–24.

Chapter 3. Hermia's Dream

1. Sigmund Freud, *The Interpretation of Dreams,* trans. A. A. Brill (New York: Carlton House, 1931), 3.

2. Ibid., 404.

3. Ibid., 245.

4. Norman Holland, *Psychoanalysis and Shakespeare* (New York: McGraw-Hill, 1966), 123.

5. Freud, *Interpretation of Dreams,* 219.

6. Norman Holland, "Hermia's Dream," in *Representing Shakespeare: New Psychoanalytic Essays,* ed. Murray Schwartz and Coppélia Kahn (Baltimore: Johns Hopkins University Press, 1980), 5–11. Johannes Fabricius finds Hermia's dream an example of the "splitting of the libido" typical of "Oberon's wood": "The more passionate, subjective and imaginary their love becomes, the more irrational and schizoid it discharges itself, and the more animal-like it appears, growing ass's ears like Titania's love-object, or transforming the beloved into a snake, like Hermia's unconscious split image of Lysander. When the lovers are not imagining their libidinal objects as perfect and divine, they are invariably hallucinated into seeing them as hideous and vile animals—bears, tigers, cats, and snakes. This emotional splitting naturally influences the diction of the four lovers, who are either cooing or screaming when talking to each other" (*Shakespeare's Hidden World: A Study of His Unconscious* [Copenhagen: Munksgaard, 1989], 136).

7. C. G. Jung, *Freud and Psychoanalysis,* trans. R. F. C. Hull (Princeton: Bollingen Series, 1961), 238.

8. C. G. Jung, *Contributions to Analytical Psychology,* trans. H. G. and C. F. Baynes (London: Routledge & Kegan Paul, 1928), 361.

9. C. G. Jung, *The Structure and Dynamics of the Psyche,* trans. R. F. C. Hull (Princeton: Bollingen Series, 1969), 155.

10. C. G. Jung, *Symbols of Transformation* (Princeton: Bollingen Series, 1967), 396.

11. Ibid., 269.

12. Ibid., 397–98.

13. Ibid., 298.

14. Jung, *Contributions to Analytical Psychology*, 107.

15. C. G. Jung, *Analytical Psychology: Its Theory and Practice* (New York: Pantheon, 1968), 130–31.

16. Jung, *The Structure and Dynamics of the Psyche*, 437.

17. Edward F. Edinger, *Ego and Archetype* (Baltimore: Pelican, 1973), 18.

18. Ibid., 26.

19. Ibid., 25.

20. Marjorie Garber, *Dream in Shakespeare* (New Haven: Yale University Press, 1974), 74. On "the silence of Egeus," see Philip C. McGuire, "Intentions, Options, and Greatness: An Example from *A Midsummer Night's Dream*," in *Shakespeare and the Triple Play: From Study to Stage to Classroom*, ed. Sidney Homan (Lewisburg: Bucknell University Press, 1988).

Chapter 4. "Must There No More Be Done?": Images of Ophelia

1. Elaine Showalter, "Representing Ophelia: Women, Madness, and the Responsibilities of Feminist Criticism," in *Shakespeare and the Question of Theory*, ed. Patricia Parker and Geoffrey Hartman (London: Methuen, 1985), 77–94.

2. Lee Edwards, "The Labors of Psyche," *Critical Inquiry* 6 (1979): 36.

3. Carol Neely, "Feminist Modes of Shakespearean Criticism," *Women's Studies* 9 (1981): 11.

4. Rebecca West, *The Court and the Castle* (New Haven: Yale University Press, 1957), 18.

5. Ibid., 18–19.

6. Ibid., 18–21, 173.

7. Ibid., 25.

8. Showalter, "Representing Ophelia," 79.

9. Ibid., 92.

10. Quoted in Peter Brunette, "Towards a Deconstructive Theory of Film," *Studies in the Literary Imagination* 19 (1985): 61.

11. Jorgens, *Shakespeare on Film*, 21.

12. Robert A. Duffy, "Gade, Olivier, Richardson: Visual Strategy in *Hamlet* Adaptation," *Literature/Film Quarterly* 4 (1976): 147.

13. For the Jungian approach to *Hamlet*, see Coursen, *Compensatory Psyche*.

14. Kathleen McLuskie, "The Patriarchal Bard," in *Political Shakespeare*, ed. Jonathan Dollimore and Alan Sinfield (Manchester: Manchester University Press, 1985), 95.

15. Ibid., 97.

16. E. Ann Kaplan, "Feminist Film Criticism: Current Issues and Problems," *Studies in the Literary Imagination* 19 (1986): 9.

17. Lillian Wilds, "Richardson's *Hamlet*," *Literature/Film Quarterly* 4 (1976): 140, 138.

18. Michael Mullin, "The Richardson, Williamson *Hamlet*," *Literature/Film Quarterly* 4 (1976): 128.

19. Jorgens, *Shakespeare on Film*, 21–22.

20. Mullin, "The Richardson, Williamson *Hamlet*," 128.

21. Glenn Litton, "Richardson's *Hamlet*," *Literature/Film Quarterly* 4 (1976): 119.

22. Ibid., 118.

23. Ibid.

24. Ibid., 119.

25. Grigori Kozintsev, *Shakespeare: Time and Conscience*, trans. Joyce Vining (London: Dennis Dobson, 1967), 215–16.

26. Ibid., 234.

27. Ibid., 218.

28. Ibid., 235.

29. Ibid., 235–36.

30. Ibid., 244.

31. Ibid., 241.

32. Ibid., 244.

33. Ibid., 218.

34. Jorgens, *Shakespeare on Film*, 229. See the picture of Ophelia in her cage, 221.

35. Ibid., 228.

36. Henry Fenwick, *Hamlet* (London: BBC, 1980), 26.

37. Ibid.

38. Ibid., 26–27.

39. West, *The Court and the Castle*, 21.

40. Ibid., 24.

41. The Swedish tendency to focus on Ophelia continues in Ingmar Bergman's recent Dramaten version of the play. According to Robert Brustein, "Ophelia is witness to [the murder of Polonius], as she witnesses almost every brutal event in this brutalized court. But this is no consumptive, sensitive suffering plant. As played by Pernilla Ostergren . . . she is a somewhat chunky lass, feisty and argumentative, and, until her father's death, possessed of a strong will. . . . Ostergren plays her mad scene—in Bergman's hands a powerful study of degenerative female psychosis—in a heavy brocaded gown and marching boots, carrying the bloody handkerchief Polonius used to staunch the wound to his eye. She also carries a dangerous pair of shears, with which she cuts off large tufts of hair, and instead of offering flowers to Gertrude and Claudius, she hands out iron nails. A central character throughout, she even appears at the rainy funeral ceremony that follows her death. . . . Instead of the usual chiaroscuro, a harsh light illuminates the entire stage area, including pipes and exit signs. And Ophelia materializes at the back, in bare feet, blue slip, and flowered crown—now a ghost haunting her own burial service" ("Twenty-First Century *Hamlet*," *The New Republic*, 18 and 25 July 1988, 28).

42. Anna K. Nardo, "Hamlet, 'A Man to Double Business Bound,'" *Shakespeare Quarterly* 34 (1983): 181–99.

Chapter 5. Jacobi and the Players

1. James Atlas, "The New Canonicity," *New York Times Magazine*, 5 June 1988, 94.

2. Sheldon Zitner, "Wooden O's in Plastic Boxes: Shakespeare and Television," *University of Toronto Quarterly* 51 (Fall 1981): 9.

3. Jay L. Halio, "A New *Hamlet* Journal," *Shakespeare Quarterly* 31 (1980): 464.

4. Harry Berger, Jr., "Psychoanalyzing the Shakespeare Text: The First Three Scenes of the *Henriad*," in *Shakespeare and the Question of Theory*, 219. Berger juxtaposes "structural irony" against "the prospective mode of dramatic irony," which Hamlet sets up in his outline of "Gonzago's" possibilities.

5. As glossed in G. B. Evans, *Complete Works* (Boston: Houghton, Mifflin, 1974), 1151.

6. As glossed in David Bevington, *Complete Works*, 3d ed. (Glenview, Illinois: Scott, Foresman, 1980), 195.

7. Ibid., 307.

8. Ibid., 578.

9. Ibid., 776.

10. Cf. Harry Morris, *Last Things in Shakespeare* (Tallahassee: Florida State University Press, 1985), 311–41.

11. Meredith Anne Skura, Review of *The Whole Journey: Shakespeare's Power of Development*, by C. L. Barber and Richard P. Wheeler, *Shakespeare Quarterly* 39 (1988): 92.

12. Ibid.

13. This interpretation would link Hamlet with the "narcissist," as described by Richard Restak: "only the subjective interpretation changes . . . based on alterations in the inner representations of the experience. . . . [The] introject [that] happens to be ascendant on any given moment is all powerful [and total]. The individual is convinced, at the moment, that the other person is either a hated enemy or a valuable and loving ally. There is no room for compromise or shades of meaning in this all-or-none world. The split which exists is a total, uncompromising one, with the inner world of introjects divided into the 'all good' or 'all bad'" (quoted in Harry Cohen, "The Narcissistic Syndrome: Causes, Problems, and Solutions," *Contemporary Philosophy* 12 [1988]: 3. Cohen goes on to say, "The problem is that 'good' and 'bad' fail to merge. [The result is] fragmented and contradictory relationships and attitudes to self and others." If narcissism also involves an effort to copy the perceived externals of successful behavior (as Lasch argues), then Hamlet is trapped between the memory of his father and the realities of Elsinore. I discuss the useful coincidence of Freudian and Jungian perspectives in *The Compensatory Psyche*, 63–99.

14. Bernice Kliman, "The BBC *Hamlet*, a Television Production," *Hamlet Studies* 4 (1982): 100.

15. Marchette Chute, *Shakespeare of London* (New York: E. P. Dutton, 1949), 227.

16. Mowat, *Dramaturgy of Shakespeare's Romances*, 65.

17. Lionel Abel, *Metadrama* (New York: Hill & Wang, 1963), 51.

18. Mowat, *Dramaturgy of Shakespeare's Romances*, 36. Here, obviously, I disagree that Hamlet is "overdistanced," as she argues on pages 124–25.

19. Alexander Bakshy, quoted in Mowat, *Dramaturgy of Shakespeare's Romances*, 36.

20. Skura, 92.

21. Derek Jacobi, as quoted in *The Dial*, WNET (November 1980): 28.

22. Harold Goddard, *The Meaning of Shakespeare* (Chicago: University of Chicago Press, 1951), p. 369.

23. Skura, Review of *Shakespeare's Power of Development*, 92.

24. Eleanor Prosser, *Hamlet and Revenge* (Palo Alto: University of California Press, 1967), 153.

25. Arthur Johnston, "The Player's Speech in *Hamlet*," *Shakespeare Quarterly* 13 (1962): 27.

26. Ibid., 28.

27. Andrew Gurr, "Theaters and the Dramatic Profession," in *William Shakespeare: His World, Work, and Influence*, ed. John F. Andrews (New York: Scribners, 1985), 1:128.

28. Ira Progoff, *Jung's Psychology and its Social Meaning* (New York: Anchor Books, 1973), 54.

29. Jung, *Contributions to Analytical Psychology*, 35.

30. Jolande Jacobi, *The Psychology of Jung* (New Haven: Yale University Press, 1943), 55.

31. Ibid.

32. Cf. O. B. Hardison, "Three Types of Renaissance Catharsis," *Renaissance Drama*, n.s., vol. 3 (Evanston, Ill.: Northwestern University Press, 1969), 3–22.

33. C. G. Jung, *Two Essays on Analytical Psychology*, (New York: Pantheon, 1953), 76.

34. Ibid., 162.

35. Jung, *Structure and Dynamics of the Psyche*, 23.

36. Carolyn Heilbrun, *Toward a Recognition of Androgyny* (New York: Knopf, 1973), 32.

37. Jacques Lacan, "Desire and the Interpretation of Desire in *Hamlet*," in *Literature and Psychoanalysis: The Question of Reading: Otherwise*, ed. Shoshana Felman (Baltimore: Johns Hopkins University Press, 1982), 316.

38. Jorgens, *Shakespeare on Film*, 34–35.

39. C. L. Barber and Richard Wheeler, as paraphrased by Skura, Review of *Shakespeare's Power of Development*, 92.

40. Holland, *Psychoanalysis and Shakespeare* 238. On the point that "the audience [may] provide . . . the only valid area for the application of psychology to the art of drama," see J. L. Styan, "Psychology in the Study of Drama; the Negative and the Positive," *College Literature* 5 (1978): 77–93.

41. J. Jacobi, *Complex/Symbol/Archetype in the Psychology of C. G. Jung* (New York: Pantheon, 1959), 20. Within this construct, it is then appropriate, as Kahn says, that "King Hamlet differs from Shakespeare's other cuckolded heroes in not turning against his erring wife and accusing her of whoredom: his son performs this function for him" (*Man's Estate*, 139, n. 20).

42. Leslie Fiedler, "The Defense of the Illusion and the Creation of Myth," *English Institute Essays*, 1948 (New York: Columbia, 1949), 76.

43. Harold Rosenberg, quoted in Edith Sitwell, *A Notebook on William Shakespeare* (Boston: Beacon Press, 1961), 82.

44. On the "bonding" between Hamlet and Horatio, see Peter Erickson, *Patriarchal Structures in Shakespeare's Drama* (Berkeley: University of California, 1985), 66–80.

Chapter 6. Edmund's Nature

1. Evans, *Signifying Nothing*, 252.

2. Ibid., 253.

3. Ibid.

4. Ibid., 256.

5. "Shakespeare and the People: Elizabethan Drama on Video," *Shakespeare on Film Newsletter* 1, no. 2 (April 1977): 4.

6. On the very different techniques employed by Elliot and Miller for their television versions of *Lear*, see Hardy M. Cook, "Two *Lears* for Television: An Exploration of Televisual Strategies," *Literature/Film Quarterly* 14 (1986): 179–86.

7. Zitner, "Wooden O's in Plastic Boxes," 1–12.

8. For example, Hannah Arendt, *Eichmann in Jerusalem* (New York: Knopf, 1963); Rudolph Höss, *Kommandant in Auschwitz: Autobiographische Aufzeichnungen von Rudolf Höss* (Stutgart: Deutsche Verlags Anstalt, 1959); Joachim Fest, *The Face of the Third Reich* (New York: Pantheon, 1970); and Gitta Sereny, *Into that Darkness: 'The Mind of a Mass Murderer,'* (London: Picador, 1974).

9. Höss, quoted in Fest, *Face of the Third Reich*, 287.

Chapter 7. Lear and Cordelia

1. McLuskie, "Patriarchal Bard," 99.

2. Ibid., 101.

3. See my argument in *Compensatory Psyche*, 119–50, which from a non-feminist perspective supports the feminist position. Cf. Stanley Cavell, "The Avoidance of Love: A Reading of *King Lear*," in *Must We Mean What We Say?* (Cambridge: Cambridge University Press, 1976), 296: Lear's "let's to prison" represents "not the correction but the repetition of his strategy in the first scene,"; and Thompson, *King Lear*, 58: "Once again, Lear is simply appropriating Cordelia without thinking that she might have different and independent desires. He ignores the existence of her husband now just as he had ignored the possibility that she might love anyone other than himself in I.i."

4. Pauline Kael, "Peter Brook's 'Night of the Living Dead,' " *The New Yorker* 4. (1971): 135.

5. William Chaplin, "Our Darker Purpose: Peter Brook's *King Lear*," *Arion*, New Series 1 (1973) 1:169.

6. Kael, "Night of the Living Dead," 135.

7. See particularly Normand Berlin, "Peter Brook's Interpretation of *King Lear*: 'Nothing Will Come of Nothing,' " *Literature/Film Quarterly* 5 (1977): 299–303.

8. Jorgens, *Shakespeare on Film*, 236.

9. Berlin, "Peter Brook's Interpretation of *King Lear*," 302.

10. Ibid., 301. Recent scholarship suggests that we don't even know what the text *is*.

11. Ibid.

12. Ibid., 300.

13. McLuskie, "Patriarchal Bard," 101.

14. Barbara Hodgdon, "Two *King Lears*: Uncovering the Filmtext," *Literature/Film Quarterly* 2 (1983): 145. See also her perceptive "Kozintsev's *King Lear*: Filming a Tragic Poem," *Literature/Film Quarterly* 5 (1977): 291–98.

15. Lillian Wilds, "One *King Lear* for Our Time: A Bleak Film Version by Peter Brook," *Literature/Film Quarterly* 4 (1976): 159–64. Berlin's arguments are cogent, but he betrays his bias when he opts for the Kozintsev version. The latter shows "that a director can be both scholarly and imaginative in remaining faithful to Shakespeare" (330, n. 2). I don't believe that one can be "faithful to Shakespeare," except in having faith in one's own vision of a particular script. Brook's

version demonstrates his faith, even if it is to a play that "shatters the foundations of faith itself," as William Elton says in *King Lear: King Lear and the Gods* (San Marino: Huntington Library, 1966), 337.

16. Kozintsev, *Shakespeare: Time and Conscience*, 88.

17. Ibid., 102.

18. Ibid.

19. Cf. Waldo McNeir: "This is too reminiscent of Olivier's 'St. Crispin's Day' exhortation in *Henry V*" ("Grigori Kozintsev's *King Lear*," *College Literature* 5 [1978]: 245).

20. Kozintsev, *Shakespeare: Time and Conscience*, 102.

21. Ibid., 232. For an appreciative and excellent analysis of Kozintsev's film, see James M. Welsh, "To See It Feelingly: *King Lear* Through Russian Eyes," *Literature/Film Quarterly* 4 (1976): 153–58.

22. See, for example, Jack Jorgens, "The New York Shakespeare Festival: 1973," *Shakespeare Quarterly* 24 (1973): 425–427; Jerry Tallmer, "Central Park: A Lucid *Lear*," *New York Post*, 2 August 1973; and Michael Feingold, "Was This *Lear* Inspired by Watergate?" *New York Times*, 12 August 1973.

23. Kozintsev, *Shakespeare: Time and Conscience*, 101.

24. Jorgens, "The New York Shakespeare Festival," 423.

25. Bruno Bettelheim, *The Informed Heart* (New York: Free Press, 1960).

26. Steven Urkowitz, "*King Lear* Without Tears," *Shakespeare on Film Newsletter* 7 (1983): 2.

27. For an analysis of the techniques employed in the BBC and the Granada Productions, see Cook's illuminating "Two *Lears* for Television", 179–86.

28. For opposing views on the Granada production, see Steven Urkowitz, "Lord Olivier's *King Lear*," *Shakespeare on Film Newsletter* 8 (1983): 1, 3 (pro); Barbara Millard, "Husbanded with Modesty: Shakespeare on TV," *Shakespeare on Film Newsletter* 11 (1986): 6 (con). For other views of these productions, see Bulman, Coursen, eds., *Shakespeare on Television* (Hanover: University Press of New England, 1988). On the question of incest, see Diane Dreher, *Domination and Defiance* (Lexington: University of Kentucky Press, 1986); Judith Herman, *Father-Daughter Incest* (Cambridge: Harvard University Press, 1981); and Mark Taylor, *Shakespeare's Darker Purpose: A Question of Incest* (New York: AMS Press, 1982).

29. Paul Acker "Conventions for Dialogue in Peter Brook's *King Lear*," *Shakespeare on Film Newsletter* 4 (1979): 9–10, subsequently printed in a longer version in *Literature/Film Quarterly* 12 (1984): 219–24. See also Michael Mullin, "Peter Brook's *King Lear*: Stage and Screen," *Film/Literature Quarterly* 11 (1983): 190–96; and Robert A. Hetherington, "The *Lears* of Peter Brook," *Shakespeare on Film Newsletter* (1982): 7.

30. Kozintsev, *Shakespeare: Time and Conscience*, 215.

31. Ibid., 268.

32. Ibid., 274.

33. In that variation on *Lear*—Kurosawa's film *Ran*—Hidetora rides behind Saburo, hoping to share a few thoughts with his son as the assassin's bullet hits. Hidetora, like Siward, loses a warrior son. And Hidetora, like Pol Pot, is a mass murderer hoping for a few quiet moments by the fireside. Hidetora's career is more like Macbeth's than Lear's and more like Verdi's Macbeth—who slaughters whole choruses—than Shakespeare's. *Ran's* power emerges from its huge images, in which fire is substituted for storm, and in its powerful portrayal of Lady Kaede, who is strikingly similar to Asaji in conception—Asaji being the "Lady

Macbeth" in *Throne of Blood*. Hidetora's loss of Saburo evokes, at best, a "that's too bad." Saburo's death is consistent with negative assumptions made within and about the world, not a shattering of possibility itself.

Chapter 8. Shakespeare and History

1. Evans, *Signifying Nothing*, 253.
2. Graham Holderness, "Radical Potentiality and Institutional Closure," in *Political Shakespeare*, 197.
3. Stanley Wells, *Furman Studies: Royal Shakespeare* (Greenville, S.C.: Furman University Press, 1976).
4. Lest that remark seem as frivolous as I felt the production was, we should remember that Shakespeare does repeat himself: Bolingbroke's repetition in *II Henry IV* (3.L70–71) of Richard's lines to Northumberland (*Richard II*: 5.1.55–56) substitutes, significantly, "my cousin Bolingbroke" for "the mounting Bolingbroke." The Fool's new verse (*King Lear*: 3.2.73–76) for Feste's song (*Twelfth Night*: 5.1.376–95) seems to say, "Here's a world outside Illyria!"
5. Joseph G. Price, "Recalling Four Past RSC Productions," *Shakespeare Quarterly* 28, 2 (Spring 1977): 262.
6. James Shapiro, Paper presented at the Shakespeare Association of America Annual Meeting, Cambridge, Mass., 1 April 1988.
7. Quoted in Sally Beauman, *The Royal Shakespeare Company's Production of "Henry VI"* (Oxford: Pergamon Press, 1976), 18. See also Robert Hapgood, "The RSC's *Henry V* Treated in Depth," *Shakespeare Quarterly* 28 (1977): 264; and Richard David, *Shakespeare in the Theatre* (Cambridge: Cambridge University Press, 1978), the latter on both productions here under discussion.
8. Jonathan Dollimore and Alan Sinfield offer a sinister interpretation of Shakespeare's treatment of the Cambridge conspiracy, but one no less sinister than Shakespeare's treatment of Henry V's treatment: "All these areas of possible resistance in the play had their counterparts in Elizabethan England and the play seems, in one aspect, committed to the aesthetic colonization of such elements in Elizabethan culture; systematically, antagonism is reworked as subordination or supportive alignment. . . . Personal confession becomes simultaneously a public acknowledgement of the rightness of that which was challenged." "History and Ideology: The instance of *Henry V*," *Alternative Shakespeares*, ed. John Drakakis (London: Methuen, 1985), 216–17.
9. Norman Rabkin, "Rabbits, Duck, and *Henry V*," *Shakespeare Quarterly* 28 (1977): 279–96.
10. Ibid., 296.
11. Robin H. Wells, "The Fortunes of Tillyard: Twentieth-Century Critical Debate on Shakespeare's History Plays," *English Studies* 66 (1985): 402–3.
12. Berger, "Psychoanalyzing the Shakespeare Text," 219.
13. Raymond Durgnat, *Films and Feelings* (Cambridge, Mass.: MIT Press, 1971), 262.
14. Holderness, "Shakespeare and Television," 14–18.
15. Mark Crispin Miller, "The Shakespeare Plays," *The Nation*, 12 July 1980, 56.
16. Ibid., 59.
17. Ibid.
18. As quoted and paraphrased by Holderness, "Radical Potentiality," 196. For

the full context, see Tim Hallinan, "Jonathan Miller on the Shakespeare Plays," *Shakespeare Quarterly* 32 (1981): 134–45.

19. David Giles, interviewed by Michèle Willems, in *Shakespeare à la télévision*, ed. Michèle Willems (Rouen: L'Université de Rouen, 1987), 72.

20. Cedric Messina, "Cedric Messina Discusses 'The Shakespeare Plays,' " *Shakespeare Quarterly* 30 (1979): 137.

21. Holderness, "Boxing the Bard," 16.

22. Miller, "The Shakespeare Plays," 56.

23. Ibid., 59.

24. Jonathan Dollimore, *Radical Tragedy: Religion, Ideology, and Power in the Drama of Shakespeare and His Contemporaries* (Brighton: Harvester, 1984), 229.

25. Norman Rabkin, *Shakespeare and the Common Understanding* (New York: Free Press, 1967), 12.

26. Ibid.

27. Stuart Hall, *Resistance through Rituals* (London: Hutchinson, 1976), 285.

28. Henry Fenwick, "The Production," in *Richard II* (New York: Mayflower, 1978), 25.

29. Ibid.

30. Ibid.

31. Marshall McLuhan, *Understanding Media* (New York: McGraw-Hill, 1964), 319.

32. Peter Saccio, "The Historicity of the BBC History Plays," in *Shakespeare on Television*, 210.

33. Jack Jorgens, "The BBC-TV Shakespeare Series," *Shakespeare Quarterly* 30 (1980): 413–14.

34. Jerry Mander, *Four Arguments for the Elimination of Television* (New York: Morrow, 1978), 280–81.

35. Jane Howell, interviewed by Michèle Willems, in *Shakespeare à la télévision*, 82.

36. Zitner, "Wooden O's in Plastic Boxes," 9.

37. Ibid.

38. *Shakespeare à la télévision*, 83.

39. Gary Waller, "Decentering the Bard: The BBC-TV Shakespeare and Some Implications for Criticism and Teaching," in *Shakespeare and Television*, 28.

40. Holderness, "Radical Potentiality," 197.

41. Henry Fenwick, "The Production," in *II Henry VI* (London: BBC, 1983), 29.

42. Henry Geduld, *Filmguide to "Henry V"* (Bloomington: Indiana University Press, 1973), 33.

43. Jorgens, *Shakespeare on Film*, 127.

44. Ibid.

45. Ibid. For a negative view of Olivier's *Henry V*, see Gorman Beauchamp, *Henry V: Myth, Movie, Play*," *College Literature* 5 (1978): 228–38. Beauchamp *compares* Olivier's film to Riefenstal's *Triumph of the Will* (236).

46. Jorgens, *Shakespeare on Film*, 128.

47. The lucidity of Welle's production can be suggested by comparing my comments with those of Samuel Crowl, "The Long Goodbye: Welles and Falstaff," *Shakespeare Quarterly* 31 (1980): 379; and Andrew McLean, "Orson Welles and Shakespeare: History and Consciousness in 'Chimes at Midnight,' *Literature/Film Quarterly* 11 (1983): 201. Each sees the film, its nuances and emotional emphases, much as I do. Such agreement is rare.

48. Jorgens, *Shakespeare on Film*, 119.

49. Saccio, "The Historicity of the BBC History Plays," 210. Cf. T. F. Wharton: "[Gwillim's] rejection of Falstaff was with a look of affecting pity. And yet, here as elsewhere, the skin-deep attractiveness was designed to convey a man almost without strong identity, whose every impulse was pallid. . . . It was a very deeply studied playing, by David Gwillim, of a very shallow man" (*Henry the Fourth: Text and Performance* [London: Macmillan, 1983], 72). I think that Wharton to some extent rationalizes the inadvertence attendant upon Gwillim's sheer inexperience as actor. Since Prince Hal is also inexperienced, the subtext of inexperience served well enough but never convinced me that this Hal could turn into a warrior-king.

50. Miller, "The Shakespeare Plays," 49.

51. Ibid., 47.

52. Dollimore and Sinfield, "History and Ideology," 223.

53. Ibid., 226.

54. Arthur Colby Sprague, *Shakespeare's Histories: Plays for the Stage* (London: Society for Theatre Research, 1966), 69–70.

55. Paul Jorgensen, *Shakespeare's Military World* (Berkeley: University of California Press, 1956), 54.

56. Wharton, *Henry the Fourth*, 77.

57. C. G. Thayer, *Shakespearean Politics: Government and Misgovernment in the Great Histories* (Athens: Ohio University Press, 1983), 138.

58. Richard Corliss, "King Ken Comes to Conquer," *Time*, 13 November 1989, 120.

59. Amy E. Schwartz, "Henry Today," *Washington Post*, 6 February 1990, A.25.

60. Ibid.

61. Stuart Klawans, "Films," *The Nation* 249, no. 2, 11 December 1989, 725.

62. Ibid., 726.

63. Jonathan Yardley, "The Metamorphosis of 'Henry,' " *Washington Post*, 26 February 1990, C2. For other responses to the Branagh production, see Michael Billington, "A 'New Olivier,' " *New York Times*, 8 January 1989, H18; Vincent Canby, "A Down to Earth *Henry V*," *New York Times*, 8 November 1989, C19; Bernice W. Kliman, "Branagh's *Henry V*: Allusion and Illusion," *Shakespeare on Film Newsletter* 14, no. 1 (December 1989): 1, 9–10; Jack Kroll, "A *Henry V* for Our Time," *Newsweek*, 20 November 1989, 78; Benedict Nightingale, "Henry V Returns," *New York Times*, 5 November 1989, H17–18; and Robert Willson, "*Henry V*: Branagh's and Olivier's Choruses," *Shakespeare on Film Newsletter* 14, no. 2 (April 1990): 1–2. An excellent essay by Paul Rathbun, "Branagh's Iconoclasm: *Warriors for the Working Day*," prepared for the 1990 Shakespeare Association Meeting may have appeared by now.

64. Quoted in Nightingale, "Henry V Returns," H18.

65. Miller, "The Shakespeare Plays," 56.

66. Ibid., 59.

67. Curt Breight, " 'Treason doth never prosper': *The Tempest* and the Discourse of Treason," *Shakespeare Quarterly* 41, 1 (Spring 1990): 10.

68. Ibid., 24.

69. Zdenek Stribrny, "*Henry V* and History," in *Shakespeare in a Changing World*, ed. Arnold Kettle (New York: International Publishers, 1964), 89.

70. Thompson, *King Lear*, 81.

71. Klawans, "Films," 726.

72. Quoted in Nightingale, "Henry V Returns," 18.

73. Catherine Belsey, "Disrupting Sexual Difference: Meaning and Gender in the Comedies," in *Alternative Shakespeares*, 187.

74. Madelon (Gohlke) Sprengnether, "The Boy Actor and Femininity in *Antony and Cleopatra*," in *Shakespeare's Personality*, ed. Norman N. Holland, Sidney Homan, and Bernard J. Paris (Berkeley: University of California Press, 1989), 204. I strongly disagree with Sprengnether's point that "Shakespeare's plays . . . do not propose any serious alternative to the patriarchal understanding of woman as 'Other' " (205). The alternative is consistently presented to the male in tragedy and consistently rejected *by* the male. That alternative, however, is a formulation of Jungian psychology and its development, often by female practitioners.

75. Sprengnether (Gohlke), "The Boy Actor," 204.

76. Jean E. Howard, "Crossdressing, The Theatre and Gender Struggle in Early Modern England," *Shakespeare Quarterly* 39, 4 (Winter 1988): 435.

77. Ibid.

Chapter 9. A Space for Shakespeare

1. Zitner, "Wooden O's in Plastic Boxes," 9.

2. Stephen Hearst, "It Ain't Necessarily So," *The New Review* 5 (1978): 3–13.

3. Adrian Mitchell, "Word Masters," *The New Statesman* (25 August 1972): 265–266.

4. Hearst, "It Ain't Necessarily So," 10.

5. Elizabeth Kirkland and Joseph Papp, quoted in Arthur Holmberg, "*Shakespeare Alive*," *New York Times Book Review*, 17 April 1988, 43.

6. Holmberg, "*Shakespeare Alive*," 43.

7. Lois Potter, "Realism Versus Nightmare: Problems of Staging *The Duchess of Malfi*," in *The Triple Bond*, ed. Joseph Price (University Park: Pennsylvania State University Press, 1975), 187.

8. Rodney Bennett, quoted in Henry Fenwick, "The Production," in *Hamlet*, 18.

9. Irving Wardel, "Merchants All," *Times*, 29 April 1970, 9.

10. Roger Manvell, *Shakespeare and the Film* (New York: Praeger, 1971), 137.

11. Sedulus, "Two for the Price of One," *New Republic*, 10 February 1973, 36.

12. Day Thorpe, "Too Much Ado," *Washington Evening Star and Daily News*, 8 February 1973, 32.

13. Anthony Burgess, *Shakespeare* (New York: Knopf, 1970), 179.

14. Sedulus, "Two for the Price of One."

15. Thorpe, "Too Much Ado."

16. Gerald Clarke, "Some Ado About Quite a Lot," *Time*, 12 February, 1973, 54.

17. Edward T. Jones, "Another Noting of the Papp/Antoon *Much Ado About Nothing*," *Shakespeare on Film Newsletter* 3 (3 December 1978): 5.

18. A version of this review appeared in the *Maine Times*, April 1973.

19. Robert Speaight, "Shakespeare in Britain," *Shakespeare Quarterly* 23 (Fall 1972): 385.

20. John J. O'Connor, "TV: ABC Offering 3-Hour 'Antony and Cleopatra'," *New York Times*, 3 January 1975, 55.

21. Benedict Nightingale, "Decline and Growth," *The New Statesman*, 25 August 1972, 265.

22. Ibid.

23. Charles Shattuck, Review of "Performing *Antony and Cleopatra*," *Shakespeare Quarterly* 32 (1981): 285.

24. As I said in my review of the 1987 RSC production, "A sympathetic rendering of Caesar should not prevent Cleopatra from worming her way to victory over him" ("Shakespeare's Scripts and British Directors," *Shakespeare Bulletin* 6 [1987–88]: 33).

25. O'Connor, *New York Times*, 55.

26. John J. O'Connor, "Irate Viewers," *New York Times*, 9 January 1975, 69.

27. *Pulse* (Channel 10, Lewiston, Maine: 1975).

28. Leonard Buckley, *London Times*, 4 August 1974, 31a.

29. A version of the review appeared in *Pulse* (Channel 10, Lewiston, Maine: April 1975) and in *Shakespeare on Film Newsletter* 12 (April 1988): 5.

30. Jack Kroll, *Newsweek*, 27 April 1981, 98.

31. *Shakespeare on Film Newsletter* (December 1979): 8.

32. Cf. *Shakespeare on Television*, 246–47.

33. Michael Long, *The Unnatural Scene* (London: Methuen, 1976), 87.

34. Ibid., 92.

35. This review appeared in *Literature/Film Quarterly* 12 (1984): 65–69.

36. McLuhan, *Understanding Media*, 312.

37. William Worthen, "*King Lear* and TV," *Shakespeare on Film Newsletter* 5 (May 1983): 11.

38. Bernice W. Kliman, "The BBC *Hamlet*," 100.

39. For a thoughtful viewpoint opposed to mine on the nature of television, see Michèle Willems, "Reflections on the BBC Series," *Shakespeare Survey* 39 (1987): 91–102. Willems usefully distinguishes between the "naturalistic" (first two seasons of the BBC series), the "pictoral" (Miller and Moshinsky), and the "stylized" (Jane Howell) approaches to production. She finds the latter—"where the visual element is used as functional or suggestive—preferable to one in which it is referential ['naturalistic'] or decorative ['pictorial']" (100), and here we agree completely.

40. A. C. Bradley, *Shakespearean Tragedy* (New York: Meridian Books, 1955), 145.

41. H. R. Coursen, "The Bard *Othello*," *Marlowe Society Newsletter* 8 (1988): 7–8. For a review that finds Moody less effective than did I, see Ann J. Cook, "The Bard *Othello*," *Shakespeare on Film Newsletter* 12 (1987): 1. For an article that supports the Bard concept of the equation between Brabantio and Othello, see Janet C. Stavropoulos, "Love and Age in *Othello*," *Shakespeare Studies* 19 (1987): 125–41.

42. *Shakespeare on Film Newsletter* 13, no. 2 (April 1989): 3.

43. Kliman, "Branagh's *Henry V*," 1.

44. Brook, *The Shifting Point*, 41.

45. Mona Wilson, ed. *Johnson* (Cambridge, Mass.: Harvard University Press, 1951), 616.

46. Terry Hawkes, ed. *Coleridge's Writings on Shakespeare* (New York: Capricorn, 1959), 163.

47. Roy W. Battenhouse, *Shakespearean Tragedy: Its Art and Christian Premises* (Bloomington: Indiana University Press, 1969), 255.

48. See Bernice Kliman's fine new book, *Hamlet: Film, Television, and Audio*

Performance (Cranbury, N.J.: Fairleigh Dickinson University Press, 1988). See also Jorgens, *Shakespeare on Film;* Bulman and Coursen, eds., *Shakespeare on Television;* and *Literature/Film Quarterly* 1 (1973) and 4 (1976) for further reviews and comments on these productions.

49. Kenneth Rothwell, "The Shakespeare Plays: *Hamlet* and the Five Plays of Season Three," *Shakespeare Quarterly* 32 (Autumn 1981).

50. This is an excerpt from a paper presented to the Shakespeare Association of America Seminar on Revenge, 1989.

51. Alan C. Dessen, "The Supernatural on Television," *Shakespeare on Film Newsletter* 11, no. 1 (December 1986): 1, 8.

52. Cf. *Shakespeare on Film Newsletter,* 14, no. 1 (December, 1989): 8.

Chapter 10. *The Tempest* on TV

1. I am excluding from this discussion productions "based on" *The Tempest.* These include the films *Forbidden Planet* (1956, with Walter Pidgeon, Anne Francis, and Leslie Nielsen), *The Stuff of Dreams* (1979, directed by John Carroll and John Scagliotti), *The Tempest* (1980, directed by Derek Jarman), *The Tempest* (1981, with Molly Ringwald as Miranda and Raul Julia as Kalibanos), and the splendid ballet version by the San Francisco Ballet Company aired several years ago on public television. The latter is the only extant television version excluded from this discussion.

2. Jack Gould, *New York Times,* 4 February 1960, 63.

3. Cf. Jorgens, *Shakespeare on Film,* 65.

4. Virginia Vaughan, "The Forgotten Television *Tempest,*" *Shakespeare on Film Newsletter* 9 (December 1984): 3.

5. Ralph Berry, "Stratford Festival Canada, 1982," *Shakespeare Quarterly* 34 (Spring 1983): 96.

6. Ibid., 95.

7. Maurice Charney, "Shakespeare Anglophilia," *Shakespeare Quarterly* 31 (1980): 290.

8. Cecil Smith, *Los Angeles Times,* 7 May 1980, 4, 8.

9. Stanley Reynolds, "The Tempest," *Times,* 28 February 1980, 9.

10. Quoted in Henry Fenwick, "The Production," *The Tempest* (London: BBC, 1980), 26.

11. Charney, "Shakespeare Anglophilia," 290.

12. Smith, *Los Angeles Times,* 4, 8.

13. Geoffrey Cauley, quoted in Fenwick, "Production," in *Tempest,* 22.

14. See Fenwick, "Production," in *Tempest,* 17–21.

15. Ibid., 17.

16. John Gorrie, quoted in Fenwick, "Production," in *Tempest,* 17.

Works Cited

Abel, Lionel. *Metadrama*. New York: Hill & Wang, 1963.

Acker, Paul. "Conventions for Dialogue in Peter Brook's *King Lear.*" *Shakespeare on Film Newsletter* 4 (1979): 9–10.

Ansen, David. "Scaling the Bard." *Newsweek*, 24 April 1979, 108.

Arendt, Hannah. *Eichmann in Jerusalem*. New York: Knopf, 1963.

Atlas, James. "The New Canonicity." *New York Times Magazine*, 5 June 1988, 24–26, 72–94.

Auerbach, Nina. *Romantic Imprisonment: Women and Other Glorified Outcasts*. New York: Columbia University Press, 1986.

Banham, Martin. "BBC's Dull Shakespeares." *Critical Quarterly* 22 (1980): 31–40.

Barber, C. L. *The Whole Journey: Shakespeare's Power of Development*. Berkeley: University of California, 1986.

Barber, Lester. "Great Lakes Shakespeare Festival." *Shakespeare Quarterly* 29 (1978): 246–49.

Barton, John. "Rehearsing the Text." LD 259. BBC Playing Shakespeare. Films for the Humanities (cassette). #4.

Battenhouse, Roy. *Shakespearean Tragedy: Its Art and Christian Premises*. Bloomington: Indiana University Press, 1969.

Beauchamp, Gordon. "*Henry V*: Myth, Movie, Play." *College Literature* 5 (1978): 228–638.

Beauman, Sally. *The Royal Shakespeare Company's Production of Henry V*. Oxford: The Pergamon Press, 1976.

Belsey, Catherine. "Disrupting Sexual Difference: Meaning and Gender in the Comedies." In *Alternative Shakespeare*, edited by John Drakakis. London: Metheun, 1985.

Berger, Harry, Jr. "Text Against Performance: The Example of *Macbeth.*" *Genre* 15 (1982): 49–79.

———. "Psychoanalyzing the Shakespeare Text: The First Three Scenes of the *Henriad.*" In *Shakespeare and the Question of Theory*, edited by Patricia Parker and Geoffrey Hartman. New York: Methuen, 1985.

———. *Imaginary Audition: Shakespeare on Stage and Page*. Berkeley: University of California, 1989.

Berlin, Normand. "*Macbeth*: Polanski and Shakespeare." *Literature/Film Quarterly* 1 (1973): 291–98.

———. "Peter Brook's Interpretation of *King Lear.*" *Literature/Film Quarterly* 5 (1977): 299–303.

Berry, Ralph. "Stratford Festival: Canada." *Shakespeare Quarterly* 33 (1982): 199–202.

Bert, Edmund. *An Approved Treatise of Hawkes and Hawking.* London, 1891.

Bettelheim, Bruno. *The Informed Heart.* New York: Free Press, 1960.

Bevington, David, ed. *The Complete Works of Shakespeare.* Glenview, Ill.: Scott, Foresman, 1980.

Boxill, Roger. "Shakespeare in New York City." *Shakespeare Quarterly* 37 (1986): 508–11.

Bradley, A. C. *Shakespearean Tragedy.* New York: Meridian, 1955.

Braunmuller, A. L. "Shakespeare in Los Angeles." *Shakespeare Quarterly* 29 (1978): 259–67.

Breight, Curt. " 'Treason doth never prosper': *The Tempest* and Discourses of Treason." *Shakespeare Quarterly* 41 (1990): 1–28.

Brockbank, Philip, ed. *Players of Shakespeare.* Cambridge: Cambridge University Press, 1985.

Brook, Peter. *The Shifting Point.* New York: Harper & Row, 1987.

Brown, John R. *Free Shakespeare.* London: Heineman, 1974.

Brunette, Peter. "Towards a Deconstructive Theory of Film." *Studies in the Literary Imagination* 19 (1985): 55–71.

Brustein, Robert. "Twenty-First Century *Hamlet.*" *New Republic,* July 1983, 28.

Bulman, James, and Coursen, H. R. *Shakespeare on Television.* Hanover: University of New England Press, 1988.

Burgess, Anthony. *Shakespeare.* New York: Knopf, 1970.

Camus, Albert. "Reflections on the Guillotine." In *Resistance, Rebellion, and Death.* New York: Knopf, 1951.

Carr, Virginia M. "Boston Shakespeare Company." *Shakespeare Quarterly* 29 (1978): 231–32.

Cavell, Stanley. "The Avoidance of Love: A Reading of *King Lear.*" In *Must We Mean What We Say?* Cambridge: Cambridge University Press, 1976.

Chaplin, William. "Our Darker Purpose: Peter Brook's *King Lear.*" *Arion,* n.s. I (1973): 165–79.

Charney, Maurice. "Shakespeare Anglophilia." *Shakespeare Quarterly* 31 (1980): 287–92.

Chute, Marchette. *Shakespeare of London.* New York: Dutton, 1949.

Clarke, Gerald. "Papp's *Much Ado.*" *Time,* 12 February 1973, 54.

Clayton, Thomas. " 'Should Brutus Never Taste of Portia's Death But Once?': Text and Performance in *Julius Caesar.*" *Studies in English Literature* 23 (1983): 237–55.

Cohen, Harry. "The Narcissistic Syndrome: Causes, Problems and Solutions." *Contemporary Philosophy* 12 (1988): 2–4.

Cohen, Michael. *Hamlet: In My Mind's Eye.* Athens: University of Georgia, 1989.

Colley, John Scott. "Drama, Fortune, and Providence in *Hamlet.*" *College Literature* 5 (1978): 48–56.

Cook, Ann J. "The Bard *Othello.*" *Shakespeare on Film Newsletter* 12 (1987): 1, 4.

Cook, Hardy. "Two *Lears* for Television: An Exploration of Televisual Strategies." *Literature/Film Quarterly* 14 (1986): 179–86.

Corliss, Richard. "King Ken Comes to Conquer." *Time,* 13 November 1989.

Coursen, H. R. "*Love's Labour's Lost* and the Comic Truth." *Papers on Language and Literature* (1970): 316–22.

———. "Shakespeare in Maine: 1973." *Shakespeare Quarterly* 25 (1974): 430–432.

———. "The Papp-Sherin *King Lear.*" *Channel Ten Pulse* (1974): 4.

———. "Trevor Nunn's *Antony and Cleopatra* on TV." *Channel Ten Pulse* (1975): 7.

———. "Polanski's *Macbeth*: A Dissent." *Dayton Review* 14 (1980): 95–97.

———. "Why *Measure for Measure?*" *Literature/Film Quarterly* 12 (1984): 65–69.

———. *The Compensatory Psyche.* Washington: University Press of America, 1986.

———. "Two D. C. Comedies." *Marlowe Society Newsletter* 6 (1986): 8.

———. "The Bard *Othello.*" *Marlowe Society Newsletter* 8 (1988): 7–8.

———. *Shakespeare on Television.* Hanover: University Press of New England, 1988.

———. "Shakespeare's Scripts and British Directors." *Shakespeare Bulletin* 5/6 (1988): 33–35.

———. "Theories of History in *Richard II.*" *Upstart Crow* 8 (1988): 42–58.

———. "The Renaissance Theatre's *Twelfth Night* on Television." *Shakespeare on Television Newsletter* 13 (1989): 3.

———. "Special Effects on Television." *Shakespeare on Film Newsletter* 14 (1989): 8.

———. "The Decisions a Director Makes." *Shakespeare Bulletin* 8 (1989): 26–29.

Crowl, Samuel. "The Long Goodbye: Welles and Falstaff." *Shakespeare Quarterly* 31 (1980): 369–80.

Dash, Irene. "The Shakespeare Plays on TV." *Shakespeare on Film Newsletter* 6 (1982): 3.

David, Richard. *Shakespeare in the Theatre.* Cambridge: Cambridge University Press, 1978.

Dessen, Alan. "The Supernatural on Television." *Shakespeare on Film Newsletter* 11 (1986): 1, 8.

Dollimore, Jonathan. *Radical Tragedy: Religion, Ideology, and Power in the Drama of Shakespeare and His Contemporaries.* Brighton: Harvester, 1984.

Dreher, Diane. *Domination and Defiance.* Lexington: University of Kentucky Press, 1986.

Duffy, Robert A. "Gade, Olivier, Richardson: Visual Strategy in Hamlet Adaptation." *Literature/Film Quarterly* 4 (1976): 141–152.

Durgnat, Raymond. *Films and Feelings.* Cambridge, Mass.: MIT Press, 1971.

Edinger, Edward F. *Ego and Archetype.* Baltimore: Pelican, 1973.

Edwards, Lee. "The Labours of Psyche." *Critical Inquiry* 6 (1979): 32–44.

Elton, William. *King Lear and the Gods.* San Marino: Huntington Library, 1966.

Engler, Balz. "Shakespeare in Switzerland." *Shakespeare Quarterly* 30 (1979): 303–304.

Erickson, Peter. "Review." *Shakespeare Quarterly* 37 (1986): 516–520.

Evans, Bertrand. "Afterword to *A Midsummer Night's Dream.*" In *The College Shakespeare.* New York: Macmillan, 1973.

Evans, G. B. *Complete Works of Shakespeare.* Boston: Houghton, Mifflin, 1974.

Evans, G. L. "Interview with John Barton: Directing the Problem Plays. *Shakespeare Survey* 25 (1972): 63–71.

Evans, Malcolm. *Signifying Nothing.* Athens: University of Georgia, 1986.

Fabricius, Johannes. *Shakespeare's Hidden World: A Study of His Unconscious.* Copenhagen: Munksgaard, 1989.

Fehernbach, Robert J. "Virginia Shakespeare Festival." *Shakespeare Quarterly* 30 (1979): 197–200.

Fenwick, Henry. "The Production." In *Richard II.* New York: Mayflower, 1978.

———. "The Production." In *The Tempest.* New York: Mayflower, 1980.

———. "The Production." In *Hamlet.* New York: Mayflower, 1982.

———. "The Production." In *II Henry VI.* London: BBC Books, 1983.

Fest, Joachim. *The Face of the Third Reich.* New York: Pantheon, 1970.

Fiedler, Leslie. "The Defense of the Illusion and the Creation of Myth." *English Institute Essays: 1948.* New York: Columbia University Press, 1949.

Fielding, Henry. *Tom Jones.* New York: Random House, 1950.

Fineman, Joel. "The Turn of the Shrew." *Shakespeare and the Question of Theory.* London: Methuen, 1985.

Forker, Charles. "Shakespeare's Theatrical Symbolism and its Function in *Hamlet.*" *Shakespeare Quarterly* 14 (1963): 215–225.

Freud, Sigmund. *The Interpretation of Dreams.* New York: Carlton House, 1931.

Frye, Charles. "Shakespeare in Seattle." *Shakespeare Quarterly* 32 (1981): 274–77.

Garber, Marjorie. *Dream in Shakespeare.* New Haven: Yale University Press, 1974.

Garner, Shirley Nelson. "*The Taming of the Shrew:* Inside or Outside of the Joke?" In *Bad Shakespeare,* edited by Maurice Charney. Cranbury, N.J.: Associated University Presses, 1988.

Geduld, Henry. *Filmguide to "Henry V".* Bloomington: Indiana University Press, 1973.

Gilbert, Miriam. "Re-viewing the Play." *Shakespeare Quarterly* 36 (1985): 609–617.

Godshalk, W. L. "The Shakespeare Festival of Cincinnati." *Shakespeare Quarterly* 30 (1979): 210–212.

Gohlke (Sprengnether), Madelon. "'I Wooed Thee with my Sword': Shakespeare's Tragic Paradigms." In *Representing Shakespeare: New Psychoanalytic Essays,* edited by Murray Schwartz and Coppélia Kahn. Baltimore: Johns Hopkins University Press, 1980.

———. "The Boy Actor and Femininity in *Antony and Cleopatra.*" In *Shakespeare's Personality,* edited by Norman Holland, Sidney Homan, and Bernard Paris. Berkeley: University of California, 1989.

Goldberg, Jonathan, "Shakespearean Inscriptions: The Voicing of Power." In *Shakespeare and the Question of Theory,* edited by Patricia Parker and Geoffrey Hartman. New York: Metheun, 1985.

Goldman, Michael. *The Actor's Freedom.* New York: Viking, 1975.

———. *Acting and Action in Shakespearean Tragedy.* Princeton: Princeton University Press, 1985.

Greenblatt, Stephen. *Renaissance Self-Fashioning: From More to Shakespeare.* Chicago: University of Chicago Press, 1980.

Gushust, Bruna. "Polanski's Determining of Power in *Macbeth.*" *Shakespeare on Film Newsletter* 13 (1989): 7.

Hageman, Elizabeth. "Shakespeare in Boston and Cambridge." *Shakespeare Quarterly* 32 (1981): 190–93.

———. "Shakespeare in Massachusetts: 1983." *Shakespeare Quarterly* 35 (1984): 222–25.

Halio, Jay L. "A New *Hamlet* Journal." *Shakespeare Quarterly* 31 (1980): 462–64.

Hall, Stuart. *Resistance through Rituals*. London: Hutchinson, 1976.

Hallinan, Tim. "Jonathan Miller on the Shakespeare Plays." *Shakespeare Quarterly* 32 (1981): 134–45.

Hapgood, Robert. "The RSC's *Henry V* Treated in Depth." *Shakespeare Quarterly* 28 (1977): 264–66.

Hardison, O. B. "Three Types of Renaissance Catharsis." *Renaissance Drama*, n.s. 3 Evanston, Ill.: Northwestern University Press, 1969.

Haring-Smith, Tori. *From Farce to Melodrama: A Stage History of 'The Taming of the Shrew': 1594–1983*. Westport, Conn.: Greenwood Press, 1985.

Hawkes, Terry. *Coleridge's Writings on Shakespeare*. New York: Capricorn, 1959.

Hearst, Stephen. "It Ain't Necessarily So." *The New Review* 5 (1978): 3–13.

Heilbrun, Carolyn. *Toward a Recognition of Androgyny*. New York: Knopf, 1973.

Herman, Judith. *Father-Daughter Incest*. Cambridge: Harvard University Press, 1981.

Hetherington, Robert A. "The *Lears* of Peter Brook." *Shakespeare on Film Newsletter* 7 (1982): 7.

Hibbard, G. R. *The Taming of the Shrew*. New York: Penguin, 1968.

Hodgdon, Barbara. "Two *King Lears*: Uncovering the Filmtext." *Literature/Film Quarterly* 2 (1983): 143–51.

———. "Parallel Practices, or the *Un*-necessary Difference." *Kenyon Review* 7 (1985): 57–65.

Holderness, Graham. "Radical Potentiality and Institutional Closure." In *Political Shakespeare*, edited by Jonathan Dollimore and Alan Sinfield. Manchester: Manchester University Press, 1985.

———. "Boxing the Bard." In *Shakespeare on Television*, edited by James Bulman and H. R. Coursen. Hanover: University of New England Press, 1988.

Holland, Norman. "Hermia's Dream." In *Representing Shakespeare: New Psychoanalytic Essays*, edited by Murray Schwartz and Coppélia Kahn. Baltimore: Johns Hopkins University Press, 1980.

Holmberg, Arthur. "Shakespeare Alive." *New York Times Book Review*, 17 April 1988, 43.

Hoss, Rudolf, *Kommandant in Auschwitz: Autobiographische Aufzeichnungen von Rudolf Hoss*. Stutgart: Deutsche Verlags Anstalt, 1959.

Howard, Jean E. "Crossdressing, The Theatre and Gender Struggle in Early Modern England." *Shakespeare Quarterly* 39 (1988): 418–40.

Jackson, Berners. "Shakespeare at Stratford, Ontario, 1973." *Shakespeare Quarterly* 24 (1973): 405–10.

Jacobi, Derek. "The BBC *Hamlet*." *The Dial*. WNET, November 1980, 26–29.

Jacobi, Jolande. *The Psychology of Jung*. New Haven: Yale University Press, 1943.

Jayne, Sears. "The Dreaming of the *Shrew*." *Shakespeare Quarterly* 18 (1966): 41–56.

Johnston, Arthur. "The Player's Speech in *Hamlet*." *Shakespeare Quarterly* 13 (1962): 25–34.

Jones, Edward T. "Another Noting of the Papp/Antoon *Much Ado*." *Shakespeare on Film Newsletter* 12 (1988): 5.

Jorgens, Jack. "The New York Shakespeare Festival: 1973." *Shakespeare Quarterly* 14 (1973): 423–27.

———. *Shakespeare on Film*. Bloomington. Indiana University Press, 1977.

———. "The BBC-TV Shakespeare Series." *Shakespeare Quarterly* 30 (1980): 413–14.

Jorgensen, Paul. *Shakespeare's Military World*. Berkeley: University of California Press, 1956.

Jung, C. G. *Contributions to Analytical Psychology*. London: Routledge & Kegan Paul, 1928.

———. *Freud and Psychoanalysis*. Princeton: Bollingen Series, 1961.

———. *Symbols of Transformation*. Princeton: Bollingen Series, 1967.

———. *Analytical Psychology: Its Theory and Practice*. New York: Pantheon, 1968.

———. *The Structure and Dynamics of the Psyche*. Princeton: Bollingen Series, 1969.

Kael, Pauline. "Peter Brook's 'Night of the Living Dead.'" *New Yorker*, 11 December 1971, 136.

———. "The Current Cinema." *New Yorker*, 5 February 1972, 76.

Kahn. Coppélia. *Man's Estate*. Berkeley: University of California Press, 1981.

Kaplan, E. Ann. "Feminist Film Criticism: Current Issues and Problems." *Studies in the Literary Imagination* 19 (1986): 7–20.

Kauffman, Stanley, "Review of Polanski's *Macbeth*." *New Republic*, 1 January 1972, 22–33.

Kennedy, Andrew. "Shakespeare in Bergen." *Shakespeare Quarterly* 32 (1981): 373–74.

Kernan, Alvin. *The Playwright as Magician*. New Haven: Yale University Press, 1979.

Klawans, Stuart. "Films." *The Nation*, 11 December 1989, 725–26.

Kliman, Bernice W. "The BBC *Hamlet*: A Television Production." *Hamlet Studies* 4 (1982): 99–105.

———. Hamlet: *Film, Television, and Audio Performance*. Rutherford, N.J.: Fairleigh Dickinson University Press, 1988.

———. "Branagh's *Henry V*." *Shakespeare on Film Newsletter* 14 (December 1989): 1, 9–10.

Knapp, Jeanette. "Virginia Shakespeare Festival." *Shakespeare Quarterly* 35 (1984):

Kozintsev, Grigori. *Shakespeare: Time and Conscience*. London: Dennis Dobson, 1966.

Kroll, Jack. "Jonathan Miller's Shakespeare." *Newsweek*, 27 April 1981, 98–101.

———. "A *Henry V* for Our Time." *Newsweek*, 20 November 1989, 78.

Lacan, Jaques. "Desire and the Interpretation of Desire in *Hamlet*." In *Literature and Psychoanalysis: The Question of Reading: Otherwise*, edited by Shoshana Felman. Baltimore: Johns Hopkins University Press, 1982.

Leek, Robert-H. "A Centenary Unobserved." *Shakespeare Quarterly* 31 (1980): 418–24.

Levin, Richard. *New Readings vs. Old Plays: Recent Trends in the Reinterpretation of Renaissance Drama*. Chicago: University of Chicago Press, 1979.

———. "Performance-Critics vs. Close Readers in the Study of English Renaissance Drama." *Modern Language Review* 81 (1986): 545–59.

———. "Feminist Thematics and Shakespearean Tragedy." *PMLA* 103 (1988): 125–138.

Libriola, Albert C., "Shakespeare in Pittsburgh." *Shakespeare Quarterly* 32 (1981): 202–10.

Litton, Glenn. "Richardson's *Hamlet*." *Literature/Film Quarterly* 4 (1976): 108–22.

Long, Michael. *The Unnatural Scene*. London: Metheun, 1976.

Lusardi, James, and Schlueter, June. "New Jersey Shakespeare Festival." *Shakespeare Bulletin* 5–6 (1987–1988): 25–26.

McGuire, Phillip. *Speechless Dialect*. Berkeley: University of California Press, 1985.

———. "Intentions, Options, and Greatness: An Example from *A Midsummer Night's Dream*." In *Shakespeare and the Triple Play: From Study to Stage to Classroom*, edited by Sidney Homan. Lewisburg: Bucknell University Press, 1988.

McLean, Andrew. "Orson Welles and Shakespeare: History and Consciousness in *Chimes at Midnight*." *Literature/Film Quarterly* 11 (1983): 197–202.

McLuhan, Marshall. *Understanding Media*. New York: McGraw-Hill, 1964.

McLuskie, Kathleen. "The Patrichal Bard." In *Political Shakespeare*, edited by Jonathan Dollimore and Alan Sinfield. Manchester: University of Manchester Press, 1985.

McNeir, Waldo. "Grigori Kozintsev's *King Lear*." *College Literature* 5 (1978): 239–248.

Mander, Jerry. *Four Arguments for the Elimination of Television*. New York: Morrow, 1978.

Manvell, Roger. *Shakespeare and the Film*. New York: Praeger, 1971.

Merrill, Gregory. "A Freudian Approach to Hermia's Dream." Unpublished paper, Bowdoin College, October, 1987.

Millard, Barbara. "Husbanded With Modesty: Shakespeare on TV." *Shakespeare on Film Newsletter* 11 (1986): 6.

Miller, Mark C. "The Shakespeare Plays." *The Nation*, 12 July 1980, 46–61.

Mills, John A. "Shakespeare in Utah." *Shakespeare Quarterly* 29 (1978): 252–257.

———. *Hamlet on Stage: The Great Tradition*. Westport, Conn.: Greenwood Press, 1985.

Mitchell, Adrian. "Word Masters." *The New Statesman*, 25 August 1972, 265–266.

Montrose, Louis. "The Purpose of Playing: Reflections on a Shakespearean Anthropology." *Helios*, n.s. 7, 1980.

Morris, Harry. *Last Things in Shakespeare*. Tallahassee: Florida State University Press, 1985.

Mowat, Barbara. *The Dramaturgy of Shakespeare's Romances*. Athens: University of Georgia Press, 1980.

Mullin, Michael. "The Richardson, Williamson *Hamlet*." *Literature/Film Quarterly* 4 (1976): 123–130.

———. "Peter Brook's *King Lear*: Stage and Screen." *Literature/Film Quarterly* 11 (1983): 190–196.

Middleton, David. "The Self-Reflexive Nature of Polanski's *Macbeth*." *Dayton Review* 14 (1980): 89–94.

Murdoch, Iris. *The Black Prince*. London: Penguin Books, 1975.

Nagler, A. M., *Shakespeare's Stage*. New Haven: Yale University Press, 1958.

Nardo, Anna K. "Hamlet, 'A Man to Double Business Bound.'" *Shakespeare Quarterly* 34 (1983): 181–99.

Neely, Carol. "Feminist Modes of Shakespearean Criticism." *Women's Studies* 9 (1981): 9–17.

Newton, Judith, and Rosenfelt, Deborah. *Feminist Criticism and Social Change.* New York: Methuen, 1985.

Nightingale, Benedict. "Decline and Growth." *The New Statesman*, 25 August 1972, 265.

Novy, Marianne. "Patriarchy and Play in *The Taming of the Shrew.*" *English Literary Renaissance* 9 (1979): 264–80.

Oliver, H. J. *The Taming of the Shrew.* Oxford: Oxford University Press, 1984.

Oruch, Jack. "Shakespeare for the Millions: 'Kiss Me, Petruchio.' " *Shakespeare on Film Newsletter* 11 (1987): 5.

Pearson, D'Orsay. Letter to author, 20 December 1987.

Perrin, Curt. "The Metadrama of *The Shrew.*" Unpublished paper, Bowdoin College, 20 November 1989.

Potter, Lois. "Realism Versus Nightmare: Problems of Staging *The Duchess of Malfi.*" In *The Triple Bond*, edited by Joseph Price. University Park: Pennsylvania State University Press, 1975.

Price, Joseph. "Recalling Four Past RSC Productions." *Shakespeare Quarterly* 28 (1977): 257–62.

Progoff, Ira. *Jung's Psychology and its Social Meaning.* New York: Anchor Books, 1973.

Prosser, Eleanor. *Hamlet and Revenge.* Palo Alto: University of California Press, 1967.

Rabkin, Norman. *Shakespeare and the Common Understanding.* New York: Free Press, 1967.

———. "Rabbits, Ducks, and *Henry V.*" *Shakespeare Quarterly* 28 (1977): 279–96.

Ranald, Margaret Loftus. "The Manning of the Haggard or *The Taming of the Shrew.*" *Essays in Literature* 1, 2 (1974): 140–68.

Rathburn, Paul. "Branagh's Iconoclasm: Warriors for the Working Day." Unpublished paper. Shakespeare Association of America, 1990.

Reihle, Wolfgang. "Shakespeare in Austria." *Shakespeare Quarterly* 33 (1982): 506–8.

Roberts, Jeanne. "Metamorphoses in *The Taming of the Shrew.*" *Shakespeare Quarterly* 34 (1983): 159–71.

Rothwell, Kenneth. "Roman Polanski's *Macbeth*: Golgotha Triumphant." *Literature/Film Quarterly* 1 (1973): 343–51.

———. "The Shakespeare Plays: *Hamlet* and the Five Plays of Season Three." *Shakespeare Quarterly* 32 (1981):

Rutter, Carol. *Clamorous Voices: Shakespeare's Women Today.* London: Woman's Press, 1989.

Saccio, Peter. "The Historicity of the BBC Shakespeare Plays." *Shakespeare on Television.* Hanover: University Press of New England, 1988.

Schlueter, June. "Review." *Choice*, March 1990.

Sedulus. "Two For the Price of One," *New Republic*, 10 February 1973, 36.

Sereny, Gitta. *Into That Darkness: 'The Mind of a Mass Murderer.'* London: Picador, 1974.

Seymour, Jill. "The Falcon Metaphor in *The Taming of the Shrew*." Honors thesis, Bowdoin College, Spring, 1990.

Shank, Theodore. *The Art of the Dramatic Art*. New York: Delta-Dell, 1969.

Shapiro, James. "The Hotspurs of the North." Shakespeare Association of America, 1988.

Shattuck, Charles. "Performing *Antony and Cleopatra*." *Shakespeare Quarterly* 32 (1981): 281–86.

Showalter, Elaine. "Representing Ophelia: Women, Madness, and the Responsibilities of Feminist Criticism." In *Shakespeare and the Question of Theory*, edited by Patricia Parker and Geoffrey Hartman. London: Methuen, 1985.

Shrimpton, Nicholas. "Shakespeare in Performance: 1985–1986." *Shakespeare Survey* 40 (1988): 169–83.

Sitwell, Dame Edith. *A Notebook on William Shakespeare*. Boston: Beacon Press, 1961.

Skura, Meredith A. Review of Barber/Wheeler, *The Whole Journey: Shakespeare's Power of Development*. *Shakespeare Quarterly* 39 (1988): 90–94.

Sorelius, Gunnar. "Shakespeare in Sweden." *Shakespeare Quarterly* 32 (1981): 369–70.

Speaight, Robert. "Shakespeare in Britain." *Shakespeare Quarterly* 23 (1972): 383–87.

Sprengnether, Madelon (Gohlke). "The Boy Actor and Femininity in *Antony and Cleopatra*." In *Shakespeare's Personality*, edited by Norman N. Holland, Sidney Homan, and Bernard Paris. Berkeley: University of California Press, 1989.

Stavropoulos, Janet C. "Love and Age in *Othello*." *Shakespeare Studies* 19 (1987): 125–41.

Stearne, Richard L. *John Gielgud Directs Richard Burton in "Hamlet"*. New York: Random House, 1967.

Stodder, Joseph H., and Wilds, Lillian. "Shakespeare in Southern California and Visalia." *Shakespeare Quarterly* 31 (1980): 254–74.

Stribrny, Zdenek. "*Henry V* and History." In *Shakespeare in a Changing World*, edited by Arnold Kettle. New York: International Publishers, 1964.

Styan, John. "Psychology in the Study of Drama: The Negative and the Positive." *College Literature* 5 (1978): 77–93.

Taylor, Mark. *Shakespeare's Darker Purpose: A Question of Incest*. New York: AMS Press, 1982.

Thayer, C. G. *Shakespeare Politics: Government and Misgovernment in the Great Histories*. Athens: Ohio University Press, 1983.

Thompson, Ann. *King Lear*. Atlantic Highlands, N.J.: Humanities Press, 1988.

Thompson, Marvin and Ruth. *Shakespeare and the Sense of Performance*. Newark: University of Delaware Press, 1989.

Trewin, J. C. *Going to Shakespeare*. London: George Allen & Unwin, 1978.

Urkowitz, Steven. "*King Lear* Without Tears." *Shakespeare on Film Newsletter* 7 (1983): 1.

Vaughan, Virginia. "The Forgotten Television *Tempest*." *Shakespeare on Film Newsletter* 9 (December 1984): 3.

Vos, Josef de. "Shakespeare in Belgium." *Shakespeare Quarterly* 33 (1982): 519–22.

Walch, Eva and Gunter. "Shakespeare in the German Democratic Republic." *Shakespeare Quarterly* 32 (1981): 380–82.

Waller, Gary. "Decentering the Bard: The BBC-TV Shakespeare and Some Implications for Criticism and Teaching." In *Shakespeare on Television*. Hanover: University Press of New England.

Wells, Robin H. "The Fortunes of Tillyard: Twentieth-Century Critical Debate on Shakespeare's History Plays." *English Studies* 66 (1985): 402–3.

Wells, Stanley. *Furman Studies: Royal Shakespeare*. Greenville, S.C.: Furman University Press, 1976.

Welsh, James M. "To See It Feelingly: *King Lear* Through Russian Eyes." *Literature/Film Quarterly* 4 (1976): 153–58.

West, Rebecca. *The Court and the Castle*. New Haven: Yale University Press, 1957.

Wexman, Virginia. "*Macbeth* and Polanski's Theme of Regression." *Dayton Review* 14 (1980): 85–88.

Wharton, T. F. *Henry the Fourth: Text and Performance*. London: MacMillan, 1983.

Wilds, Lillian. "One *King Lear* for Our Time: A Bleak Film Version by Peter Brook." *Literature/Film Quarterly* 4 (1976): 159–64.

———. "Schell's Most Royal *Hamlet*." *Literature/Film Quarterly* 4 (1976): 134–40.

———. "Shakespeare in Southern California." *Shakespeare Quarterly* 32 (1981): 250–62.

———. "Shakespeare in Southern California." *Shakespeare Quarterly* 33 (1982): 382–87.

Willems, Michèle. *Shakespeare a la télévision*. Rouen: L'Université de Rouen, 1987.

———. "Reflections on the BBC Series." *Shakespeare Survey* 39 (1987): 91–102.

Williamson, Jane. "The Duke and Isabella on the Modern Stage." In *The Triple Bond*, edited by Joseph Price. University Park: Pennsylvania State University Press, 1975.

Willson, Robert. "*Henry V*: Branagh's and Olivier's Choruses." *Shakespeare on Film Newsletter* 14 (1990): 1–2.

Wilson, John Dover. *What Happens in "Hamlet."* Cambridge: Cambridge University Press, 1935.

Wilson, Mona. *Johnson*. Cambridge: Harvard University Press, 1951.

Worthen, William. "*King Lear* and TV." *Shakespeare on Film Newsletter* 5 (1983): 7.

———. "The Player's Eye: Shakespeare on Television." *Comparative Drama* 18 (1984): 193–202.

———. "Deeper Meanings and Theatrical Techniques: The Rhetoric of Performance Criticism." *Shakespeare Quarterly* 40 (1989): 449–59.

Zitner, Sheldon. "Wooden O's in Plastic Boxes: Shakespeare and Television." *University of Toronto Quarterly* 51 (1981): 1–12.

Index of Actors, Directors, and Productions

General Index